Cover Art: "Our Lady of Chivalry" by Cecilia Lawrence
www.lordshadowblade.deviantart.com

MARY'S APOSTOLIC MISSION AND OURS

by

Emile Neubert, S.M.

ACADEMY OF THE IMMACULATE
NEW BEDFORD, MA
2011

MARY'S APOSTOLIC MISSION AND OURS is a
book prepared for publication by the Franciscans of the
Immaculate [marymediatrix.com], POB 3003,
New Bedford, MA 02741-3003.

Translated from the French:

LA MISSION APOSTOLIQUE
DE MARIE ET LA NÔTRE
par E. NEUBERT, Marianiste
Editions Alsatia
17, rue Cassette
Paris, 1956

Translated by

Joseph Stefanelli, SM
Cupertino, California
2008

© 2011 Franciscans of the Immaculate
All rights reserved

Cum permissu superiorum

The permission of the superiors is a declaration of the
Roman Catholic Church that a work is free from error
in matters of faith and morals, but in no way does it
imply that she endorses the contents of the book.

ISBN: 978-1-60114-055-5

MARY'S APOSTOLIC MISSION AND OURS

Emile Neubert, SM
Marianist

Translator's Note

The translation of this work corresponds exactly to the French original of Fr. Neubert, composed over a half-century ago in 1956. When the author refers to the present, the reader must keep in mind that he does not mean the beginning of the third millennium, but the middle of the twentieth century. In a few places the footnotes have been completed in order to facilitate consultation of the author's sources by readers no longer acquainted with his methodology. But no attempt has been made to change his method of citing sources. Some extra phrases have been added to the text by the translator to facilitate identification of persons and places no longer familiar. Such additions are found between brackets of this kind {}. Notes added by the translator appear between the same type of bracket {}. Simple translations of Latin or French phrases in the text are within parentheses (). In the footnotes mere translations of titles in French not available in English are found within parentheses () immediately after the title. Where a French work cited has been translated into English, the English title is found at the end of the note between brackets of this kind [].

Contents

Doctrinal Precisions

Relationships Between Mary's Functions
and Her Apostolic Mission

The Weapons of the Marian Apostolate

Preface

Almost from the beginnings of Christianity, the faithful sensed that the name of "Queen of Apostles" given to the Virgin is more than simply an honorary title, and that it corresponds to a true role of Mary in the Church of Christ. Consequently, they loved to involve Mary in all their apostolic works.

How is it though, that theologians who have been so engrossed in her other grandeurs — sometimes for centuries — never even gave a thought to writing a treatise, or at least a chapter, on her apostolic mission?

Their silence on this matter, it is true, has not been absolute. Father Paul Verrier, SM, at the Mariological Congress of Brussels in 1921, gave a presentation on "Mary, Source of Every Apostolate." At the International Mariological Congress of Rome in 1950, Father Godfried Geenen, OP, read a Dutch report on "The Mission of Mary in Her Triumph Over All the Enemies of God."[1] It is, above all, Archbishop Suenens, in his work entitled "Theology of the Apostolate"[2] (whose publications

---

[1] Acts of the Mariological Congress, vol. XI. *De zending van Maria in Haar Triump over alle Vijunden Gods.*

[2] {*Théologie de l'apostolat de la Légion de Marie*, Paris 1951 [English tr.: *Theology of the Apostolate of the*

xvi   MARY'S APOSTOLIC MISSION AND OURS

and translations are being disseminated at an ever-increasing rate), who often speaks of this mission of Mary and draws eminently practical consequences from it. Yet, apparently, no theologian has thought of composing a systematic treatise on the subject.[3]

From this attitude, should we assume some lack of esteem on the part of theology for this function of Mary? No, not at all! Their silence is rather an argument in favor of it. What usually leads theologians to expose and discuss a doctrine are rather the denials and deviations it produces, e.g., the discussions raised by the divine Maternity or the Immaculate Conception. Nothing like that has arisen with regard to belief in the apostolic mission of the Mother of Jesus. Christian piety and the zeal of her ministers have lived peacefully, almost unobtrusively, without having felt a need to speak of it — just as we do not think of speaking to the doctor of bodily functions that are operating normally. If they wished to single out the special

---

Legion of Mary, Cork, Ireland, 1953].}

[3] The first proofs of my text had been printed when I came to know of the appearance of *Marie et notre Apostolat,* (tr. Mary and Our Apostolate) by Lucien Dilharre, of the Apostolate of Prayer. The subject is broad enough and important enough that a great number of books would not exhaust it. Mary is part, a most excellent part, of the treasure from which the head of the household draws forth the new and the old, *nova et vetera.*

efficacy of Mary's apostolic action, they have been content to mention it under the general term of "Mary's mediation."[4]

At the present time, though, when this mission of the Virgin is so clearly obvious, there is a two-fold reason to examine it more closely: first of all, in order to glorify the Mother of God, so dear to all the children of holy Church who are always happy to proclaim her glories. *Dignare me, laudare te, Virgo sacrata!* — secondly, in order to inspire her servants, who are more and more numerous and active, to resolutely follow the providential indications laid out for them in this mission of their Mother. The word of God is "spirit and life."[5] We are not only to accept the truths of our Faith, we are to live them. Living out our belief in Mary's apostolic mission, means being determined to become apostles to help her in this mission. It means to carry out our apostolate with unlimited confidence since it is not a matter of our interests, but of Mary's interests. With Mary, success is assured!

E. Neubert.

---

[4] I have touched on this subject in most of the books I have written on the Blessed Virgin. I did not discover it by myself. I inherited it from Father Chaminade who saw in it the reason for the existence of the two Marian societies he felt called to found.

[5] Jn 6:64.

Introductory Letter

From His Excellency Paul Richaud
Archbishop of Bordeaux

Feast of the Holy Rosary
Sunday, October 7, 1956

Dear Father Neubert,

It is always a grace for me to read your work. You excel in clear and simple words which contain a solid and profound teaching. Our dear Father Chaminade, apostle of the regions of Bazas and Bordeaux, has bequeathed to you a real charisma for speaking of the Blessed Virgin. Drawing close to Mary under your guidance means to approach the very channel of all grace with ease and in complete security.

May you then be praised for the new volume which your filial pen has dedicated to the Mother of Jesus. It is not simply a repetition of the other works; rather, it underscores an aspect of devotion to the Blessed Virgin which, perhaps, has not been sufficiently emphasized and which, in either case, responds to the concerns of present-day Christians in a most suitable way.

They are aware of the urgent need to present Christ to a world that is crumbling every day, due to the very fact that it has neither received the Good News, nor is it really faithful to it. The apostolate is inscribed in the most compelling logic of contemporary faith. Your merit will have been to show the chosen and irreplaceable role which Mary holds in any apostolic endeavor.

Your work makes no claim to be exhaustive nor is it, strictly speaking, a theological dissertation or an historical study. However, you do establish, with the necessary nuances, the foundations of the cult rendered to the Queen of Apostles. The overview which you give of the influence of devotion to Mary in the overall apostolic action of the Church down through the ages, provides an argument from experience. This is a very impressive argument for convincing all those who might wish to communicate the message of Christ that, in order to do it effectively and wisely, they cannot exclude the one whom Jesus Himself and His chosen workers willed to include.

Above all, you have rendered a great service to the apostles of Christ through the final chapters of your work where you reveal what I may dare call the "Marian technique" of the apostolate. Obviously, these are suggestions that might have been read elsewhere, but the fact that they are attached to the words and attitudes of Mary makes them especially persuasive. Whatever is considered in the light of the Blessed Virgin is suffused in a clarity which delights and astounds! It then appears so simple and so natural, even in regard to the most supernatural realities, that we are amazed at not having thought of it earlier or, at least, of not having seen it so clearly. What else would one expect? The Mother is there! So many issues are put into their true perspective when discussed with our Mother! So many undertakings are no longer impossible when performed under the watchful eye of our Mother!

When treating of the "dispositions required of the Virgin's apostle," you present us with the most common prescriptions of the apostolate, but those sometimes most forgotten. You restore, within the operative perspectives of both the priest and the activist, the great principles of the evangelization begun by Jesus Christ: "Do whatever he tells you." It is only His Mother who can make us attentive and responsive to His directives.

The apostolate is an art. Everything depends on the way it is done. It is only the Mother of Jesus who knows the ways of Jesus.

The apostolate presumes a spirit, a breath. It is only the Spouse of the Holy Spirit who can assure us of acting, not according to our spirit, but under the breath and the guidance of the Holy Spirit.

The apostolate is a sublime and eternal form of parenting. It is only the Mother of souls, the most humble of the little children of God, who can obtain this fecundity for us.

I anticipate, dear Reverend Father, the greatest possible diffusion of your words. In writing them, you have once more manifested yourself to be the true and indefatigable apostle of Mary. Kindly accept, I implore you, this expression of my esteem and devotion.

+ Paul Richaud,
Archbishop of Bordeaux

Part One

MARY'S APOSTOLIC MISSION

CHAPTER ONE

The Meaning of "Mary's Apostolic Mission"

We find the word "apostle" for the first time in the Gospels with reference to the choosing of the Twelve, as recorded by Saint Luke. "In those days," he says, "he departed to the mountain to pray, and he spent the night in prayer to God. When day came, he called his disciples to himself, and from them he chose twelve, whom he also named apostles" (i.e., those sent).[1]

Usually these Twelve are considered to be the first apostles. But, in reality, the first Apostle was Christ himself. In fact, before returning to the Father, He says to the Twelve: "As my Father has sent me (made

---

[1] Lk 6:12-13.

me an Apostle), so I send you (make you apostles)."[2]
The entire Holy Trinity was involved in sending
this first Apostle: the Father sent, the Son was
sent; the Holy Spirit, by rendering Mary fruitful,
gave the Son the humanity indispensable for the
accomplishment of His apostolic mission.[3] This
mission was to ransom humanity from sin and to
make of humans other children of the Father and,
thereby, to glorify God outraged by our crimes. In
order to carry it out, the Christ had to evangelize
people and to offer His life as a Victim of expiation.

Before leaving this world, Christ passed this mission
on to the Twelve: "As my Father has sent me, so
I send you. ... All power in heaven and on earth
has been given to me. Go, therefore, and make
disciples of all nations, baptizing them in the name
of the Father and of the Son and of the Holy Spirit,
teaching them to observe all that I have commanded
you. And, behold, I am with you always, until the
end of time."[4] The Twelve, therefore, were only
associates in the apostolic work confided by the

---

2 Jn 20:21.

3 Lk 1:35. Since the Incarnation is a work of God *ad
extra*, it was decided upon and carried out by the Three
Divine Persons. (Denziger 284, 429 {DS 535, 801};
Summa, III, q. 3, a. 4). It is only by "appropriation"
that the work of the Incarnation is attributed to the
Holy Spirit.

4 Jn 20:21; Mt 28:18-20.

Father to Christ. Their mission was a participation in His, a prolongation of His own mission, from which theirs drew its entire efficacy. He alone remained the Apostle *par excellence*: in His name, they were to teach; in His name, to dispel demons and to work miracles.

Like the apostolate of Christ, theirs consisted in freeing men from the tyranny of Satan to make of them children of the heavenly Father. They, too, in order to accomplish their mission, were to preach and to suffer all sorts of persecutions, sometimes even death.[5] Their successors were to continue this apostolate: "Behold, I am with you always, until the end of the age." [6]

The concept of "apostolate," therefore, contains three ideas: that of being *sent*, as indicated by the word itself, but sent by God; that of freeing men from Satan in order to make them children of God; that of devoting one's self, to the achievement of that goal, without counting the cost. Nowadays, the word "apostle," employed in a non-religious sense, often only indicates a person filled with ardor in spreading some idea, even without having been "sent" by anyone in particular.

---

5 Jn 16:1-4.

6 Mt 28:20.

Did Mary also receive an apostolic mission? Tradition supposes so. God wished to make of her the "New Eve," the Associate of Christ. We would, therefore, also expect her to participate in His apostolic mission.

Is this mission identical to that of the other apostles or to that of her Son? It is identical to neither. But, as we shall see, though her mission is a participated one, it is, for many reasons, more similar to that of Jesus than to that of the other apostles.

We shall examine what is said of it in Holy Scripture (both the Old and the New Testaments), in Tradition, in the Liturgy, and in the Magisterium of the Church. After that, we shall see the precisions and explanations brought forth in theology.

The mission conferred by Christ on His apostles includes, in addition to administering Baptism, the double objective of preaching the doctrine of salvation: "Go, teach all nations," and practicing the Christian life, "teaching them to observe all that I have commanded you!" Mary's apostolic mission embraces both Christian doctrine and Christian living.

FROM HOLY SCRIPTURE

CHAPTER TWO

In The Old Testament

The Prophecy from Genesis

At the very beginning of the history of the human race we find the famous curse that God hurled against the serpent: "I will put enmities between thee and the woman, and thy seed and her seed: she shall strike at thy head, and thou shall strike at her heel."[7] Who is it that the inspired author referred to as "the

---

[7] {Gn 3:15. Vulgate text.}

woman"? Is it Eve, or "woman" in general, or the Mother of the Messiah? The exegetes discuss it but they apparently are not ready to concur. However, it does seem that they tend more and more to agree on seeing in Eve an allusion to Mary, but actually of little importance to our purpose here. In editing the book of Genesis, Moses was only the secretary; God was the author. That the secretary does not always understand what his master dictates, so it is that we often see Jesus in the New Testament speaking words which His disciples will only understand after the fact.

God confided the authentic interpretation of Scripture to either another inspired writer or to his Church. In Revelation, Saint John teaches us that the dragon of whom he speaks is the "ancient serpent."[8] The child who conquers is Christ. As to the woman, mother of the child, she sometimes stands for Mary, sometimes for the Church, sometimes for both Mary and the Church.

The Church, in her liturgy, and especially in the Office of the Immaculate Conception, recognizes in the woman victorious over the serpent, Mary victorious over Satan. It is precisely this text that Pope Pius IX cites in his Bull, *Ineffabilis Deus*, which

---

8 Rev 12:9.

defines Mary's privilege. If the Virgin's victory is applied in these documents to the mystery of the Immaculate Conception, it is not limited to this mystery. The victory of the Immaculate over Satan was only the first of an uninterrupted series of victories she was to have over the enemy of the human race until the final judgment when he will have been banished forever into the depths of hell.

The Hebrew text points out the posterity of the woman as destined to crush the head of the serpent, and not the woman herself. That does not affect the conclusion drawn: it is clear to all Catholics that it is not of herself, but through her Son, that Mary achieves the defeat of Satan. The sacred text shows us two enemy groups fighting one another: on one side, the Woman and her posterity; on the other, Satan and his posterity. "I will put enmities between thee and the woman, and thy seed and her seed:" i.e., Mary on one side with her Son, Jesus, and her other children; Satan on the other side, with his fallen angels and his earthly cohorts. The victory belongs to Mary and her posterity.[9]

---

[9] It will not be won without wounds: the serpent strikes at the heel of the woman's posterity — the humanity of Christ crucified, His brothers and sisters persecuted by Satan. But the enemy will be able to strike only at the heel of the woman, while he himself will have his head crushed.

The Prophecy of Isaiah, 7:14

The Old Testament has another famous prophecy relative to Mary, that of the Virgin who is to give birth to Emmanuel. "The virgin shall be with child, and bear a son, and shall name him Emmanuel": a Hebrew word signifying "God with us." Saint Matthew applied this text to the virginal conception of Mary.[10] To be the cause of God's being with a soul is evidently to perform a work of apostolate. To be the cause of God's being with us is to perform a work of universal apostolate.

This second prophecy complements the first. The first shows us what might be called the negative aspect of Mary's apostolic mission: to snatch souls from Satan. The second has us see her engaged in a positive apostolate which is the goal of the first: to restore divine life in souls won over from Satan.

---

10 Mt 1:23.

CHAPTER THREE

In the New Testament

The Annunciation

The Old Testament gave us a foretaste of that which the New Testament gives us a clear vision. On the first page which places us in the presence of the Virgin, we witness a scene whose importance is impossible to fathom. Saint Luke gives an account:

> In the sixth month (after the announcement of the expected birth of John, the precursor) the angel Gabriel was sent from God to a town in Galilee called Nazareth, to a virgin betrothed to a man named Joseph of the house of David, and the virgin's name was Mary. And coming to her, he said, 'Hail, full of grace, the Lord is with you. Blessed are you among women.' But she was greatly troubled at what was said and pondered what sort of greeting this might be. Then the angel said to her, 'Do not be afraid, Mary, for you have found favor with God. Behold, you will conceive in your womb and bear a son, and you shall name him Jesus. He will be great

and will be called Son of the Most High, and the Lord God will give him the throne of David, his father, and he will rule over the house of Jacob forever, and of his kingdom there will be no end.' But Mary said to the angel, 'How can this be, since I know not man?' And the angel said to her in reply, 'The Holy Spirit will come upon you, and the power of the Most High will overshadow you. Therefore, the child to be born will be called holy, the Son of God. And behold, Elizabeth, your relative, has also conceived a son in her old age, and this is the sixth month for her who was called barren; for nothing will be impossible for God.' Mary said, 'Behold, I am the handmaid of the Lord. May it be done to me according to your word.' Then the angel departed from her.[11]

Mary raises a question, and she expects some clarification. God's messenger provides it. She knows well that her Son will be the Messiah, the Liberator announced by the prophets and awaited by all the people. Gabriel told her that He will be called Jesus, i.e., "Yahweh saves." God gives greater understanding to her than to Joseph that the Child will bear this name because He will save mankind

---

11 Lk 1:26-38.

from their sins. The redemptive mission of her Son implies a collaboration of supreme anguish on her part. If, as she knows from the prophets, particularly from Isaiah, that He is to be called "a man of sorrows," she understands that she is to be a mother of sorrows. God owes it to himself, and is duty-bound to Mary, to allow her to glimpse the consequences; otherwise, in asking her consent, he would have "deceived her," so to speak.

He is, therefore, the only true Apostle who is to be born of her. The entire apostolate of the world depends on the will of the Virgin: the apostolate of Christ who, depending on her response, will or will not come to save us, and the apostolate of His disciples who can only be apostles through Him.

She gives her *fiat*! She gives the world its Redeemer and the multitude of co-redeemers who, after Him, will work for the salvation of the human race until the end of time. The world will be redeemed because on that day (on an unknown date), in the little town of Nazareth, a young girl of fifteen consented to say "yes" to the divine proposal.

As we shall see, Mary will be an apostle during her entire life. Sometimes she will do it with greater sorrow than at Nazareth, but never again will she posit an act having the impact of Nazareth. Had she not been present at Calvary, Christ would have ransomed us anyway. But He could not have been Christ, the Redeemer, if Mary had not given her consent at Nazareth. This is why we can say that Mary's response to Gabriel is the origin of the entire Christian apostolate: that of Christ's and of His disciples, until the consummation of the ages.

The Visitation

The Gospels are sparse of details on Mary but almost every time she is mentioned, we see her accomplishing some apostolic work.

Gabriel revealed to Mary that her cousin, Elizabeth, would become a mother in her old age. He presents this unexpected maternity as proof of the one, even more extraordinary, which he announces to her. Mary understands however that, in reality, he is inviting her to go to her cousin in view of a mission. It would have been natural for the young Mother to want to remain in her solitude to savor in peace the infinite marvel of possessing the Son of God within herself. But Jesus wishes to use her help in the accomplishment of His mission. Therefore, she rises "in all haste" — as the Evangelist remarks — to undertake a journey of three or four days to bring the Messiah to her relative.

Mary begins with a salutation to her cousin; but at her first words, the Holy Spirit comes upon Elizabeth and her son. Elizabeth senses herself being filled with the Spirit from above and exclaims "in a loud voice" (sign of her being possessed by the Spirit): "How does this happen to me that the mother of my Lord should come to me?" So it is that she suddenly learns her cousin is also a mother, Mother of her "Lord." In the Old Testament, the word "Lord" always refers to God. In the very chapter in which we find Elizabeth's question, the name "Lord" is cited another fifteen times and always with the meaning of "God." That is especially true of Elizabeth's greeting: "How does this happen to me that the mother of my Lord should come to me? ... Blessed are you who believed that what was spoken to you by the Lord would be fulfilled."[12]

What a marvelous grace Mary brings to her cousin! And a grace no less marvelous is brought to her cousin's child! John leaps for joy in his mother's womb! Like her, he is filled with the Holy Spirit; he is purified of original sin; he is prepared to become the greatest of the prophets!

---

12 See E. Neubert, *Marie dans le dogme*, 3rd ed., p. 48. [English tr.: *Mary in Doctrine*, Milwaukee 1954]

And the father, Zachariah, will also become beneficiary of the double grace of a miracle and of the gift of prophecy. At the time of Mary's arrival, he is mute as punishment for his unbelief. But the Virgin-with-Child remains in his house for three months, and the old priest greatly benefits from her presence. When the day of John's birth arrives, Mary is still there. Saint Luke implies this by mentioning that it was in the sixth month of Elizabeth's pregnancy when the angel came to visit Mary, and she remained with her cousin three months.[13] Behold! Zachariah is suddenly filled with the Holy Spirit! His tongue is loosed and he begins to prophesy, proclaiming the arrival of the Messiah-Redeemer and announcing the mission of John, precursor of the Messiah.

The First Revealing of Jesus to the World

Jesus is a mere new-born Babe when He reveals Himself to the world; and He does it through Mary.

It is first of all to the Jews, in the persons of the shepherds of Bethlehem, that He announces His coming. They find the Infant laying in the manger and, next to Him, His young Mother, not in a reclining posture, but standing up, smiling,

---

13 See E. Neubert, *Vie de Marie* (*Life of Mary*), 2nd ed., pp. 59-63.

welcoming them, and recounting to them all that discretion allows her to reveal about this little Messiah. They, in their turn, make themselves apostles of the New-born. The Gospel says: "They made known the message that had been told them about this child. All who heard it were amazed by what was told them."[14]

Then, it is to the pagans, in the persons of the Magi, to whom the Messiah reveals Himself. They, too, according to Matthew's text, "found the child with Mary, his mother, and prostrating themselves did him homage."[15]

It is again in the arms of Mary where the old man, Simeon, and Anna, the prophetess, find Him. Luke mentions that Anna "gave thanks to God and spoke about the child to all who were awaiting the redemption."[16]

The Wedding at Cana

Mary did not follow Jesus in His Public Life. But Saint John shows us that she is very close to Him on two occasions: at the beginning and at the end of His life.

---

14 Lk 2:17-18.

15 Mt 2:11.

16 Lk 2:38.

The first is the episode of the wedding at Cana. Who has not admired the attentive and delicate charity of the Mother of Jesus? But what has perhaps been less emphasized is that this charity — while having as discreet objective, the relief of a material need — also exercised a work of spiritual apostolate. Saint John, who recounts for us the event to which he was a witness, concludes: "Jesus did this as the beginning of his signs at Cana in Galilee and so revealed his glory, and his disciples began to believe in him."[17] Mary's intervention had, for effect, to attract the attention of the guests to the supernatural power of her Son and to confirm faith in Him on the part of His first disciples, among whom were Peter, John, and Andrew.

On Calvary

The second occasion, incomparably more worthy of our consideration here, is the presence of Mary on Calvary. Calvary, like Nazareth, presents one of the two grand foundations of Jesus' apostolic mission. At Nazareth, her *fiat* wins for us the future Redeemer; on Calvary, she cooperates with Him in our Redemption.

---

[17] Jn 2:11.

It is at the hour of the Passion that Jesus pays the price of our ransom and there purchases, in principle, the supernatural life of the whole human race. From that moment, all those who desire it have the means of freeing themselves from Satan's yoke to become children of God. But God has willed that Mary cooperate in our Redemption through Christ. By a title inferior to that of her Son and in total dependence on Him, she contributes to our salvation by her union of will and suffering, and by the abdication of her maternal rights. We can, therefore, say that we are born to the supernatural life thanks to Jesus and to her. She therefore participates in a unique way in the apostolic work of the one who is Apostle *par excellence.*[18]

Because it is at Calvary that she gives birth to us, it is there that Jesus Christ proclaims her Maternity in our regard by giving her to us in the person of Saint John.[19]

Every mother is the first apostle of her child. But our spiritual Mother — because she is spiritual — is

---

[18] E. Neubert., *Marie dans le Dogme*, 3rd ed., pp. 141-143.

[19] E. Neubert, *Marie dans le Dogme*, 3rd ed., pp. 110-111.

Mother in an incomparably superior manner, for her Maternity conjoins to her apostolic mission.[20]

It is John, the well-beloved disciple, become a priest the previous evening at the institution of the Eucharist, to whom Jesus directly confides His Mother. Every priest is an apostle by a special title, a title more sacred than that of lay apostles. On Calvary, Mary especially becomes Mother *par excellence* of her Son's apostles.

Mary at the Cenacle

Before dispersing to begin their mission, the apostles gathered in the cenacle to prepare themselves, through recollection and prayer, for the coming of the Spirit from on high which the Master had promised them. Mary was also there,[21] praying with them and for them.

And then, the divine Spirit who had already descended upon her, also came upon the apostles and transformed them into new men who went forth full of courage and strength to conquer the world for Christ. Here, as elsewhere, by her prayer and maternal influence, the Virgin caused Jesus

---

20 E. Neubert, *Marie dans le Dogme*, 3rd ed., pp. 221-222.
21 Acts 1:14.

to be better understood, and she prepared other missionaries for Him.

Mary and the Evangelists, Luke and John

The presence of Mary in the cenacle is the last, explicit, scriptural record of the Mother of Jesus. But the inspired text allows us to infer, even to affirm, other influences on her part.

The initial preaching of the apostles seems to have been limited to proclaiming and to proving that Jesus was the true Messiah, Son of God; that He had shed His Blood to ransom us from sin and death; that He had resurrected and gone to Heaven to merit for us to rise in our turn and to join Him in the presence of the Father. Yet, quite naturally, their disciples wanted to know more about the life of the Savior. As to His Public Life, many witnesses could instruct them; hence, the origin of our four Gospels.

But the Public Life was limited to two years, or three at most. What had taken place before that? In particular, how did the Son of God come into this world to become a human being? An altogether legitimate curiosity prompts these questions. Saint Matthew satisfies them in part. He relates that the angel of the Lord had appeared to Saint Joseph in a dream and revealed to him that what was in Mary had come from the Holy Spirit.[22] Matthew's account is centered on Saint Joseph. Matthew probably received this information from the Mary whom Scripture identifies as the mother of James and Joseph, wife of Cleophas who was the brother of Saint Joseph.[23]

If it was by the working of the Holy Spirit that Mary had become Mother, how did this issue come about? The short passage from Saint Matthew does not entirely satisfy the curiosity of the faithful. Saint Luke, however, having researched all the sources,[24] provides the answer, and gives us a detailed account of the beginnings of John the Baptist and of Jesus. He takes great care to imply his source. Twice,[25] he comments that Mary kept these things in her Heart and pondered them. Did he receive this information directly from the lips of the Virgin, or from some confidant to whom she had revealed the treasures stored in the silence of her Heart for so many years, until the moment willed by God? We do not know;

---

22 Mt 1:20.
23 Cf. Mt 27: 56. E. Neubert, *Vie de Marie,* chaps. 11-13.
24 Lk 1:3.
25 Lk 2:19, 51.

but there is no doubt that she was the source of the facts.[26]

These remembrances of Mary are of supreme importance. They are the foundation of Marian dogma and of devotion to her. Without them, hundreds of thousands of Hail Marys would not ascend to the Mother of Jesus from the mouths of the countless faithful, day and night without interruption, from all corners of the world. Without the Virgin's recollections, Jesus Himself would be less known to us, less close to us; we would not go to Him with the simplicity, confidence, and love which we experience at the sight of the humble Virgin of Nazareth listening to the message of the angel and pronouncing her *fiat*.

May we also assume Mary's influence in the Gospel according to Saint John? He composed this Gospel some thirty or forty years after Mary's death. But John certainly had recounted to Mary all of Jesus' actions and words contained in his Gospel, as she desired to know everything in reference to her Son so as to meditate upon it. And whenever John gave an account of some action or teaching of the Master, Mary's reflections and reactions must have no doubt led him to penetrate many times, even

---

[26] E. Neubert, *Vie de Marie,* chaps. 13-16.

more deeply, into the hidden meaning of Jesus' lessons and gestures. The fourth Gospel delves into the mystery of Christ more profoundly than do the other three. Besides, he whom Jesus calls "son of thunder" — who had wished to call down fire from heaven onto the village of Samaria, and who had heard himself addressed by the Master with this reproach: "you do not know of what spirit you are,"[27] — is more concerned than the others to emphasize the commandment of fraternal love. Is it rash to opine that this profound penetration and this spirit of charity are due in part to his closeness to the Mother of Jesus?

May we not also suppose that the other apostles we find in Jerusalem — Peter, his first bishop; James, successor to Peter and nephew of Mary; Paul also, perhaps, and some of the other ten of whom Acts tells us nothing — owe something of their apostolic action to the influence of her who is Mother of the Church? The formation of apostles will always be one of the tasks of predilection in centuries to follow.

---

27 Mk 3:17; Lk 9:55 {Vulgate text; some English versions have: "turned and rebuked them."}

FROM TRADITION

A. Mary, Guardian of the Faith

We said above that the apostolic mission of Mary extends to both Christian doctrine and to Christian life.

The apostolate of doctrine is twofold: negative and positive. It consists in defending the orthodox doctrine against falsification, and in propagating it throughout the entire world.

CHAPTER FOUR

Mary, Logical Argument
Against Heresies[28]

Mary's victorious action may be viewed under different aspects. There is, first of all, an argument from reason, given that there is a logical opposition between her functions and privileges, and the affirmations of heresy. This aspect is especially evident in the struggle of the early Fathers against the Christological heresies of their times.

---

28 The program of the International Mariological-Marian Congress of Lourdes, Sept., 1958, treated, among other topics, "Mary and the Defense of the Dogmas of Faith."

The True Humanity of Christ and the Human Maternity of Mary

The first heretics the Church encountered were the Gnostics (philosophers and mystics, or who claimed to be such) who saw an absolute incompatibility between the spirit and the flesh. The latter, being evil in itself, could not have been assumed by Christ. Other heretics, the Marcionists (not preoccupied with speculation but with practical living), taught the same doctrine about the flesh and the nature of Christ. The issue in the struggle was indeed a capital one: at stake was the truth of the human nature of Christ and, consequently, of the Redemption. The innovators were generally wise and learned men, eloquent, influential, and clever. One of them, Valentine, ascended to the seat of Saint Peter for a time. The great task of the Fathers and the theologians of that period was to defend the truth of the humanity of Christ.

Their greatest argument, of course, was His being born of Mary. Saint Ignatius of Antioch had already written to the Trallians: "Stop up your ears if someone speaks to you of another doctrine than that of Jesus Christ, who is of the race of David,

who is of Mary, who was truly engendered."[29]
Following Ignatius — Irenaeus of Lyons, Clement
of Alexandria, Tertullian of Carthage, Hippolytus
of Rome, and others, invariably based the reality of
the humanity of Jesus on His being born of Mary:
of Mary, and not *through* Mary, as was claimed by
the Valentinians, who accorded Him only a body
formed of astral matter which did nothing more
than pass through the womb of the Virgin.[30]

The Divinity of Christ and the Virginity of Mary

It was to be expected that belief in the divinity of
Christ should encounter adversaries from the very
beginnings of Christianity.

First, it was the Jews. They were awaiting as
Messiah, someone to whom an extraordinary degree
of God's power would be given, but not a divine
Messiah. During those early centuries, they were the
most obstinate and the most hateful deniers of the
divinity of Jesus.

---

29 *Ad Trailianos*, 9.
30 See E. Neubert, *Marie dans l'Eglise Anténicéene* (*Mary in the Antinicene Church*), pp. 3-56.

There was also a Judeo-Christian sect which, while admitting the messiahship of Jesus, denied His divinity. These were the Ebionites.

Among the Gnostics, we can distinguish two chief adversaries of the divinity of Christ: Cerinthius, whom it seems Saint John aimed at in his letters,[31] and Carpocratix. Both saw in Jesus only a superior man, born like other humans.

All these deniers of the divinity of Jesus deny, at the same time, His virginal birth. That is why the defenders of His divinity were determined to defend the virginity of His Mother.

Saint Ignatius had already mentioned "the virginity of Mary, with [the truth of] His birth and the death of Christ, as one of the three mysteries that should be loudly proclaimed, but which was accomplished in the silence of God."[32]

The Fathers {of the Church} who come after him are not content with affirming Mary's virginity; they seek to establish it by a variety of arguments. Justin, Irenaeus, Tertullian, Origen, Hippolytus, Lactantius ardently and eloquently devoted themselves to this end.

---

[31] I Jn, chaps. 1, 2, 4, 5; II Jn: verses 9, 11.
[32] *Ad Ephesianos*, 19.

Among the Gnostics, we have mentioned only Cerinthius and Carpocratix as direct deniers of Mary's virginity because they were deniers of her Son's divinity. But the struggle between other Gnostics who saw a divine being in Jesus also led the Fathers to insist on the virginal conception. That was because all the Docetists, whatever their individual theories, rejected the humanity of the Savior so as to better guarantee His divinity. Their adversaries, while maintaining the humanity of Jesus, had to show that they did not, by that fact, deny His divinity. The solution to the difficulty was found in the supernatural birth: though Jesus was human because He was truly born, He was more than simply human because He was born of a virgin. So, the same Fathers cited above as defending the divinity of Jesus through Mary's virginity, can be cited as defending the possibility of the union of His divinity with His humanity through the explanation of Mary's virginity.[33]

In summary, both heretics and orthodox drew on the principle that a God can be born only of a virgin and that, from a virgin, only a God can be born. From an ontological point of view, the principle is not absolutely uncompromising, but from a

---

33 E. Neubert, *Marie dans l'Eglise Anténicéene*, pp. 57-120.

psychological point of view it expresses an exigency of the religious soul.

This is the same principle we find implied in the attitude of certain modern heretics. Around the middle of the 19th century, Doctor Pusey, progressive Anglican theologian, had mentioned, in a book entitled *Eirenicon* (Peaceful), the conditions under which the Anglican Church might unite with the Catholic Church. He had particularly stated the abandonment of the Catholic Church's idolatrous cult of Mary. Cardinal Newman, his former friend, answered him in a letter, a veritable treatise, which perhaps constitutes the most beautiful writing of the 19th century on devotion to Mary. Pusey had claimed that the cult we render to Mary must necessarily relegate her divine Son into the shadows. Newman first asks that the statement be proven. Then he adds: "There is another fact — one that speaks very loudly, it seems to me. If we cast a glance over Europe, what do we see? In fact, the countries and the peoples who have lost faith in the divinity of Christ are precisely those who have abandoned devotion toward his Mother. Those, on the contrary, who have more especially honored her, have preserved their orthodoxy. Compare, for example, the Greeks with the Calvinists, France with northern Germany, or the Catholics with the Protestants in Ireland." It is still a fact that the countries and the peoples who have lost their faith in the divinity of Christ are also those who have rejected the virginity of Mary.

Around the year 1900, there were some heated discussions among Protestant theologians in Germany with regard to the Creed. Some rejected the article: "Who was born of the Virgin Mary"; others wanted to retain it at all costs. These latter were not necessarily devotees of Mary, but they saw that the stakes were less a privilege of Mary than the divinity of her Son.

Shortly thereafter, in the name of progress in exegetical knowledge, the modernists in France also worked in an underhanded manner to demolish faith in the divinity of Christ. Rome had not yet spoken. Amidst these discussions, a magazine article appeared, undermining belief in Mary's virginity. It opened the eyes of a great number of their well-intentioned disciples who had trustingly followed them, and it drew them back to a traditional faith. The article was denounced by the Archbishop of Paris. The condemnation of Modernism by Pius X followed shortly after.

Personal Union of the Two Natures in Jesus: Virginal Conception; Divine Maternity

The Gnostic doctrines exposed above, admitted only a very tenuous union between the humanity and the divinity of Jesus. According to them, there was a divine being and a more-or-less real human being in Him. This was not Christ, at once and indissolubly God and man, the Christ who slept from fatigue in the boat and who then, with a word, calmed the turbulent waves.

Defenders of the traditional doctrine all applied themselves to showing the unity of person in the duality of natures. Their decisive argument was, again, the virginal conception of Mary. The one Christ was truly human because He was born of Mary; and truly God because He was born of her virginally. Saint Ignatius of Antioch is very explicit on that point. For example, he wrote to the Ephesians: "Our doctrine is one of flesh and of spirit, engendered and non-engendered, God made flesh, in death true life, of Mary and of God."[34]

The same doctrine, explained in greater detail, is found in Justin, Irenaeus, Tertullian, Origen, and Hippolytus. Tertullian, for example, writes: "God

---

34 *Ad Ephesianos*, 7.

is born of Mary,"[35] which is the exact equivalent of: "Mary is Mother of God." The word *Theotokos*, Mother of God, must have been used from the end of the third century, for it is found in the oldest prayer to Mary, the Greek *Sub tuum*. The text was recently found in a papyrus dated at the beginning of the fourth century at the latest. It was popular in the fourth century and even known to the pagans who made jest of it.

Then, in the fifth century, around 430, Nestorius, bishop of Constantinople, publicly banned the use of this title of the Virgin, under pretext of finding an Arian or Apollinarian meaning in it. What, in reality, was Nestorius' view of the union of the two natures in Jesus? He did not define it. It would seem that he admitted only a kind of moral union of the two natures, a perfect accord between the wills and the activities of the two natures and, consequently, of special honors for the humanity, but not a truly substantial union by means of which the actions of the two natures belong to the same "I," to the divine "I." By calling Mary, Mother of God, *Theotokos,* a substantial (in the Greek: "hypostatic") union of the two natures was affirmed. The Council of Ephesus, 431, condemning Nestorius, not only safeguarded the Virgin Mary's greatest title of

---

35 *Adversus Praxeam*, 27.

honor, but safeguarded the orthodox doctrine about the person of Christ and the traditional doctrine of the Redemption; for the immolation of the body of Christ could only save us if it was the body of a God.

These facts which we have presented suffice to show, in Mary, the decisive response to all the Christological heresies. The mystery of the Incarnation is the central mystery of Christianity. All the teachings of our Faith more or less directly depend on it and, in one way or another, Mary enters into the refutation of other heresies which would emerge in the course of centuries. History could point this out; but that would take us off course here. Besides, the proof has been presented by many other authors.[36]

The refutation of Nestorius not only provided an occasion for giving an especially illuminating proof of the function of Mary as guardian of the Faith, but also for presenting an explicit affirmation of that function. A homily Saint Cyril is said to have given the evening of the condemnation of the heresiarch contains the following acclamation: "We

---

[36] J.-B. Terrien, SJ, *La Mère de Dieu*, vol. 1, chap. 3. Paul Sträter, *Katholische Marienkunde*, vols. 1 and 2. P. G. Geenen, OP, *De Zending van Maria in haar triomp over alle Vijnden van God.*

salute you, *Theotokos*, true treasure of the universe, inextinguishable flame, crown of virgins, scepter of orthodoxy!" However, this homily was mistakenly attributed to this great adversary of Nestorius. In fact, it was "pronounced at Ephesus on the return of the seven delegates to the Council, after the meetings of Chalcedon and the election of Maximian of Constantinople (October 25th) — therefore, in November 431. At that time, Cyril had already returned to Alexandria."[37] But it matters little for our purpose whether it was Cyril or some theologian of his party who actually gave the homily. It shows that at that moment in history, there was already an awareness of Mary's role in the preservation of Catholic orthodoxy. The affirmation by an ordinary theologian has an even greater chance of presenting a common belief than the pronouncement of a genius.

Little by little, this awareness of Mary's role became more precise. In the East, at the beginning of the eighth century, we find the following statement from the pen of Saint Germain of Constantinople (d. 733): "From Our Lady flows the most pure and limpid water which submerges the entire host of

---

37 René Laurentin, *Court Traité de Théologie Mariale*, 166. [English tr.: *Queen of Heaven. A Short Treatise on Marian Theology*, Dublin-London 1956]

heresies."[38] Toward the middle of the same century, in the West, we find this responsorial: *Gaude, Maria, Virgo cunctas haereses sola interemisti in universo mundo.*[39] It seems to have been first used in southern Italy; from there, it was transmitted to Gaul and then to the other Christian countries.[40] By the fact that it is a liturgical text repeated at every feast of the Virgin, it must have had great influence in disseminating faith in Mary's mission as Guardian of the Faith.

---

[38] *PG,* vol. 98, col. 305B.

[39] {Rejoice, O Mary, Virgin, you alone have overcome all heresies throughout the entire world.}

[40] L. Brou, OSB, *Marie destructrice de toutes les heresies* in *Ephemerides Liturgicae* (1948) and *Addendum* in the same review of 1951. The Mariological-Marian Congress of 1958, Lourdes, presented a report on the origin, history, and true significance of the cited responsorial.

CHAPTER FIVE

Mary, Argument of the Heart

Christian faith is not a metaphysical system. Jesus did not say: "My word is true philosophy." He said: "My word is spirit and life…"[41] If we must "seek out the truth with all our heart," it is with all our heart that we must seek out the divine Truth above all else. To how many individuals has experience — perhaps painful experience — proven Pascal's words to be true: "God is sensed by the heart and not by reason."

Now, if Mary is a logical argument, simple and conclusive, in the refutation of heresies, she is by far a much more convincing argument because she is an argument of the heart.

The Virgin has been so highly regarded throughout the human history of all true Catholics that she has become especially dear to each of them. The experience varies from soul to soul but, in each one, she is held in such high esteem that nothing in the world could persuade them to disavow her mediation when recalling the peace and joy of certain feasts, of certain personal events: finding

---

41 Jn 6:64.

consolation in sorrows, conquering temptations, amending transgressions, assuaging hours of anguish, overcoming hardship, curing illnesses; perhaps sentiments of rebellion against God or of despair were transformed into repentance, trust, confidence, and courage. What Catholic heart cannot recall thinking of her, of her intervention, at a particularly painful or happy moment of its existence? Even for those who no longer pray to her, she remains dear; any insult to the Virgin instinctively upsets them. Since the various teachings of the Catholic faith are linked to Marian doctrine, embracing a doctrinal error would amount to rejecting the Virgin and all that one had previously experienced, thanks to her. In her presence we sense God; any doctrine that distances us from her is surely a false doctrine.

Emotional factors certainly played a part in the distrust of Modernism which arose among many Catholics who had favored it at first — a lack of trust fomented by the magazine article (previously stated) attacking Mary's virginity. It more or less played upon the aversion of Catholics with regard to the heresies succeeding each other over the centuries. Doubtlessly, it is more difficult to prove this than to cite the arguments by which the Catholics opposed them; and this is so because it is easier to express ideas than feelings, though often what is expressed is less true than what remains unspoken.

It is true that in the early periods of Christianity, devotion to Mary was not what it is today. The Virgin was not yet "the Madonna really among us to whom we pray on our knees, who smiles and is quick to pardon."[42] Like doctrine, devotion expanded progressively but probably more quickly than doctrine, because the heart intuits much more quickly than does the mind. It can be presumed that, from the very beginning, Mary was the object of a special veneration and began to exercise a mysterious attraction over believing hearts. Already in the Gospel, we see the young Mother of the Messiah, Son of God, greeted by an archangel as "full of grace." Elizabeth, inspired by the Holy Spirit, declares her most blessed among all women. She is called blessed as her Son is blessed. She herself announces, in the name of that same Spirit, that all generations would call her blessed. Her answer determines the lot of the human race. She is so miraculously pure, so great before angels and humans and, at the same time, so small in her own eyes; so humble, so simple, and so forgetful of herself. She seeks only to serve, to be of help to Elizabeth, to the shepherds, to the magi, to Simeon

---

42 {Words of a traditional French hymn.}

and Anna, and to the guests at Cana, sacrificing her Son for all of us. She suffers because of her Son and because of us; she endures interior suffering because of false judgments against her Maternity; she is greatly afflicted at Bethlehem and in Egypt; and she undergoes extreme tribulation on Calvary. She experiences immense grief without complaint, seeking no escape from her anguish, but only the will of God — a will that exalts and deals the blow of martyrdom. We can readily understand why Adolf Harnack, the high priest of Protestant exegetes (around 1900), could say that Mariolatry had already begun with Luke's Gospel.

Soon, the frequent mention of her title, "Victress over heresies," and the role of the New Eve at the side of the New Adam, which the Fathers attribute to her, beginning in the second century, helped the faithful to better understand the place which she occupied in the history of their salvation. In addition, the increasing importance of the practice of virginity attracted the attention of the faithful with special veneration for the miraculously virginal one who was soon simply called "the Virgin," "the Blessed Virgin," "the Immaculate Virgin."

She must have been invoked early in Christian history. Private prayer remains a secret between the soul and the supernatural world and is not usually recorded in history. Yet, we do know that prayer to the Virgin existed from earliest Christianity. In his panegyric on Saint Cyprian, Saint Gregory of Nazianzen recounts that, while still a pagan, Cyprian was pursuing the virgin Justina who appealed to Mary to protect her virginity, and was heard.[43] Gregory, we now know, confused Cyprian of Carthage with a Cyprian the magician. Is he more accurate when referring to Justina's prayer to the Virgin? That makes little difference for our purpose. If he invented this detail it would be because, already from the times of the persecutions, recourse to the Virgin was instinctively natural. The invocation of Mary, therefore, did not correspond to the time of his writings (fourth century); it had to go back much earlier.

As a matter of fact, in 1917, the identification of a papyrus dating from the fourth century, and bearing a fragment of the text of the Greek *Sub tuum,* leads to the same conclusion. For this formula to have had the time to circulate, there must have already been a custom of addressing oneself to the Mother of God. There is an appeal to the protection of

43 *Oratio* 11. PG vol. 35, col. 1181.

Mary, *praesidium*. The ancient text appeals to her compassion, *eusplanchnian*. This presupposes a particularly warm relationship between the soul and the *Theotokos*.

All these facts lead us to assume that the Virgin occupied an eminent place in the mind of Christians in the first centuries. It is probable that, in their struggle for the orthodox faith, she was already not only a logical argument for them, but also an argument of the heart. This was to be verified in a striking way in the fifth century, in opposition to the defective Christology of Nestorius.

Nestorius had been raised according to the principles of the School of Antioch. Several members of that school had professed a more or less ambiguous doctrine on the union between the humanity and the divinity of Jesus. They taught that the Word had come into Jesus as into the prophets, uniting itself to Jesus by complacency or through love. Theodore of Mopsuestia, Diodore of Tarsus, his teacher, and Paul of Samosata seem to have professed this doctrine; at least, they had been accused of it. The faithful in general were hardly moved by their formularies, and left it to the doctors of the different schools to debate them. Nestorius' Christological teaching was no more shocking than theirs. But when he drew the conclusion from their principles that Mary was not the Mother of God, the entire East was suddenly aflame — simple believers, clergy of all ranks, monks of all professions, protested with indignation and cried "blasphemy"! This was not only at Constantinople, but also in Egypt, Asia, Palestine — the whole of Greek-speaking Christendom. On the evening of the day when the audacious Bishop had been condemned and deposed, Saint Cyril, who had presided over the assembly, wrote to his people in Alexandria:

> We were about two hundred bishops assembled. All the city-folk remained in suspense from morning until evening awaiting the judgment of the Holy Synod. When it was learned that the unfortunate one had been deposed — with one voice, all began to congratulate the Holy Synod and to glorify God for the fall of the enemy of the Faith! At our exit from the church, we were escorted to our residences with flaming torches. It was evening. The entire city was illuminated; women carrying bowls of incense walked ahead of us. God had demonstrated his omnipotence to those who blasphemed his name![44]

---

44 *Epistula* 24.

The joy of the people of Ephesus reverberated through the entire East. The *Theotokos* had triumphed! Nestorius' opposition had served the Virgin's cause better than the most eloquent theologian could have done. After that, the East offered a cult to the Mother of God which surpassed in enthusiasm and veneration even the official liturgical texts and whatever the Latin liturgy might chant in her honor.

How, then, could so many peoples convert to Protestantism in the 16th century, given that devotion to Mary seemed to have been generally accepted in countries that embraced the Reformation? That fact can be explained by different reasons, depending on the areas. We might point out three principal ones:

First, following the position of Father Rene Laurentin, one of the most competent historians of Mariology, we may say that from the middle of the 13th century Marian theology became so insipid among some that it no longer merited the name of theology. Devotion, such as iconography, progressively lost its Christocentrism. It displaced theology with sentimentality; it crumbled into a multiplicity of often superficial practices. Until 1577 (date of the appearance of the *De Virgine incomparabili* of Saint Peter Canisius), works intended to respond to the Marian attacks of the Protestants were rare and poorly done. The non-polemic literature was more mediocre than ever.[45]

Besides, at the beginning, the innovators did not attack veneration to the Mother of God. In 1521, the year after his revolt, Luther published a long commentary on the *Magnificat* with regard to the dignity of Mary in which he says, for example:

> This divine maternity earned for her goods so excellent, so immense, that they surpass all understanding, From it, in fact, all honor comes to her, all beauty, to the point that she is, in all the human species, the only person who is superior to all others, who has no equal, by the fact that she possesses such a Son in common with the heavenly Father. ... Thus, the very title of Mother of God contains all honor, for no one could say of her or announce to her any greater thing though one might have as many tongues as the earth

---

45 R. Laurentin, in *Maria. Etudes sur le Sainte Vierge*, 8 vols., Paris 1949-1971, vol. 3, pp. 14ff.

has flowers or blades of grass, as the sky has stars, and the sea has grains of sand.

Luther concludes his commentary with expressions of hope for light and love, and adds: "May Christ accord us these favors through the intercession and assistance of his most beloved Mother."[46] However, following a principle accepted by all Catholics, that we must not attribute to Mary what is due only to God, he insinuates traces of idolatry everywhere in the cult of the Virgin, to the extent of rendering it worthless.

In Switzerland, Zwingli, the great reformer of Zurich, became violent, it is said, when he was accused of being opposed to the veneration of the Virgin, protesting that he accepted being labeled a drunkard or any other bad name but, never, of not loving the Mother of Jesus! But he, too, in his invectives against papist superstitions, succeeded little by little in undermining the confidence of the good people in the Mother of God.

A second factor was that, for the princes who took the side of Luther, the matter was less a question of religion than it was a question of politics and greed.

---

46 Luther, *Super Magnificat*. {English tr.: "The Magnificat put into German and Explained, in P. D. Krey & P. D. S. Krey, ed., *Luther's Spirituality*, New York 2007}

It was more a matter of gaining independence from imperial power and, above all, of getting possession of the goods of the Church and of the convents. According to the acceptable principle of the time, the ruler imposed his religion on his subjects. The subjects of numerous rulers who defected to Protestantism, therefore, had no other clergy, no other cult, and no other doctrine than that of the Protestant clergy, cult, and doctrine. Though a goodly number of them remained faithful to the Virgin Mary in their hearts, their descendants gradually took on the attitude of the reformers. A similar phenomenon had taken place earlier in Africa, land of flourishing Christian churches, after the Muslims had subjugated all those regions to the religion of the Prophet Mohammed. Many Muslim fanatics of the 20th century had fervent disciples of Saint Cyprian as ancestors, many of whom shed their blood for the cause of Christ.

The fact of these forced conversions to Protestantism, therefore, proves nothing against the influence of devotion to Mary as a factor in maintaining orthodoxy. In those places where the people were free to choose, their fidelity to the Virgin assured their fidelity to the Catholic religion. Even in those places where religion was reduced to a few practices and where Protestant missionaries thought they might have free reign, the prospect of having to abandon the cult of Mary preserved the people in the Faith of their fathers. According to the testimony of Catholic missionaries:

> It was basically devotion to Mary around 1900 that preserved the inhabitants of the Philippine Islands from apostasy in the face of schism, and from falling prey to the many Protestant missionaries who came from North America laden with gold. … If the countries of South America, so lacking in priests, had not been protected, they would have no doubt succumbed, one after another, to the cold and depressing religion of Protestantism, void of Mary, being proclaimed by countless North American preachers who invaded the land, promising all sorts of material advantages. The people gratefully accepted the schools and medical services of the foreigners, but refused to adopt their fractured Christianity. Some twenty years later, similarly encountering the cult of the Virgin among the Africans, the proselytizing efforts of Protestant missionaries were dashed and they were forced to withdraw from the country.[47]

---

[47] Paul Sträter, *Katholische Marienkunde, Maria im Christenleben,* pp. 109-111.

There hardly appeared to be any defections of
Catholics converting to Protestantism except
in cases of marriages forbidden by the Catholic
Church. On the contrary, during those years, there
was a movement among many sincere Protestants
to adopt the practice of honoring and praying to
the Virgin Mary, many of whom returned to the
Catholic Church, disheartened by the void and chill
of their own religion.

CHAPTER SIX

Mary and the "Sense of Faith"[48]

We have seen how the Virgin constitutes an
argument from reason and from faith, guaranteeing

---

48 Clement Dillenschneider published, in 1954, a
remarkable work on *Le sens de la Foi et le progrès
dogmatique du mystère marial* (Academia Mariana
Internationalis, Via Merulana, 124, Rome). The
object of our chapter is not the same as that of his
work. Dillenschneider shows how the sense of faith
contributes to the dogmatic development of the Marian
mystery. Here our purpose is to show, inversely, how

the orthodoxy of our statements with regard to the mystery of the Incarnation. This mystery is the central mystery of our religion; it projects a vivifying light over all our beliefs and over all our principles of behavior. However, there are many teachings of our Faith with no apparent relationship to any thought of the Virgin. So many errors have been condemned by the Church over the course of the centuries whose refutation did not imply any mention of some Marian doctrine!

Yet, even for those teachings, Mary acts as guardian of the Faith. That is because those who habitually live in her company or, at least, voluntarily turn to her, acquire a sense, an instinct, which averts them from any doctrinal error and helps them intuit an orthodox attitude.

Teachers of a science or of an art, in order to discover what is true or beautiful in their specialty, possess, in addition to a rational method, a kind of special sense, a second nature, which enables them to immediately distinguish, without recourse to rules or principles, the true from the false, the harmonious from the unbalanced. This special sense is innate, in part, or at least presupposes innate

---

devotion to Mary contributes to the acquisition of this sense of faith.

dispositions; it is partly acquired through practice, under favorable conditions.

Faith, deposited in us with the supernatural life we have received in Baptism, can also develop and flower into a "sense of faith." This has been defined as "the supernatural intuiting of the believer, fruit of the vigor of his faith and of the gifts of the Holy Spirit by which one is enabled to discern, in communion with the Church, the implications of a revealed truth proposed as an object of faith by the Magisterium."[49]

The gifts of the Holy Spirit by which this sense of faith is exercised are, above all: the gift of understanding, which bestows the ability to sound the depths of the content of a revelation; the gift of knowledge, which enables us to discern the true from the false; the gift of wisdom, which leads us to savor and love wisdom, and develops in us a kind of con-naturality with wisdom.[50] This faith and these gifts are perfected by the intensity of the life of faith and by the presence of certain dispositions which favor their free development.

A true devotion to Mary, then, especially a life of intimacy with her, is an excellent

---

49 Dillenschneider, *Ibid.*, p. 327.
50 Dillenschneider, *Ibid.*, p. 323ff.

method — undoubtedly the best — for acquiring this sense of faith. That is because true devotion to Mary: 1) naturally supposes the constant exercise of the virtue of faith; 2) provides us, in Mary, with a great model of the life of faith; 3) constantly recalls to us the great truths which are at the basis of a life of faith; 4) creates the dispositions of humility, obedience, purity, and love which favor the gifts of understanding, knowledge, and wisdom, by means of which the sense of faith is practiced.

Devotion to Mary Implies the Constant Exercise of the Life of Faith

Mary has meaning only in the order of faith. It is from Jesus that we receive our Christian faith. But we can be interested in Jesus for a number of reasons that have nothing to do with faith. We might see in Him the prophet of a new social, or moral, or philosophical doctrine; or a hero, or a genius, or a martyr of a bountiful utopia; or a charismatic leader who attracted the crowds as no one else ever had — a type of superior humanity which arouses admiration and love.

Mary has nothing of that. From the natural point of view, she was a pious, modest, loving, young girl who became the Mother of Jesus. She lived in obscurity with her Son for thirty years in the small and unremarkable town of Nazareth. She remained there during the glorious period of her Son's life. She was present at His death and then disappeared without anyone knowing for sure where or when she died.

Mary is irrelevant to those who do not believe in the divinity of Jesus. What she is, she is only in the order of faith. Her greatness as Mother of God, her privileges, her functions at the side of her Son on earth and in Heaven, our trust, our love, all the manifestations of our devotion toward her — all these have meaning only in the order of faith. If you encounter a scholar or an artist in a great church during a solemn function, you would not know for sure whether it is faith or snobbery or art that brought him there. If you see him praying the Rosary before a statue of the Virgin, you are sure of being in the presence of a believer.

Mary, Our Model of the Life of Faith

If Mary teaches us to believe, it is not only because, near her, we necessarily find ourselves in a supernatural element, but also because she is our model and our teacher *par excellence* in the life of faith. For the other natural and supernatural virtues (except for hope), it is Jesus who is our Model and our Teacher. But He cannot be as such for faith, because He saw divine realities face to face, and such vision excludes faith. With regard to the realities which we must believe without seeing them, which we must believe because God has revealed them, our ideal exemplar is Mary.

When Mary comes to visit her cousin, Elizabeth says: "Blessed are you who have believed!" In fact, Mary had to believe in such strange realities that no saint of the Old or of the New Testaments ever had to make an act of faith of this magnitude! She had to believe that she would become a mother while still remaining a virgin; that her Son would not only be the "super-man" whom His contemporaries, the Jews, awaited as Messiah, but the very Son of God and that, consequently, she would have the same Son in common with the heavenly Father. She had to believe that, since she would be mother through a miracle of the Holy Spirit, she was to leave it to God to reveal her mysterious maternity to her fiancé. She had to believe that her Son would be seated on the throne of David though He found no housing in the city of His royal ancestor. She had to believe that He would be obliged to flee at night from the menacing usurper of His throne, and that He would have to work as a common laborer in a little town of Galilee. She had to believe, above all, that when He died, tortured on a gibbet, He would reign without end.

It would only be when she saw Him resurrected and rising into the heavens to sit at the right of the Father that she would know how truly and marvelously the prophecy of Gabriel was realized. Yet, confronted with the obscure and inconceivable realities presented to her, she did not hesitate. She only asked what God desired of her and she simply embraced his will: "Behold I am the handmaid of the Lord; let it be done to me according to your word!" When the events appear to contradict the promises so brutally, she does not complain; she does not object. She accepts the facts without understanding them; she is content with meditating upon them in her heart so as to fully enter into the divine plan. At such a school, who could not find it easy to believe God even when appearances seem at extreme variance with the affirmations of faith?

The Practice of Devotion to Mary and the Great Truths of Faith

Some manifestations of devotion to Mary are especially suited for intensifying this life of faith. There is, first of all, the Rosary, the most popular practice of devotion to Mary, the most frequently and emphatically recommended by Popes in more recent times (and by Mary herself at Fatima). It places us in a climate of faith at each decade, especially at the very mention of the most fundamental mysteries of our religion.[51] This method recalls each of the mysteries to our mind and to our heart, and awakens a consciousness of them in the various situations of life.

First, there are the Joyful Mysteries, centered on the Incarnation. They remind us that God became one of us whereas, for most people, God runs the risk of being only an abstract and distant idea. Then the Sorrowful Mysteries, which retrace the events of the Passion and Death of Jesus, and of our Redemption. They teach us that suffering, rather than distressing us, should be accepted with love for the One who wished to suffer so much for us. This should help us to contribute to our own salvation and to the salvation of those who are dear to us. And the Glorious Mysteries, which raise our sights toward Heaven where Christ has preceded us and awaits us, in order to render us infinitely happy in the company of the Father and of the Spirit and of Mary. We will be all the happier with Them

---

[51] In some regions, each mystery is recalled ten times in each decade, in the middle of each Hail Mary. Hail, Mary ... of your womb, Jesus, whom you conceived of the Holy Spirit. Holy Mary ... ; ... whom you carried to Elizabeth. Holy Mary ... ; etc.

for having suffered all the more with Them, with greater resignation and love for Them.

In summation, the fifteen mysteries of the Rosary {the five Luminous Mysteries were added only long after the death of Fr. Neubert} are precisely among the truths of our religion which are most helpful to living our Faith. All else being equal, there is certainly more tranquil, loving, vital, and active faith among the people who generally pray the Rosary than among those who have lost or never had such a practice.

Pilgrimages are another great manifestation of devotion to Mary. When making pilgrimages to her great sanctuaries, doesn't Mary also give us a particularly lively sense of supernatural realities? We do not see her; but she is there. We can, so to speak, feel her presence; the supernatural becomes natural. What pilgrim to Lourdes or to Fatima or to Banneux has not been deeply moved, and returned home with a stronger or restored faith?

Definitions of Mary's Privileges and the Institution of Her Feasts

Such exceptional facts at certain moments in the Church's history aroused an exceptionally lively renewal of faith. For example, we can cite the definition of the dogmas of the Divine Maternity in 431, the Immaculate Conception in 1854, and the Assumption in 1950.

Ages ago, in the year 431, the definition of the Divine Maternity of Mary touched the highest point of our Faith because then there was question of the very person of Jesus. The other two dogmas only had to do with the special privileges of Mary; but their effect was to revivify and strengthen the entire ensemble of essential teachings of the Catholic religion.

On December 8, 1854, in the presence of an immense crowd from all corners of the earth, Pius IX defined the dogma of the Immaculate Conception of the Mother of God. The entire Catholic world welcomed the papal declaration with respect and enthusiasm. It was, in practice, a recognition of the papal infallibility, not yet officially defined; it would facilitate the solemn definition at the Vatican Council of 1870. It is clear, of course, that the doctrinal infallibility of the Pope is one of the most powerful gifts that God has given to his Church to support the true Faith. To show this, we need only take note of the ongoing disintegration of traditional teachings among the Protestant sects.

But it is not only indirectly, by way of its proclamation but, directly, by its very object, that the dogma of the Immaculate Conception was to be a powerful support for the faith of the faithful. Toward the time of its proclamation, as a consequence of concurrent philosophical, social, political, and economic issues — materialism and rationalism were triumphant. The cult of materialism, of pleasure, of money, of the life of the senses was substituted for the worship of God preached by Christ. Secret sins (and even public ones, if they were not too shocking) were being accepted as normal. Similar situations had been seen more than once in the history of Christianity. But, formerly, sin was called sin and there was hope for repentance before appearing in God's awesome presence. Now, the very notion of sin, of a judging God, or of an afterlife, were in the process of disappearing.

Confronted, then, with this lot of humanity wishing only to acknowledge matter and striking a rebellious poise against all authority, the Pope presented to the entire world, a human being like us, but all pure and radiant, amidst the acclamations of millions of Catholic voices and transports of joy such as the world had not seen for centuries. She is such, because there is not the least shadow of sin in her; because she had always lived in the spirit; because she sought only God. And, behold, since that moment even to our days, the Immaculate Virgin continues to arouse the enthusiasm of Catholic hearts to purity and to total self-giving to God.

A little less than a century after the definition of the Immaculate Conception by Pius IX, the dogma of the bodily Assumption of Mary into Heaven was defined by Pius XII on November 1, 1950, during the Holy Year. He, himself, in words immediately preceding the text of the definition, indicated the teachings of the Faith which the definition should recall and inculcate with greater force:

1) Practical faith for peace and love among people in their union in the Mystical Body of Christ under one Mother only: "We firmly hope that this proclamation and solemn definition of the Assumption will contribute significantly to the progress of concord among the peoples, for it will render glory to the most Holy Trinity to whom the Virgin Mary is united by such special ties. …"

2) The importance of a life consecrated to God and to neighbor: "It must also be hoped that, in reflecting on the glorious examples of Mary, people may be ever more persuaded of the value of human life when it is entirely consecrated to the

accomplishment of the will of the heavenly Father and to devotedness to all our neighbors."

3) The sublime end to which our soul and our body are destined: Indeed, faith in the Assumption of Mary into Heaven affirms and renders faith in our own resurrection more real.

As to the various feasts of the Virgin, each one underlines a truth of the Faith and the help which Mary offers to human beings to live the life of faith in a more effective manner.

Dispositions Favoring the Acquisition of the Sense of Faith

For faith to grow and to achieve this sense of faith, the presence of certain favorable conditions is needed, particularly the dispositions of humility and simplicity, purity and love.

Humility and Simplicity

To believe means to accept a truth without seeing it, without having acquired it through the natural enlightenment of our own insight. Proud minds are incapable of making this admission of impotence, this submission to a superior authority. One of the most common causes for rejection of certain truths of the Faith is pride. God reveals himself only to the humble, to the simple. "At that very moment, He rejoiced in the Holy Spirit and said, 'I give you praise, Father, Lord of heaven and earth, for although you have hidden these things from the wise and the learned, you have revealed them to the childlike. Yes Father, such has been your gracious will.'"[52] Devotion to Mary pre-supposes or creates the spirit of humility and of simplicity. To honor a Woman who did nothing outstanding during her lifetime; to have recourse to her in order to go to God instead of addressing ourselves directly to the Most High — these are acts of humility and of simplicity natural to the child of Mary.

Besides, the entire life of this Woman was but a continuous act of submission to truths she did not understand and to commands stranger than reason. Near her, we learn to love humility and blind submission to the word of God.

Purity

Matters of purity are also intimately tied to matters of faith. "Blessed are the pure of heart, for they shall see God."[53] They shall see him face to face after this

---

52 Lk 10:21.
53 Mt 5:8.

life; but even in this life, they see him in a certain manner through the light of faith.

Among Christian peoples, so long as youth remains pure, there are generally no difficulties with regard to faith. But if they regress and commit faults against chastity, although faith in God is undoubtedly not lost, the sense of the supernatural weakens little by little. Perhaps, by reason of companions or readings or studies, the notion that there is no God suggests itself to the mind. Though generally rejected at first, it runs the risk of gaining ground and may lead to temptations against faith. As long as there are only faults of weakness, sincerely rejected at the time of confession, the evil scarcely goes much further. But, if the will makes its choice in favor of a life of sin, faith becomes a nuisance to be silenced, while seeking to question its rights. Living only in and for the realm of matter, we would no longer have a sense of the divine and would try to persuade ourselves that we are only dealing with a prejudice from the past. Would we still believe? We could not be sure and, soon, we would run the risk of ending up not believing at all.

On the contrary, those who take the means suggested by religion for conserving or recovering purity have much greater ease in preserving their faith, even in the midst of incredible temptations. Among these means, one of the most effective and universally recommended is having recourse to Mary. The thought of the Virgin most beautiful, most pure, most radiant in her purity—whom Christ has given to them as Mother to help them remain faithful to Him—gives them a sense and a love of purity. They invoke her and find out that, in the most dreadful temptations, they emerge victorious. They sense that a more-than-human strength supports their weakness; they have an experience of the divine. Their awareness of living a pure life, a life of profound peace amidst a world that is almost universally corrupt and which proclaims purity to be impossible, is tangible proof to them of the existence of God. They do not believe as formerly, when they had no reason to deny God; they believe because they have had an experience of him.

Love

Our faith, to be true and effective, must be a living faith. To believe is to believe in love.

Those who see in the Christian faith only a philosophy, a *Weltanschauung*—a morality that is primarily negative, made up of prohibitions and threats—understand nothing of our religion. God is love; all his mysteries are mysteries of love: the Incarnation, the Redemption, the coming of the

Holy Spirit, the indwelling of God, eternal life — all these mysteries are mysteries of love, up to and including the mystery of suffering, for it allows us to love more purely and more effectively on earth, and more intensely in Heaven.

To help us to admit not only with reason, but to realize with all our being that our religion is a religion of love, Jesus has given us His Mother as our Mother. Close to her, we sense how God is our Father; how Jesus Christ is our Brother; how the Holy Spirit is a Spirit of love; how our neighbor is also our brother or sister in Jesus and in Mary; how to observe the Commandments. We understand how to love God and neighbor. We learn how suffering purifies us and makes us happy through the union of our sufferings with those of Christ and His Mother. With Mary, our piety is expanded. We work with greater joy; we carry out our duties with greater success. We suffer with greater peace and love. Our faith becomes more consoling, more spontaneous, more sublime, more triumphant! In this way, both faith and experience help us to understand how Mary gives us a "sense of faith" to the ultimate degree.

CHAPTER SEVEN

Miraculous Interventions by Mary in the Support and Diffusion of the Faith

The various aspects which we have so far discussed of the Virgin's activities in favor of the support and propagation of the Faith, enable us to render an account of this Marian activity in a natural way, at least to some extent. But there is another aspect, a directly supernatural one, a miraculous one. Doubtlessly, since faith is a grace and all graces come to us through the Mediatrix of all graces, we may affirm that every act of faith produced by a believer supposes, at its origin, an intervention of the Virgin. But we do not see this intervention; we believe it. Here, we wish to speak of certain authentic interventions of Mary which are altogether miraculous from the outset.

There seems to be no doubt about many of these interventions. A rendition of certain others may have been embellished with legendary details. Yet they, too, are valid testimonies, if not of the facts presented, at least of the tradition which attributes to the Mother of God an efficacious role in the defense and progress of the true Faith.

Saint Gregory Thaumaturgus {Miracle worker; also know as St. Gregory of Neocaesarea}

The oldest of these interventions is mentioned by Saint Gregory of Nyssa in his account of the life of Saint Gregory Thaumaturgus. It seems he heard this story from his grandmother, Blessed Macrina, who had known Gregory Thaumaturgus in his episcopal city of Neocaesarea. Gregory of Nyssa recounts that, one night when Thaumaturgus was reflecting on some controversial points of the Catholic faith, he saw a venerable old man. Frightened at first from the experience, the Saint regained his composure; but then the old man showed him

> … another apparition: a feminine figure of super-human appearance. Frightened once more, he averted his eyes, troubled by the vision and quite unable to look at it … The two apparitions began to speak to one another on the subject of his doubt. In this way, not only was Gregory instructed on the true doctrine of the Faith, but he also learned the names of the two persons, for they were addressing one another by their titles. It was thus, he said, that he learned that the feminine apparition was begging John the Evangelist to open up the mystery of religion to the young

man; and John answered that he was ready to
satisfy the Mother of the Lord, for this would
give him great satisfaction. Gregory put down
in writing the Trinitarian formula dictated by
John; it is the Trinitarian Creed which bears
his name.[54]

In the Middle Ages we have the Order of Our
Lady of Mercy for the Redemption of Captives,
the first religious family of men, it would seem,
giving mention to the Virgin in its name. It had
been founded to ransom Christian slaves from the
Turks, for they were in great danger of losing their
faith. According to the Breviary,[55] it owed its origin
to an apparition of Mary to Saint Peter of Nola. The
Saint had come to make a pilgrimage to the Virgin
in her sanctuary of Montserrat. There, while he was
praying before her statue, Mary appeared to him and
expressed her ardent desire for him to establish an
Order that would undertake this work. Peter went to

---

54 *De Vita S. Gregorii Thaumaturgi.* PG vol. 46, col.
909, 912. The authenticity of St. Gregory's panegyric
is generally admitted. But some doubt on the matter
has been raised more recently (Laurentin, *Court traité
de théologie mariale*, p. 161 [English tr.: *Queen of
Heaven. A Short Treatise on Marian Theology*, Dublin-
London 1956]). In any case, the remark made earlier
applies also to this story. It proves, at the least, that in
the 4th or 5th century, a miraculous intervention of the
Virgin in favor of orthodoxy was seen as quite natural.

55 Jan. 28.

consult his confessor, Saint Raymond of Penyafort, who had just received the same message from the Mother of God. Together they went to King James I of Aragon whose cooperation they would need. He, too, had received an identical message from Mary. This is how the Order originated. In addition to the three ordinary vows of religion, the Mercedarians took a vow to be made captives themselves, as ransom, should funds to free the Christians be in default.

This account seems to be an "embellished legend of an established fact which, perhaps, can be simplified as enlightenment to Saint Peter of Nola from the Mother of God. The mission to found an Order was confided to him for the release of Christian captives, with the vow of rendering up his own life, as Christ had done for the human race."[56]

The Order contributed greatly to preserving the faith of a large number of Christians who had fallen into the hands of the Turks.

Our Lady of Bourguillon, Guardian of the Faith

The following is another intervention of Mary which favorably upholds the true Faith, and equally contains something of the miraculous.

---

56 *Maria. Etudes sur le Sainte Vierge*, vol. 2, p. 726.

On the promontory dominating the city of Fribourg {Switzerland} on the east, there is a beautiful little chapel called Our Lady of Bourguillon. No matter what time one might go there, the faithful will be found in prayer, eyes raised to a lighted niche above the main altar. A statue of the Virgin holding her Son on her left arm, and a scepter in her right hand, is enshrined there. We can distinctly see the head of Mary and that of her Child, both wearing crowns of gold, and the body of the statue vested in brocaded garments.

Mary's face is serious, yet illuminated by a gentle, maternal smile. It is turned slightly to the left, gazing at her children in prayer before her.

The base of the niche is covered with gilded hearts, military medals, and other such objects. In arch-form above the Virgin is the inscription, *Gardienne de la Foi* (*Guardian of the Faith*). If we look at the walls of the nave, we see that they are completely covered to the ceiling with ex-votos of various sizes in white marble, expressing gratitude to Mary in a number of different languages.

In the Middle Ages, this site had been utilized as a leprosarium. It was the chapel for lepers. One of them had sculpted the Virgin in the niche. But the inscription around the Virgin's head recalls a more recent event.

In the 16th century, Protestantism had junctured from Germany to Switzerland and was making menacing strides. The original cantons had remained faithful to the traditional Faith, but almost all the others had transitioned to the Reformation. The Canton of Fribourg had remained Catholic; but there was great danger that it might follow the example of the other cantons surrounding it on all sides. To the north was Basle and Berne nearby, to the east; Lausanne and Geneva to the south; Neuchâtel to the west. And the circle was growing ever tighter. Besides, the religious practice of the Fribourgeois (citizens of Fribourg) was much affected by the laxity of the times. In the city of Fribourg barely twenty Catholics fulfilled their Easter duty.

The magistrates, who held to the Faith of their ancestors, became worried. What could be done? They had maintained their confidence in Mary and they took a vow that, weather permitting, the citizens of Fribourg would go in procession every two weeks to the sanctuary of Our Lady of Bourguillon. The good Virgin heard their supplication: Protestantism was halted at the borders of the canton!

In 1580, she sent them Saint Peter Canisius, her most illustrious servant of that period, whose great work on the Mother of God, *De Virgine Incomparabili*, had just appeared. He spent the remainder of his life in Fribourg and died there in 1597. From the very beginning, the Saint felt attracted to the holy chapel of Bourguillon. He made it a ritual to go there every day and to preach often, with forceful conviction, on the goodness and the power of the Virgin. He assured the pilgrims who came to pray there, that "Mary works miracles in this shrine."

He founded three Sodalities of the Blessed Virgin in the city of Fribourg: one for men, called the Bourgeois; one for women, called the Ladies; and one for students.

The Guardian of the Faith suggested to him yet another means of strengthening the faith of his beloved Fribourgeois in their loyalty to the Catholic faith. He founded a school, entrusted to the priests of the Society of Jesus (the celebrated *Collège St-Michel*), which was to assure the Catholic education of all the governing classes of the canton. Almost all the future priests, religious, magistrates, officers, writers, and scholars of the Canton of Fribourg since then, and even today, were educated in that school according to the doctrine and spirit of the Catholic Church.

The Saint dreamed of an even more powerful work for the defense and expansion of the Faith: a Catholic university. His desire would be realized by one of the greatest magistrates ever produced from the canton: Georges Python. This latter, in 1889, despite the poverty of the area, succeeded in providing this locale with a university, one almost unique in its kind: it is at once a state university, a Catholic university, and an international university. Not only the professors of the Faculty of Theology, confided to the Dominicans, but those of the other faculties as well are Catholics, recruited from among scholars of different European countries, and even elsewhere. Many of them enjoy a worldwide reputation.

The enrollment, as well, is not limited to students from Fribourg or the surrounding Swiss cantons only. They come from all over the world to study under Catholic teachers in a Catholic spirit. Scholars and leaders, proud to have been formed at the University of Fribourg, may be found in positions of high rank in all centers of the old and the new worlds.

It is also at Fribourg that international religious, scientific, or social congresses are frequently held. In 1884, even before the foundation of the University, Bishop Mermillod founded *l' Union*

Catholique d'Etudes Sociales de Fribourg (The Fribourg Catholic Union of Social Studies). "It undertook the development of a complete Catholic social doctrine, and its work was later revived by the Sovereign Pontiff. In 1891, *Rerum Novarum* was an official statement of Catholic doctrine on the rights of the individual."[57]

The city of Fribourg was scarcely more than a village in the 16th century and the capital of a canton whose size was less than a third of the bordering {French} territory of Doubs. Yet, because its magistrates, fearful of the growth of the Reformation, had entrusted it to the Virgin of Bourguillon, Guardian of the Faith, it not only became the unconquerable bastion of the Catholic faith in its own small region, but a hearth radiating light and Catholic practice throughout Switzerland, Europe, and the entire world; it became a "second Rome," as it has been called, not without reason. Is it not the Guardian of the Faith who worked this miracle?

Origin of the Society of Mary (Marianists)

The ancient enemies of the Catholic Church still professed a certain faith in a divinity: the Turks adored a unique God and rendered him a faithful

---

57 Jean Valarche, in *Hommages aux Catholique suisses*, [1954.]

cult; the Protestants laid claim to Jesus Christ. Other enemies of the Church had arisen, determined to remove from the human race all faith in a revealed God. In the 18th century, there was the clique of self-proclaimed *philosophers*, continually spewing ridicule on all supernatural religion. Moreover, there was the Great Revolution with its bloody battle against all religious inclinations.

It was then that the Virgin Mary once again intervened in raising up new religious societies as added weapons in defense of the Faith which seemed about to disappear from the face of the earth.

Kindly permit me to give special mention to one among them: the Society of Mary, in whose foundation, the goal of helping the Virgin in her mission as Guardian of the Faith appeared with particular clarity and perception.

Its founder, William Joseph Chaminade, sensed being called to the religious life early on, but he had not given the least thought to founding a new order. In fact, several times he had sought to enter some society with which he was familiar. But, at each attempt, it was evident to him that God did not want him there. In the meantime, he had been ordained to the priesthood several years before the beginning of the Great Revolution, and devoted himself to the education of youth. In 1791, he rejected the schismatic oath and resolved to carry on his sacred ministry in hiding in the city of Bordeaux until 1797, when he was forced into exile.

He went to Saragossa {Spain}. There he passed long hours before the miraculous Virgin in the sanctuary of Our Lady of the Pillar, asking her to show him the means of reviving the Christian faith in his fatherland. In some extraordinary way, he received special insights from her which could be condensed to the following three: 1) It was Mary's mission to lead the battle against Satan and his followers, and this mission would manifest itself in an especially notable way in the new era which had just begun. 2) For the accomplishment of this mission, she desired the cooperation of two new religious societies of men and women which would be dedicated to her without reserve, and would fight in her name for the triumph of Christ and His Church. 3) It was he whom Mary had chosen to muster up both of these elite troops.

The founder would express these ideas in a circular letter on the occasion of the first approbation of his work by the Holy See {1839}:

> Every period in the history of the Church has its record of the combats and glorious victories

of the august Mother of God. Ever since
the Lord sowed dissension between her and
the serpent, she has constantly vanquished
the world and the powers of hell.[58] All the
heresies, the Church tells us, have been
subdued by the Blessed Virgin Mary and,
little by little, she has reduced them to the
silence of oblivion.

This is Mary's apostolic mission in general and,
behold, her special mission in current times as well:

In our own day the great prevailing heresy
is religious indifference that dulls the souls
of individuals, and reduces them to a state
of torpid egoism and moral stagnation. …
The divine torch of faith is burning low
and dying in the heart of Christendom;
virtue is becoming increasingly rare and
is disappearing, while vice is rampant and
spreading with horrific fury. It seems that
the time is near when we will witness general
defection and all but universal apostasy, as has
been foretold.

And yet, this sad but true picture of our times
does not discourage us by any means. Mary's
power has not been lessened. It is our firm

---

58 {See Gn 3:15, Vulgate version.}

belief that she will subdue this heresy like all the others, for she continues to be, as ever, the incomparable Woman, the Woman of promise who is to crush the head of the infernal serpent. Jesus himself, who in His public utterances always addressed her by this great name, would thereby teach us that she is the hope, the joy, and the life of the Church, and the terror of hell. To her, therefore, is reserved a great victory in our day, for to her belongs the glory of saving the Faith from destruction with which we are being threatened.

Practical Conclusion: Let Us Go to Help Her in This Mission!

We, who have come to understand this providential design, have hastened to offer our feeble services to Mary in order to labor under her direction and to combat at her side. We have enlisted under her banner as her soldiers and her ministers, and we have bound ourselves by a special vow of *stability* to assist her with all our strength until the end of our life, in her noble struggle against the powers of hell. And, just as an eminent religious order has chosen the name and standard of Jesus, so we have enrolled under the name and standard of Mary; and we are willing to go wherever she may send us to spread her cult and, through it, the kingdom of God in souls.

This is really the distinguishing mark and family trait of our two Orders. We are in a particular manner the auxiliaries and the missionaries of the Blessed Virgin in the great work of the reform of morals and in the preservation and propagation of the Faith.[59]

In addition to the vow of stability, Father Chaminade had given his new religious a fifth vow, expressing even more clearly their mission to teach and to propagate the Faith under the direction of Mary, called "the vow to teach the Faith and Christian practice."[60]

---

59 Chaminade, *Letter* no. 1163.

60 Since Rome no longer authorized a fifth vow of religion (and , a fourth, only with difficulty!) the vow of teaching was denied the Society of Mary in 1864 by the Sacred Congregation of Bishops and Regulars. The vow of stability was conceded only because of its very special Marian sense.

B. Mary and the Apostolate of Life

More extensive and even more constant than Mary's role as Guardian of the Faith is her mission as Mother and Educator of souls. However, we can only infinitesimally know how this mission is carried out. Most of the time, in fact, everything occurs in the secret of the heart, between the soul and Mary. The soul itself is often only slightly aware of the influence it receives from its Mother in Heaven.

CHAPTER EIGHT

During the First Centuries: Mary, Model, and Helper

Mary, Model

This more or less obscure awareness of Mary's action upon the soul was often the case in the first centuries of the Christian era when focus on the Mother of Jesus was mostly occasioned by Christological heresies. However, at that time, we can already recognize her twofold influence on the Christian life, as Model and as Helper.

The high esteem placed on the practice of virginity during the first Christian centuries naturally drew attention to Mary whose virginity had been preserved through a singularly, miraculous intervention, while conceiving and giving birth to the Son of God. It was to honor Him that generous persons embraced a life of complete chastity. As Origen already said in the third century: "It was logical that the first fruit of a life of purity should be Jesus among men and Mary among women. For it would be unbecoming to attribute the title 'first among virgins' to someone other than Mary."[61]

We know that Saint Ambrose outlined a visibly striking image of the Virgin Mary in order to present her to Christian virgins as Model of the virtues they should emulate. In shaping this profile, Ambrose took inspiration from an earlier document attributed to Saint Athanasius who had already presented Mary as ideal Exemplar for those who consecrated their virginity to Christ.

Here again, it is a matter of influence reserved for chosen souls. Later, after the image of the Virgin had become more familiar to the Christian people, such influence would become more prominent and widespread.

Mary, as Helper

There is another sanctifying influence which the Virgin exercised in earlier centuries on all categories

---

61 *Commentaria in Mattheo.*, X, 17.

of Christians: her favorable intervention for those who invoked her.

We have already seen that the invocation of Mary dates from those first centuries, as evidenced by Saint Gregory of Nazianzen's story about the virgin, Justina, and the fragment of papyrus containing the *Sub tuum*.[62]

The intercessory power of the Mother of Jesus is often mentioned by the Greek Fathers, particularly on the occasion of their homilies on her Assumption. Saint Germain of Constantinople and Saint John Damascene often revert to it in impassioned terms. In the West, the Latin Fathers were teaching it from the eighth century with Ambrose Autpert (d. 784);[63] this was four centuries before Saint Bernard. We know well with what eloquence and persuasion the Abbot of Clairvaux exhorted his listeners to have recourse to the Star of the Sea in all their difficulties.

Confidence in the all-powerful, heavenly Mediatrix naturally leads to appealing to her. This appeal to Mary, with a view to obtaining pardon from sin, strength to overcome temptation, grace to make

---

[62] See chap. 5, above. {On the *Sub tuum* cf. Mother Maria Francesca Perillo, F.I., *Sub Tuum Praesidium. Incomparable Marian Praeconsium*, in *Mary at the Foot of the Cross IV*, New Bedford MA 2004, pp. 138-169.}

[63] *Maria. Etudes sur le Sainte Vierge*, vol. 2, p. 551.

progress in virtue, imitating her and her divine Son — even abstracting from the reality of her intercessory power — works psychologically on those who address themselves to Mary. Such a prayer greatly helps to leave sin behind, to live a truly Christian life, and to resolutely strive for holiness, because it presupposes or creates the will to correct oneself and to make progress. In other words, for those who believe in the reality of Mary's mediation, it is evident that the power of grace is added to the initial good intention of Mary's clients.

CHAPTER NINE

Mary and the Formation of Religious Apostolic Societies

Qualified Apostolic Workers

In Christ's Church, people are not left to their own personal initiative in working out their conversion and sanctification. Before His Ascension, Jesus confided to the apostles and to their successors the charge of ministering to the faithful in His place. That charge consists of instructing them, directing them, and procuring for them special graces in view of certain particular needs by way of the Sacraments. It is the pope, the bishops, the priests, the religious who are charged with this very special, apostolic mission; in great part, the ruin or the resurgence of innumerable souls depends upon the fidelity of the appointed ministers.

It is easily understood that the Virgin has a special interest in these official apostles of the Church and that, on the other hand, it is extremely important for them to have her intervention in their apostolic work.

Why Begin With the Religious?

Until more recent centuries, we have relatively little by way of specific documentation on the place appropriated to the Virgin in the movement of the diocesan clergy among the faithful. There is a great deal more documentation on religious, and for various reasons. The action of the parish clergy is generally made on a person-to-person basis and is not inscribed in historical records. That of religious orders is more of a special undertaking, carried out in a sense, as an army preparing for battle {to win souls}. It is almost uniquely the religious who have left writings on their activity. There is also, undoubtedly, the fact that they tend to be (both because of their vocation and the facilities available to their way of life) more concerned with intimacy with our Lord and His Mother. They seem to have more quickly and more enthusiastically understood Mary's role in their twofold spiritual and apostolic activity.

We begin, therefore, with a consideration of the role which the Virgin has played in the activity of religious with regard to others. Also, since the religious have exercised a sometimes considerable influence on the diocesan clergy within their area, it will later be easier for us to see the place she occupied in the apostolate of the parish clergy.

Is There a Distinction Between Explicitly Marian Orders, and Others?

With regard to the role attributed to Mary's intervention by diverse religious orders in their apostolic activity, it might at first seem that we should separate them into two categories: orders whose very names proclaim their belonging to Mary, and those who have names with no allusion to the Mother of Jesus. But such distinction has, in fact, little basis. There are orders, such as the Society of Jesus or the Society of the Redemptorists, who have given such an importance to the Marian apostolate that it might well be asked whether any religious society directly placed under the name of Mary has done as much.

We can say that, from the tenth century onward, and perhaps even earlier, all the religious families distinguished themselves by a special devotion to the Mother of Jesus, and for various reasons. Most of them were founded by saints, great servants of Mary as are all the saints, who bequeathed their spirit to their disciples. Or, in some cases, it was Mary herself who asked a particular servant of God to found a new order and, naturally, the members of such an order are pleased to remember this origin. Or the order might have produced a saint, a great servant of Mary, who created a tradition of Marian devotion within the religious family. Perhaps, at some moment in its history, the order was solemnly consecrated to Mary.

Besides, the religious of every order are obliged to tend to perfection, i.e., to the closest possible union with Christ, and will have understood early on, through personal experience, that Mary is a marvelously effective help for realizing such union. Already in the seventh century, Saint Ildephonse spoke of service to Mary in terms of such tenderness that we find them entirely natural from the mouth of Saint Louis Marie de Montfort a thousand years later, "With what ardor," Ildephonse wrote, "I desire to become the servant of this Lady; what joy I find in the yoke of this service! … I wish her to command me so that I may be the servant of her Son. I wish to serve her that her Son may command me … For whatever we do for the Handmaid, we do for the Master. What we give to the Mother redounds to the Son. To serve the Queen is to honor the King."[64]

Those who have experienced the exceptional efficacy of recourse to Mary in their personal life, will naturally have recourse to her in their apostolic activity. Not only will they invoke her assistance but, to the people they evangelize, they will recommend the same recourse to the Virgin in all the difficulties of life, for example, as Saint Bernard did. Those most devoted to the Virgin will do it more frequently — out of the abundance of the heart, the mouth speaks — and their examples and successes will stimulate their confreres to employ the same methods.

As to the religious societies that chose to take Mary's name as their own, they are numerous since the

---

[64] *Liber de virginitate perpetua Mariae.* PL, vol. 96, col. 108.

beginning of the 19th century. "From 1820 until the present day, there are more than 700, counting only those of women; and the year 1950 saw as many as sixteen new foundations."[65] Obviously, it was in great part the Marian movement, aroused by the definition of the Immaculate Conception, which contributed to this fact.

It goes without saying that the members of these societies depend in a special way on the Mother of God, both for their work of personal sanctification and for their apostolic enterprises, and that they feel obliged to contribute to the diffusion of Mary's cult. Some of these societies seem to only see a general relationship between their work and their apostolate; others see deeper relationships between their consecration to the Coredemptrix and their apostolic mission.

It is clearly impossible to underline the role which each of these various orders and congregations of religious women and men attribute to Mary in their work among the faithful. We can find precious information on that subject in the directives of the various religious families on devotion to Mary, published in volumes two and three of *Maria*. Here,

---

65 R. Laurentin, in *Maria. Etudes sur le Sainte Vierge*, vol. 3, 19.

we must be satisfied to note briefly the particular means employed by some of them, as well as the predominant character of their Marian apostolate.

The Order of Saint Benedict[66]

The oldest of the religious orders in the West, the Order of Saint Benedict, is naturally the first which distinguished itself by its cult of Mary. The Benedictine monks have contributed greatly to the study of the mystery of the Mother of God. The names of the great mariologists before the 13th century — Autpert, Pascasus Radbert, Rupert of Deutz, Saint Anselm — are all names of Benedictine monks. If they have reveled in the grandeurs of the Virgin, it is because the very person of Mary attracted them. We especially know of Saint Anselm's tender devotion to the Virgin.

One branch of the Benedictine family, that of Cîteaux,[67] is specially noted for its love for the Mother of Jesus and its zeal in spreading devotion to her. The most illustrious chanter of the Virgin during the Middle Ages was Saint Bernard, a Cistercian.

---

66 J. Leclercq, in *Maria. Etudes sur le Sainte Vierge*, vol. 2, 547ff.

67 J. B. Auniord, in *Maria. Etudes sur le Sainte Vierge*, vol. 2, 579ff.

The study and preaching of the grandeurs and the goodness of Mary were not the only means of Marian apostolate for the Benedictines. Through their composition of hymns, and their collections of prayers and of miracles attributed to Mary's intercession, as also through works of art, the monks and nuns — for instance, Saint Gertrude and Saint Mechtilde — contributed much to spreading a loving and trusting devotion to the Mother of God and, in consequence, to the sanctification of others.

The Order of the Friars Preachers[68]

From early in the 13th century, new great orders arose in the Church. The two most illustrious were the Franciscans and the Dominicans. The founder of the latter, Saint Dominic, and his first disciples, were noted servants of Mary. The lives of the saints and of the blessed of the Order illustrate their devotion to the Virgin and the favors, authenticated or not, they are said to have received from her.

The Dominicans propagated certain Marian practices, like the repetition of the Hail Mary hundreds of times a day and, eventually, the rosary with meditation on its mysteries, thanks especially to Blessed Alan de la Roche. Saint Pius

---

68 Andre Duval, in *Maria. Etudes sur le Sainte Vierge*, vol. 2, 737.

V, the Dominican Pope, granted them the exclusive privilege of directing confraternities of the Holy Rosary. Through the diffusion of that prayer, the disciples of Saint Dominic exercised, and continue to exercise, great influence on the faith and the religious life of the faithful. We are well aware of how often and with what conviction the more recent Popes, especially Leo XIII, Pius XI, and Pius XII recommended its recitation, and how Mary herself insisted on it at Fatima.

The Franciscan Order[69]

A simple, enthusiastic, impassioned soul, the "soul of a poet and of a knight," Saint Francis of Assisi was instinctively drawn toward the Virgin Mary.

His followers inherited his simple and ardent devotion to the Mother of Jesus and find their happiness in speaking of her grandeurs and her goodness. They invented and disseminated various practices of devotion to her, such as the Angelus, the Saturday consecrated to Mary, and a "seraphic Rosary" {Seven Joys of Our Lady}.

Their forcefulness in defending the Immaculate Conception naturally enlivened their zeal for

---

69 Jean de Dieu, OFMCap, in *Maria. Etudes sur le Sainte Vierge*, vol. 2, 783ff.

devotion to Mary. They founded confraternities of the Immaculate Conception. In the 16th century in Spain, they spread the devotion of the "holy slavery," which Saint Louis Marie de Montfort would preach with great enthusiasm in France, a century later.

After the founding of the great apostolic orders of the 16th century, it is very difficult to form a precise idea today of the immense influence exercised by the Franciscan Order in Europe and in the missions. Among the reasons for their success, devotion to Mary occupied, and still occupies, a place apart. The great Franciscan proselytizer of the 18th century, Leonard of Port-Maurice, acknowledged that sinners who remained impenitent following his sermons on such frightening truths as death, judgment, and hell, were transformed when he began to speak to them of the Blessed Virgin.

The Order of the Servites of Mary[70]

This order, also founded in the 13th century, recognized only the Most Blessed Mary as its founder. "She herself explains the reason why she raised up this order: for her service, for her glory, for her glorification." Its principal object is "to share especially in her sorrows." Its rule orders its

---

70 G. M. Roschini, OSM, in *Maria. Etudes sur le Sainte Vierge*, vol. 2, 883ff.

preachers never to fail to speak of Mary and, when they conduct a series of sermons, to always give one on her sorrows. It was by preaching on Mary that they exercised a very fruitful apostolate from the beginning, and restored peace to the province of Tuscany which was torn apart by adverse factions. Especially in these later times, the Servite Order has distinguished itself by encouraging the study and development of Marian dogma.

The Society of Jesus[71]

It is the name of Jesus that Saint Ignatius gave to the Order he founded. But the members of this Order have so distinguished themselves by their zeal for the glory of Mary that "it is rightly said" — and other than Jesuits have said so — "that the Society of Jesus could just as legitimately be called the Society of Mary. ... The very enemies of the Society and of the Church reproach it for its Mariology. ... When Pius IX contacted all the dissident sects and invited them to the Vatican Council in 1868, the theologians of Groninque [University of Groningen in the Netherlands] rejected the invitation alleging, among other complaints, that the Roman Church

---

[71] E. Villaret, SJ, in *Maria. Etudes sur le Sainte Vierge*, vol. 2, 935ff.

had allowed Christianity to degenerate into Marianism due to Jesuit influence."

Even before his conversion, Ignatius, "like other knights of his day, had found the Lady of his dreams ... 'She was neither a countess nor a duchess,' he related, 'but of a much more elevated status.'"

He visited the sanctuary of Montserrat {Spain}. "It is there that he made his 'armed watch'; it was there that he hung up his sword at the altar of the Madonna and consecrated himself definitively to the service of the Mother of God." He wrote his *Exercises* there, under Mary's inspiration, often citing her as Helper and Model.

He founded his Society of Jesus on the morning of the Assumption in 1534 at Montmartre {Paris}, in a church dedicated to Mary's sorrows.

"Following the spirit of its founder, [the Society of Jesus] chose Mary for its Lady ... It has recourse to Mary as one who introduces another to Jesus ... It makes Mary the inspiration and the patroness of its activity and of its struggles in the service of Christ. ... It celebrates the feast of the Blessed Virgin Mary, Queen of the Society of Jesus," under the rite of a first class feast.

The Society of Jesus has been the forerunner in what concerns the study and diffusion of Marian dogma. Saint Peter Canisius, after fifteen years of careful research, produced the first great work on the life and privileges of Mary, *De Virgine Maria Incomparabili*, to refute the attacks of heretics against Catholic doctrine about Mary. A systematic work on the collection of questions on Marian theology earned Suarez, another Jesuit, the title of "father of Mariology." It was Passaglia, a Jesuit, whom Pius IX charged with the preparatory work for the definition of the Immaculate Conception. Still another Jesuit, Terrien, around the year 1900, composed the most complete treatise up to that time on the grandeurs of Mary, *La Mère de Dieu et la Mère des Hommes* (*The Mother of God and the Mother of Men*). And it was under the direction of another Jesuit, Hubert du Manoir, that the great Marian encyclopedia, *Maria. Etudes sur le Sainte Vierge,* of the 20th century, was published in five {when completed in 1971, eight} large volumes.

As to their Marian apostolate among the faithful, the Jesuits, according to the expression of Benedict XIV, "brought the name of Mary, together with that of Jesus, to all the shores of the world." Saint Francis Xavier wrote to Saint Ignatius: "I have found that people reject the Gospel whenever I present the

Cross of the Savior but fail to mention the presence of His Mother."

As to the practice of ordinary devotions, the Jesuits have been outstanding in propagating the devotions of the Rosary, the Scapular of Mount Carmel, the Little Office of the Immaculate Conception, the month of Mary, and "holy slavery." There is no doubt that Montfort was introduced to this devotion at their College of Rennes where he made his studies.

As to a special Marian apostolate, the foundation of sodalities of the most Blessed Virgin is due to the Jesuits. These sodalities were to exercise such an apostolic influence that, if they had devoted themselves to no other Marian work, they would still merit a place of honor among the Virgin's apostles.

The Clerks Regular of the Mother of God[72]

Some fifty years after the foundation of the Jesuits, Saint John Leonardi founded the Order of Clerks Regular of the Mother of God, in Lucca {Italy}. The members of that Order preach to the people about

---

[72] Leodegario Picanyl, SP, in *Maria. Etudes sur le Sainte Vierge*, vol. 2, 915ff.

the Blessed Virgin. The sanctuaries of the Virgin are under their tutelage as hearths of Marian piety.

The apostolic zeal of Saint John Leonardi led him to be equally concerned with infidels. He laid the foundation of what would later become the "Propagation of the Faith."

Congregation of the Mother of God[73]

This Society, founded by Saint Joseph Calasanctius was, at first, a branch of the preceding Society. It is dedicated to founding and directing "religious schools," strongly insisting on devotion to the Mother of God in the formation of little children. Pius IX had been one of its pupils.

The Bérullian School[74]

The 17th century was the "great century" for France, not only from the point of view of literature and the other arts, and of political glory, but equally so with regard to the spirituality and the apostolic spirit of its priests. The influence of Cardinal de Bérulle, at the beginning of that century, would be felt by all the great spiritual personages of that period and

---

73 Leodegario Picanyl, SP, in *Maria. Etudes sur le Sainte Vierge,* vol. 2, 925ff.

74 André Rayez, SJ, in *Maria. Etudes sur le Sainte Vierge*, vol. 3, 31ff.

beyond; it continues even now, and will no doubt continue for a long time to come.

Bérulle, theologian of the Incarnation, contemplated the state and the grandeurs of the Word Incarnate with love, and at great length. But it was from Mary that the Son of God wished to take our nature, and He wished to make His Mother like Himself as much as a mere creature can resemble an incarnate God. So, "to speak of Mary is to speak of Jesus, and to honor Mary is to honor Jesus. It is even to honor Jesus in the greatest of His works, for she is the most exalted effect and ornament of the power and preference of Jesus in the order of grace."

Jesus is perpetuated in the priest; but then, Jesus was constituted priest in Mary's womb and wished to associate His Mother in His priestly mission. Therefore, in the formation of priests, Bérulle and his disciples took pleasure in insisting on the intimate and constant relationship which the priest should have with the Mother of Jesus.

If Bérulle and his immediate successors do not seem to have spoken expressly of the Marian apostolate, i.e., an apostolate undertaken directly under the auspices and for the glory of Mary, they have contributed much to it. People like Olier, John Eudes, Grignion de Montfort, and Chaminade are the heirs of his Marian doctrine. It involved a priesthood which necessarily preached Mary and which exercised its apostolate in the name of Mary.

Saint John Eudes and the Congregation of Jesus and Mary[75]

Having entered the Oratory on March 25, 1623, John Eudes took the vow of slavery to Jesus and Mary on March 25th of the following year. Like Bérulle, his teacher, he insists on the intimate unity of Jesus and Mary. "Jesus and Mary are so closely knit together," he said, "that whoever sees Jesus sees Mary; whoever loves Jesus loves Mary; who ever has devotion to Jesus has devotion to Mary."

He especially loved to speak of the Heart of Mary. For him, the Heart of Mary "is the whole mystery of Mary seen under the aspect of love; and devotion to the Heart of Mary is one's entire devotion to the Virgin."

The purpose of this devotion is "to have but a single heart with Jesus and Mary to accomplish the divine will in everything." In a prayer formula which he composed for his Institutes, "he addresses himself to the Hearts of Jesus and Mary in the singular,

---

[75] L. Barbe, in *Maria. Etudes sur le Sainte Vierge*, vol. 3, 163ff.

so intimate is Their union in his eyes. *Ave, cor sanctissimum; Ave, cor mitissimum ...*"[76]

In his missions, he aroused the crowds when preaching of the Heart of Mary. He instituted confraternities destined to perpetuate devotion to that Heart. In 1641, he founded the Order of Our Lady of Charity (women religious); and in 1643, the Congregation of Jesus and Mary, a society of priests — foundations in which, and through which, he continued to spread the devotion so dear to his heart. "Above all," he said to the members of the second group, "I beg of you, my dearly beloved sons, to honor and to have honored in all possible ways, our very good and most lovable Mother, the most holy Mother of Jesus, the well-beloved of God."

He had recourse to another means of spreading devotion to the Heart of Mary: the liturgy. He composed a liturgical office in her honor and, little by little, he was able to have it adopted by all the dioceses of France and many religious orders. On the occasion of his beatification, Pius X proclaimed him "Father, Doctor, and Apostle" of the liturgical cult of the Sacred Hearts of Jesus and Mary.

---

76 {Most Sacred Heart, Most Humble Heart}

Father Olier and Saint-Sulpice[77]

Like his teacher, Cardinal de Bérulle, Father Olier saw everything in religion from the point of view of Our Lord, and he saw the Blessed Virgin indissolubly united to her Son. "It is above all the spiritual life of Jesus in Mary that is the object of Sulpician devotion. Jesus is in Mary in a permanent way through the fullness of His Spirit which He has superabundantly poured out upon her. Every time Olier writes about the Blessed Virgin, and that is very often, he describes this interior life with a tenderly filial love and he explains the means to esteem it and to participate in it."

Through this devotion, we empty ourselves of all that is inordinate within us so that the Spirit of Jesus who lives in Mary may take possession of our soul that we might remain closely united to the Blessed Virgin. The prayer composed by Olier: "O Jesus, living in Mary, …" expresses these dispositions.

There is no question of a Marian apostolate in all of this. But it is clear that a priest, apostle by his very vocation, who becomes another Jesus under the guidance of Mary, will be an eminent apostle.

---

[77] Pierre Pourrat, PSS, in *Maria. Etudes sur le Sainte Vierge*, vol. 3, 153ff.

Saint Vincent de Paul and
the Lazarists {Vincentians}[78]

Saint Vincent de Paul always professed a profound veneration and entire confidence in regard to the Mother of God. He honored her Immaculate Conception in a special way.

He recommended this same attitude to his missionaries: Abelly could, in all truth, affirm of Monsieur Vincent: "The devotion of this holy man toward the Mother of God was abundantly clear in the sermons he gave in her honor and in the missions where he preached. He encouraged his disciples to do the same, and to carefully instruct the people on the obligation of all Christians to honor, serve, and invoke this most blessed Mother of God, and to have recourse to her in their needs and concerns."

"The various works and foundations of Monsieur Vincent took inspiration from the same Marian spirit." These works were numerous confraternities of charity and, especially, the Daughters of Charity, particularly devoted to the mystery of the Immaculate Conception from their very foundation. At the request of the foundress, Louise de Marillac,

---

78 Edmond Crapez, in *Maria. Etudes sur le Sainte Vierge*, vol. 3, 95ff.

Saint Vincent composed an act of consecration to Mary Immaculate for them which, ever since then, they renew every year on December 8th. Notable is the expression: "Most holy and glorious Virgin Mary ..., we beg you most humbly to accept the irrevocable offering of our souls and of our persons, which we dedicate and consecrate to your service and to your love on this feast day, for the remainder of our life and for eternity. We propose to lead others to honor, serve, imitate, and invoke you so as to find favor with God."

It was from among the Daughters of Charity that Mary Immaculate chose her confidant, Saint Catherine Labouré, to reveal devotion to the Miraculous Medal to the world and, in that way, to convert and sanctify millions of souls, as well as create the Sodality of the Children of Mary, an immense army of lay apostles which we will again speak of later.

In the foreign missions of the Lazarists, preaching has always had an important role. "The Blessed Justin de Jacobis, C.M., who died in Africa in 1860 after a fruitful apostolate, wrote to one of his confreres ... "Gratitude to the Immaculate Heart of Mary makes it a duty for me to declare to you what long experience taught me with the greatest certainty. It is that whenever some progress occurs as rapidly and as unexpectedly in the Catholic missions, the Church owes it to the intercession of this pure Virgin who has so much power in Heaven and on earth, and who takes a most lively interest in the extension of the reign of her divine Son."

Saint John Baptist de la Salle and the Brothers of Christian Schools[79]

"Convinced that love for the Son inspires love for His Mother," writes Belain, biographer and friend of de la Salle, "he had at heart a supreme devotion to the most holy Virgin. One of his great pleasures was to defend it and to spread it; his joy was to see Mary's honor increase in the kingdom of Jesus."

He took great care to inculcate this devotion in the Congregation of the Brothers, of which he was Founder; and he expected them, in turn, to continue its development among their students. To this effect, he provided his Congregation with meticulous counsels on the varied ways of teaching the youth to know, honor, invoke, love, and serve their heavenly Mother.

His sons have remained faithful to the spirit of their father. They have composed excellent handbooks

---

79 Georges Rigault, in *Maria. Etudes sur le Sainte Vierge*, vol. 3, 206ff.

designed to give their pupils a solid devotion to Mary. Several of them have merited to be ranked among the most eminent servants of Mary in current times, such as the two Mutien Brothers (uncle and nephew), and Brother Leonard.

If the Brothers of Christian Schools have constituted one of the largest and most flourishing religious societies of men today, and form Christians of solid, active faith throughout the world, it is certainly due in great part to their Marian apostolate.

Saint Louis-Marie de Montfort and the Society of Mary[80]

Born of a profoundly religious family, Louis-Marie Grignion de Montfort, distinguished himself for his piety from his earliest years. While still young, he already showed signs as the future missionary of the rosary. "By means of little gifts and beautiful promises, he drew his little sister, Louise, to reciting the rosary with him."

He took up his studies in the college of the Jesuit Fathers at Rennes; it was there, no doubt, that he was introduced to the devotion of "holy slavery." In 1693 he went to Paris to complete his clerical

---

80 J. M. Hupperts, SMM, in *Maria. Etudes sur le Sainte Vierge*, vol. 3, 251ff.

formation at the seminary of Saint-Sulpice where he encountered the spirituality of Bérulle. Among the seminarians, he organized the Confraternity of Holy Slavery to Mary.

He was ordained in 1700 and embraced the missionary life. He was confirmed in this choice by Pope Clement XI with whom he had consulted, and who conferred upon him the title of Apostolic Missionary.

"Like every missionary, he would teach the Christian life, giving due place to the Blessed Virgin in the supernatural world. If he hoped to elicit contrition, he would point out that devotion to Mary was essential to reparation; if he called the wretched to sanctify their sufferings, he showed Mary standing at the foot of the Cross to sweeten their bitterness with the kindness of her maternal love. To souls dedicated to loving God, he urged them to practice the love of God through the mediation of the Mother of the Head, Mother of the members, Advocate and Mediatrix. To insure their perseverance, he invited them to make a consecration to Mary."

To all sinners and faithful Christians alike, he preached consecration to Mary and the rosary. A Third Order member of the Dominicans, authorized to receive into the confraternity of the rosary all those who desired it, he preached and encouraged the practice of the rosary with incredible conviction, ardor, and success; and he developed extraordinary ways of inculcating this devotion. Immense crowds followed him and were converted. "Never," he said, "has a sinner resisted me when I grabbed him by the collar with my rosary."[81]

He recommended the daily recitation of the rosary as means of perseverance for converted sinners and as means of perfection for faithful souls. As another means of perfection he recommended above all the practice of "holy slavery." By such preaching, he evangelized the western provinces of France and implanted that solid spirit of faith there, which continues to distinguish them in our day {c. 1955}.

In the final years of his life, he put his Marian teachings into writing, particularly in a little untitled work which was later called the *Treatise on True Devotion to Mary*, in which he explained "holy slavery." This manuscript was discovered and published in 1842, and was widely circulated, especially since the beginning of the 20th century, having been translated into practically all the

---

81 By this the Saint meant not that he physically grabbed the sinner, but used the power of the rosary to persuade him.

languages of the world and printed into millions of copies.

In a famous passage at the outset of this work, the Saint describes, in apocalyptic terms, the very special role of Mary in these last days:

> It is through Mary that the salvation of the world began, and it is through Mary that it will be consummated ... In these final times, God wishes to reveal and disclose Mary, the Masterpiece of his hands ... Mary must shine more than ever in mercy, in strength, and in grace in these final times ... She must be terrible to the devil and his henchmen in these end times!

He attributed to Mary the original prophecy of the Woman crushing the head of the serpent and decried the growing rage of the demon against the children of the Virgin:

> But to these children, Mary distributes abundant graces. They will be great and will rise in sanctity before God, superior in zeal to every creature, animated and so strongly dependent on divine help that, in union with Mary, they will crush the head of the devil

with their lowly heel, and cause Jesus Christ
to triumph.

Then, in fiery words, he described the apostles of
these last times and then concluded: "When and
how will this happen? … God knows! It is for us to
be silent, to sigh, and to wait, *exspectans exspectavi*
(expectantly I awaited)."[82]

The universal dissemination of this *Treatise on True
Devotion* advanced the marvelous Marian apostolate
of Saint Louis-Marie de Montfort and continues to
increasingly spread the conviction of Mary's role in
the Christian apostolate.

De Montfort had wanted to found a society of
missionaries that would continue his work. At
his premature death—he was only 43—it was
comprised of only two priests and seven coadjutor
brothers. It developed little by little, exercising
its ministry in the west of France, hindered by
governmental restrictions. In 1821, it began to
prosper. With the discovery of the manuscript on
"holy slavery," it became better known, especially
during the 20th century. It was Father Morineau,
a Montfortian religious, who founded the French
Society of Marian Studies which would be followed

---

82 Chap. 1, art. 2, par. 3.

by the foundation of similar societies in various countries of the old and new worlds.[83]

Saint Alphonsus Liguori and the Redemptorists[84]

"Whatever good has happened to me," said Saint Alphonsus in his prayer to Mary which prefaces the *Glories of Mary*, "my conversion, my holy vocation, and so many other graces — I acknowledge all as having come to me through your intercession."

It was also the Blessed Virgin, appearing to the Saint in the grotto of Scala, who helped him with her advice in founding and organizing the Institute of the Redemptorists. His followers, too, after their profession of religious vows, credited Mary for their perseverance and, as testimony to their gratitude, they not only promised her their perpetual service and special love and cult, but also their constant endeavor to extend her love and cult.

The Marian activity of the Redemptorists is exercised by word and pen.

The Marian Apostolate of the word

---

83 De Montfort was canonized in 1947. Today, the Society of Mary has more than 1500 religious, in most Christian countries and in missionary areas under the direction of seven bishops or apostolic vicars.

84 P. Hitz, CSSR, in *Maria. Etudes sur le Sainte Vierge*, vol. 3, 275-305.

In the missions and retreats that they preach, sermons on the Blessed Virgin and prayer to Mary play roles of primary importance. They are considered the most accessible and the most effective means for conversions and perseverance. Saint Alphonsus was insistent on this point from the Congregation's very inception. By order of the General Chapter, it was decided ... that, in the missions and retreats, one must always preach a sermon on the Blessed Virgin since experience has proven this to be the most beneficial sermon.[85]

To preach of Mary and of confidence in her intercession is what the salvation of souls depends on. ... We can assert in all truth that, most often, none of our preaching produces as much fruit of salvation and compunction than the sermon on the loving-kindness of Mary.[86]

The sons of Saint Alphonsus have been faithful to their father's recommendations, "so much so, that, in a great many areas, the Christian people call the

---

85 P. Hitz, CSSR, in *Maria. Etudes sur le Sainte Vierge*, vol. 3, 282.

86 P. Hitz, CSSR, in *Maria. Etudes sur le Sainte Vierge*, vol. 3, 283.

Redemptorists 'the priests who preach the most about the Blessed Virgin.'"[87]

The Marian Apostolate of the Pen –

> Here, too, Saint Alphonsus himself gave the example in his *Glories of Mary*, which appeared in 1750. ... He had worked on it for sixteen years. Published during the height of Jansenism and Voltairian unbelief, its success was enormous, especially in France. During the 19th century, new editions appeared every year or two. Little by little the book was translated and published in the principal languages of the world. By 1950 there had been some eight hundred different editions.[88]

From the 19th century and on, the disciples of Saint Alphonsus devoted themselves to imitating their holy founder in his writing apostolate. They have produced great numbers of Marian publications. Most of them are devotional books and brochures. Others, especially in more recent years, are solid historical or theological works on the Mother of God and her cult.

---

[87] P. Hitz, CSSR, in *Maria. Etudes sur le Sainte Vierge*, vol. 3, 284.

[88] P. Hitz, CSSR, in *Maria. Etudes sur le Sainte Vierge*, vol. 3, 284.

{Blessed} William Joseph Chaminade[89] and the Society of Mary (Marianists)

We have already mentioned Father Chaminade and the Society of Mary, with reference to Mary as Guardian of the Faith.[90] However, since the chief object of the Society he founded is to assist Mary in "her mission to preserve and increase faith," the total object of the Society of Mary constitutes a universal Marian apostolate, as we shall indicate.

We have seen that Father Chaminade based Mary's apostolic mission on Sacred Scripture: "She shall crush your head," and on the liturgy: "You alone have conquered all heresies in the entire world." He did not pretend to be original in this view; however, he is original in his repeated affirmations that this mission of Mary's was to break forth brilliantly with unprecedented power in the new age, beginning after the French Revolution of 1789. Saint Louis-Marie de Montfort had also foreseen the times of Mary's triumph. But he ended his prophecy with these words: "When and how will this come about? … God knows! It is for us to be silent, to sigh, and to wait."[91]

---

89 {Chaminade was beatified Sept. 3, 2000.}

90 Chap. 7.

91 *Treatise de la vraie Dévotion*, no. 59 [English tr.: *True Devotion to Mary*].

Chaminade declared: "The time is now! A great victory is promised to Mary **in our day**." We are aware of five different and solemn circumstances when he made this declaration—even in a document to Pope Gregory XVI in which he must have carefully weighed every word, as his request for the approbation of his two Foundations was inclusive. Such forthrightness in declaring his conviction, with such clarity and without the least hesitation or reservation, of Mary's special role in the new age, is all the more astonishing in that, at the time the founder expressed it, there were no signs as yet of the revival of Marian fervor which made of the 19th and 20th centuries the centuries *par excellence* of Mary.

In fact, all prognostications seemed to anticipate a period of very great relaxation in the devotion of the faithful toward the Mother of God. In his evaluation of the different periods in the history of Mariology, Father Laurentin says of the most recent one which began in the 19th century: "From a Marian point of view, the 19th century projects a singular physiognomy. It begins with a most extreme negativity. During the first thirty years, the rarity and mediocrity of Marian literature is reduced to its lowest level ever, even below that of the 15th century."[92]

As for devotion, if there were any fervent souls (as proof: those who would found Marian societies), general piety toward the Virgin was strongly influenced by the Jansenism of the 17th century as witnessed by Monsignors d'Hulst, Trochu, Baunard, and the findings of the Curé of Ars.[93] It seems almost impossible, therefore, to explain in some satisfactory way the crystal clear affirmations of Chaminade, except to say that he must have received special illumination from Mary at her sanctuary in Saragossa.[94]

It was, therefore, this conviction about the apostolic mission of Mary, especially in the approaching new age, and the mandate he had received at her

---

92 *Court traité de théologie mariale*, p. 59 [English tr.: *Queen of Heaven. A Short Treatise on Marian Theology*].

93 Cited by Dillenschneider in *La Mariologie de S. Alphonse de Liguori, son influence sur le renouveau de doctrines mariales et de la piété catholique après la tourmente du protestantisme et du jansénisme*, Fribourg en Suisse, 1931.

94 Chaminade could not have been influenced by the preaching of de Montfort. All Chaminade's Marian teachings predate 1842, the date of the discovery of the *Traité de la vraie devotion* (*True Devotion to Mary*). Besides, Montfort speaks of an unknown time; Chaminade, of the present times.

sanctuary in Saragossa, that determined Father Chaminade to found two societies of women and of men who would place themselves completely at the disposal of Mary to help her in her providential mission.

It should be remarked — and this seems to be a second original point of Chaminade's Marian doctrine — that, in his Foundations, the Virgin does not intervene to help her children in their apostolate; it is her children who give themselves to help her in her own apostolate. It is for this very reason that they have come together in religious societies. Their profession is, in fact, a consecration to Mary, Queen of Apostles.

In order to better mark their total belonging to the Virgin in view of her providential mission, they add a vow of **stability** to the three vows of poverty, chastity, and obedience which takes on a special Marian sense for them: that of perseverance in the service of Mary. It is defined in the Constitutions as follows: " ... This vow is specifically a dedication to the Blessed Virgin with the pious design of propagating knowledge of her and perpetuating love for her and the cult due her as much as possible, through self and others, in whatever circumstance of life."[95]

It was their filial piety toward Mary that moved these new religious to "give themselves to Mary with all their possessions and all the talents of their being, that she might make of them whatever pleased her for the greater glory of her Son!" A follower of the Berullian school, Chaminade faithfully charged his students with the obligation to imitate Jesus. Consider then, "that Jesus is born of Mary. Nurtured and educated by her, He was subject to her; He associated her to all His works, to all His sorrows, to all His mysteries. Devotion to Mary (i.e., dedication to the ultimate degree) is, therefore, the most striking aspect of the imitation of Jesus Christ."[96]

> We have committed ourselves to Mary but, in what way? In all that a child should feel and do for a good mother: love her, respect her, obey her, and assist her. Oh! We have, above all, committed ourselves to the culminating effect of filial love, assistance, and active goodwill: we have made the commitment to

---

95 Constitutions 1839, art. 19.
96 Constitutions 1839, art. 5.

publicly proclaim the name of Mary and to have her honored everywhere![97]

The apostolate of the religious of Mary has become as universal as that of their Mother, for it is a participation therein:

> Among the many congregations that sprang into existence in succeeding ages and in various parts of the world, some were called to one particular form of work, some to another. And last of all, we believe that we too have been called by Mary herself, to assist her with all our might in the struggle against the great heresy of our times. To this end, we have taken for our motto, as declared in our Constitutions, these words of the Blessed Virgin to the attendant at Cana: "Do whatever he tells you" (Jn 2:5). We are convinced that our particular mission, despite our weakness, is to perform all the works of zeal and of mercy for the welfare of our neighbor. It is for this reason that, under the general title of teaching Christian morals, we employ all the means at our disposal for preserving our neighbors from the contagion

---

97 *Esprit de notre Fondation* (The Spirit of Our Foundation), vol. 1, p. 127

of evil, and restoring those who have fallen under its sway.[98]

The principal work of the Society of Mary is teaching and is, most assuredly, the most essential and fruitful. But no other work of zeal is excluded from its program. From another point of view, the three categories of the Society of Mary — priests, professional laymen, and laymen engaged in various trades — are equally called to this apostolate undertaken in the name of Mary, each following its appropriate function. Its founder would say that the Society of Mary "is essentially apostolic in its universal membership."

The religious of Mary are keenly aware that the work they perform in Mary's mission is not their own but hers; likewise, they do not act in their own name but in the all-powerful name of Mary to whom God has promised victory over the serpent, thus equipping them with invincible confidence! "With Mary's protection, we should have the confidence to convert the entire world," Chaminade would often repeat.

This is the same intensely Marian and apostolic spirit, (intensely apostolic because proceeding from Mary, Queen of Apostles), that the founder

---

98 Chaminade, *Letter* no. 1163.

strove to instill in the Daughters of Mary, the feminine branch of his foundation. He wrote to the foundress {Adèle de Trenquelléon}: "As to what should distinguish you from other orders, it is zeal for the salvation of souls … Your community will be composed of missionary religious."[99]

No other founder seems to have had such clear ideas on the relationships between the apostolate of his disciples and the apostolic mission of Mary. It is true that, concerning Chaminade, I have been able to consult all his works, even those unpublished; while for the greater part of other founders of orders, their ideas are known to me only from the necessarily brief notices given in volumes two and three of *Maria*.

For the rest, I willingly make Chaminade's remark my own, with regard to a similar comparison. After raising the objection that "all the religious orders have honored Mary in a special way and take glory in belonging to her," he wrote:

> By no means do we claim the cult of the Blessed Virgin as our exclusive portion. That would indeed be a foolish pretension; for who has ever loved the Son without loving the Mother?

---

99 *Esprit de notre Fondation*, vol. 3, 297.

Then he continues:

> What I regard as a really distinctive trait of our two Orders, and what seems to me to be without precedent in all the religious orders I know of, is the fact that we embrace the religious life in the name and for the glory of the Blessed Virgin, and for the sake of devoting ourselves to her — that is to say, our bodies and all that we possess, in order to make her known, loved, and served — totally convinced that we shall not bring others back to Jesus except through His most holy Mother.

He concludes with a remark that should appease any objectors in that event:

> I would again respond that if other religious orders have this trait in common with us, we ought to compliment them, bless them, and invite them to vie with us in zeal and love to spread far and wide the august name of Mary and the knowledge of her ineffable bounties.[100]

---

[100] Three citations from Chaminade, *Letter* no. 1163.

Society of the Catholic Apostolate:
Pallottine Fathers

Like Father Chaminade, Saint Vincent Pallotti had the conviction of Mary's role in the apostolate, especially urgent in modern times, as the inspired idea for the foundation of his Society. He loved to consider the Virgin as Queen of apostles, and his disciples as Mary's instruments. The feast of Mary, Queen of Apostles, is the patronal feast of his Congregations.

The Pallotine Society (official name: *Societas apostolatus catholici*, more popularly known as Pallotines) developed rather slowly in Italy at first, then in Germany, and somewhat departed from the clear vision of its Marian mission. But, in 1912, a young priest {Fr. Joseph Kentenich} understood that belonging to the Queen of Apostles should doubtlessly be more than a mere act of piety; it involved a program of apostolic action. He was able to communicate his ideas and enthusiasm to a group of young members of the Society, and he began to envisage an apostolate undertaken in the name and for the glory of Mary.

After the First World War, he created a center for Marian retreats near the house of studies for young religious at Schönstadt, near Coblenz. This was the beginning of the "Apostolic Movement of Schönstadt." Some of the older religious found the young priest's ideas a bit too novel. But the publication of the founder's writings after 1922, showed that these innovators were only reverting to the focus which had initially motivated the very foundation of the Society.

In 1926, the "Sisters of Mary," a new religious society different from the Pallotine Sisters, was founded at Schönstadt and developed rapidly. Until 1940, Schönstadt was the center of an extremely intense Marian apostolic activity. Then the war broke out and the founder of the center — not an avowed Nazi — was sent to a concentration camp. Through nothing short of a miracle, Fr. Kentenich later emerged safe and sound. With the collapse of Hitler's regime, the activity of the Marian apostolate resumed even stronger. Retreats are given uninterruptedly to all ages and all classes of society, but preferentially to priests, and to men and women teachers. Each category is grouped into leagues comprising hundreds of members. It is indeed the "Marianization" of all those who, by their very professions, are called to the exercise of a greater apostolic influence.

Besides, the entire Pallotine Society has profited from this conscious reawakening of its Marian

apostolic mission. Since the beginning of the
movement at Schönstadt, it has more than tripled
in membership. Its occupations are the same:
administration of schools, internal and external
missions, various works of the sacred ministry. But
because its members maintain the awareness of
being Mary's instruments, the results are remarkably
different.[101]

The first half of the 20th century has seen the
emergence of a considerable number of other
religious societies of men explicitly placed under the
name and auspices of Mary.

The Society of Mary (Marists)
Venerable Jean-Claude Colin[102]

This Society, according to the testimony of its
founder, also owes its origin to a direct intervention
of Mary. It especially seeks to reproduce the spirits
of humility and recollection of its Mother. It is
involved in education and in the missions.

---

[101] {Fr. Kentenich (1885-1968) was removed as head of
the Schönstadt Movement and transferred in 1952 to
Milwaukee, WI, where he remained until 1965, when
he was permitted to return to Schönstadt and resume
his activities. This movement, with Father Kentenich
as head, was then separated from the Pallotines by
decree of the Holy See.}

[102] *Maria. Etudes sur le Sainte Vierge*, vol. 3, 349ff.

The Little Brothers of Mary
of Blessed M. Champagnat[103]
{Champagnat has since been canonized.}

A disciple of Father Colin, Father Marcellin Champagnat founded a branch of the Marist Brothers especially dedicated to education, which formed an independent society after a few years. It has grown very much, and exercises its apostolate under the auspices of Mary in numerous countries of the Old and New Worlds. For some time, it has produced excellent handbooks to make Mary known, loved, and served by the thousands of young people to whom it provides a Christian education.

The Missionary Oblates of Mary Immaculate
of Bishop Mazenod[104]
{Mazenod has since been canonized.}

This Society, which received both its name and its investiture from Leo XIII, was founded at Aix in Provence, in 1816, by Bishop Mazenod. The Oblates exercise their apostolate of evangelization to the poor under the auspices of Mary Immaculate, in both Christian and pagan lands, particularly in northern Canada. In addition, they also direct a

---

103 *Maria. Etudes sur le Sainte Vierge*, vol. 3, 351.
104 *Maria. Etudes sur le Sainte Vierge*, vol. 3, 355ff.

large number of sanctuaries dedicated to Mary, and preach retreats and parish missions in which they devote themselves to "giving special attention to the salvific role of Mary."

Especially over the past few years {the early 1950's}, the Oblates of Mary Immaculate have also devoted themselves to the study of the mystery of Mary. They have published many works on the Blessed Virgin and furnish the Canadian Society of Marian Studies with a social headquarters and secretarial staff.

Venerable Jacob Liebermann and The Congregation of the Holy Spirit and of the Immaculate Heart of Mary[105]

The son of a rabbi from Saverne, Jacob Liebermann converted to Catholicism in 1826 at the age of twenty-four. "When the waters of Baptism flowed over my Jewish head," he revealed, "**at that moment, I loved Mary** whom I had previously detested."[106] He entered the seminary of Saint Sulpice where he connected with the writings of Olier; he felt attracted to contemplating "the interior of Jesus and

---

105 H. Barre, CSSp, in *Maria. Etudes sur le Sainte Vierge*, vol. 3, 379-401.

106 H. Barre, CSSp, in *Maria. Etudes sur le Sainte Vierge*, vol. 3, 382.

of Mary." "The life of Mary in Jesus and of Jesus in Mary is one of his favorite meditation themes."[107]

Little by little, a particular devotion to the Immaculate Heart of Mary was formed and developed in him. Two seminarians, Eugene Tisserant and Frederic le Vavasseur, members of the Confraternity of the Immaculate Heart of Mary (which Father Desgenettes, pastor of Notre-Dame des Victoires {Our Lady of Victories}, had just created) conceived the idea of founding a society devoted to the evangelization of the Blacks. They spoke of it to Liebermann, who approved their project. He then understood the Virgin's desire to devote himself to this very project.

From the beginning, he said to Desgenettes, "all our trust was in the goodness of our most Blessed Mother." He went to Rome to submit the project to the Congregation for the Propagation of the Faith. Without even waiting for a response, he set to work "laying out the process to be followed" in his undertaking. However, it amounted to nothing and he found "his mind a total blank."

> Only Tisserant was of the opinion that we should consecrate our work to the most

---

107 H. Barre, CSSp, in *Maria. Etudes sur le Sainte Vierge*, vol. 3, 383.

Holy Heart of Mary. Le Vavasseur and I did not think that an apostolic work should be consecrated to the Immaculate Heart of Mary, even though our full confidence was in that most Holy Heart.[108]

This was a strange but providential attitude. The Blessed Virgin wished to show that it was not mere sentimental devotion that would lead the apostles to seek her intervention in their works in favor of souls. Devotees of the Virgin naturally do this in their many varied activities. It was rather that intimate and essential ties were to exist between her and the entire apostolic work. The narration continues:

I thought that the Society should find in its consecration all its devotions and a perfect model for all the fundamental virtues of the apostolate. I do not know why **I didn't have the least idea** that we would perfectly find this in devotion to the holy and Immaculate Heart of Mary.

I settled, therefore, on another idea toward this end. I put quite an effort into drawing up the plan in question but was unable to come up with a single idea: I found my

---

108 H. Barre, CSSp, in *Maria. Etudes sur le Sainte Vierge*, vol. 3, 390.

mind a total blank. Then I paid a visit to "the seven churches" and I also went to visit some churches dedicated to the most Blessed Virgin. With that — **having no idea why** — I found I had decided to consecrate the work to the most Holy Heart of Mary.

I returned to my residence and immediately began to resume the plan in question. It was all so clear that, at a single glance, I foresaw it in its entirety with all the developments in all their details. It was inexpressible joy and consolation for me!

This orientation is affirmed from the very first pages of the "Provisional rule of the Missionaries of the Most Holy Heart of Mary."

What distinguishes us from all the other workers who labor in the vineyard of the Lord, is the very special consecration which we make of our whole Society, of each of its members, and of each of their works and undertakings, to the most Holy Heart of Mary, an **eminently apostolic Heart,** totally afire with desire for the glory of God and the salvation of souls.[109]

---

[109] H. Barre, CSSp, in *Maria. Etudes sur le Sainte Vierge*, vol. 3, 390-391.

We consider her Heart as a perfect model of the zeal which should consume us, and as an abundant and ever-accessible source from which we can draw.

In order to facilitate its missionary efforts, the Society of the Most Holy Heart of Mary united itself to a society founded in the 17th century for an apostolate among the Blacks, under the name of Society of the Holy Spirit. With it came its civil and religious approbations. It seemed that devotion to the Immaculate Heart of Mary might be relegated to second place to the devotion to the Holy Spirit. In fact, as Libermann explained to his uneasy disciples, "Mary is to bring the Holy Spirit to us so that we, like her, might be filled with the superabundance of his holiness."[110]

Saint Anthony Mary Claret
and the Congregation of the Sons of the
Immaculate Heart of Mary[111]

Born in 1807, Anthony Mary Claret distinguished himself at an early age by his ardent devotion to Mary. She saved him from mortal danger on the

---

110 H. Barre, CSSp, in *Maria. Etudes sur le Sainte Vierge*, vol. 3, 399.

111 N. Garcia-Garces, in *Maria. Etudes sur le Sainte Vierge*, vol. 3. See also Barrios-Moneo, *La Espiritualidad cordi-mariana de S. A. M. Claret.*

beach of Barcelona, and from even greater dangers to his honor and his soul. She granted him the gift of perfect chastity after a victorious combat, and both the ordinary and extraordinary graces of mystical union. His preferred devotions were the rosary (he recited the fifteen decades every day, even in the midst of the most absorbing apostolic works), and visits to Mary in one of her sanctuaries.

Ordained to the priesthood in 1835, he went to Rome to offer his services to the Congregation for the Propagation of the Faith, from whom he was given the title of Apostolic Missionary, and went on to preach in Catalonia and the Canary Islands (1840–1849). His missions were completely Marian. He invoked Mary before starting out, and he was sure of success since it was she, and not he, who acted. He spoke of her endlessly, of her goodness and of her mercy. In the name of Mary, he freed the possessed and healed the sick. Sinners converted in great numbers. At the end of his missions, he spent up to fifteen hours {a day} in the confessional, and often had to ask for help from a dozen other confessors.

In 1849, he founded the Congregation of the Missionaries, Sons of the Immaculate Heart of Mary.

In 1850, Pius IX named him Archbishop of Santiago in Cuba. In the accomplishment of that task, he showed himself as both a great Bishop and an ardent missionary. Immense crowds were converted at hearing him speak of Mary. Hundreds, sometimes thousands, followed him on foot or on horseback in his apostolic travels.

He returned to Madrid in 1857 as confessor to the Queen and used her influence to propagate devotion to Mary in Spain. His most powerful apostolic arm was the rosary. He was its apostle in both the spoken and written word. He taught the crowds how to recite it; he distributed millions of leaflets to make the practice known to all Christians.

Hounded by Masonic persecution, he was exiled by the First Spanish Republic and died in France in 1870.

He communicated his spirit and his Marian apostolate to the members of the Society he had founded: Missionaries, Sons of the Immaculate Heart of Mary. Their spirit is essentially a filial spirit toward the Heart of Mary, i.e., of Mary in her love, the principle of divine and human maternity; of her mission as Coredemptrix and Distributrix of all graces; of her universal apostolic mission; and they share in her apostolic spirit. "A son of the

Immaculate Heart of Mary," said their Founder "is a man who burns with divine love, and who desires and uses all possible means to set the world on fire with it."

Bishop Claret's sons are conscious of the mandate received from their Founder. They seek out the means to carry out his apostolate for and through the Virgin: erection of sanctuaries in honor of the Immaculate Heart of Mary; foundation of chairs of Mariology in faculties of theology; consecration of families to the Heart of Mary; devotion of the first Saturday; various Marian associations for the different social classes; publication of valuable Marian magazines and books, etc. They have contributed greatly to the foundation and success of the Spanish Society of Marian Studies.

Other Marian Missionary Societies[112]

There are a great many other missionary societies whose very names indicate their consecration to Mary: Congregation of the Immaculate Heart of Mary, from Scheut; Augustinians of the Assumption; Missionaries of La Salette; Missionaries of the Holy Family; Priests of Saint Mary of Tinchebray, etc.

---

112 *Maria. Etudes sur le Sainte Vierge*, vol. 3, 354-378; Paul Sträter, *Katholische Marienkunde*, vol. 3, pp. 177-184.

There are many missionary societies that do not have the name of Mary in their title, but do have it in their heart and in their apostolate. All would doubtlessly be ready to apply to themselves the words written in 1662 by Bishop Fallon, founder of the Paris Foreign Mission Society:

> The more I think of it, the more I am convinced that our mission is a work of this Mother of Mercy who cares for the coming of her Son into the hearts of peoples with as much love as she had here on earth ... I am more than ever convinced that the Most Blessed Virgin has been the chief promoter of our dear mission and that she wishes to have full direction and sway over it.

Religious Societies of Women

At the side of the men religious exercising their apostolate in the name of Mary, we must mention the even more numerous women religious. There are over 700 societies, of which 269 are from France. Their apostolic activities are of the most varied: care of infants, education and instruction of children and adolescents, reform of souls who have strayed, care of the poor, dedication to those who are ill, etc.[113]

What has been said above about the Marian inspiration and effectiveness of men religious consecrated to the Virgin applies also to women religious, many of whom, in great numbers, form the feminine branch of an order or congregation of men previously mentioned, with identical spirituality.

Besides the feminine societies whose titles carry an allusion to Mary, there is an even greater number that belongs to her by some indication of their rule or some official consecration or some tradition. They, too, think of Mary in their apostolate as inspiration, as model, as all-powerful helper.

In some areas or at certain times, it is thanks to them that the people remain deeply attached to the cult of Mary despite critical or minimizing tendencies of a clergy touched by Protestant or rationalistic influences. By nurturing, with a living devotion to Mary, the future mothers of the families they will rear, they prepare homes imbued with a solid and fruitful faith. It is often thanks to them that, despite a father who is marginal or non-practicing, the children, boys as well as girls, are raised with deep

---

113 *Maria. Etudes sur le Sainte Vierge*, vol. 3, 473.

Christian values. In addition, there are thousands, millions of souls won or led to Christ who could not be reached by the priests. These women religious are Mary on earth in that they exercise in all ways the kind, simple, obscure, but all-powerful action of their Mother and Model.

People generally recognize the apostolic influence exerted by women religious dedicated to the active life. But unbelievers, and even a certain number of Christians, are less aware of the reason for the existence of contemplatives. When there is so much work to be done, why selfishly enclose oneself in a monastery to be preoccupied only with self and forgetful of others? — Such an attitude reflects a misunderstanding of the vocation of these cloistered women religious. They do not forget that the duty of love is twofold: love for God and love for neighbor. And the second should mirror the first.

They, too, think of others, of those others who remain in the world and who have need of help. And they offer help to them every day, through their prayers and immolations. In our big cities, they are what the "ten just" would have been for Sodom and Gomorra: compensation for the evil committed and bulwark against the chastisements requited for so many crimes.

They also provide tremendous help to the apostolic workers. Saint Teresa {of Avila} had been profoundly struck by the need to come to the aid of priests. Without the prayers and sacrifices of contemplative women religious, the priests themselves were at risk of being lost and of losing innumerable souls confided to their care. Pius XI gave another young contemplative, Saint Therese {of Lisieux}, as principal patroness to missionaries, along with Saint Francis Xavier.

This desire to help priests by their prayers and sacrifices is, of course, also dear to a great number of women religious engaged in the active life. They highly esteem the sublimity of the priesthood. Having been prevented from aspiring to it because of their sex, they wish to at least compensate by providing supernatural assistance to the priests.

CHAPTER TEN

Mary and the Apostolate of the Secular Clergy

The apostolate of secular priests was not set forth (for reasons given above in Chapter Nine) by historians as readily as that of the religious. And it is equally difficult to render account of what place the Mother of God held in the apostolate of secular priests, as opposed to religious priests. We strongly assert, however, that she did have an important place — and this is verifiable.

First of all, we know that, for many long centuries, the faithful loved to pray and to sing of the Virgin Mary's holiness. Statues, paintings; chapels, churches, and cathedrals; pilgrimages, confraternities of the rosary and others; collections of miracles; vows pronounced in her name — all of these presuppose a deep and trusting devotion to the Mother of Jesus. And such devotion was certainly inspired, in great part, by priests in whose parishes where it was active.

Moreover, almost all the founders of religious orders and societies, which we have just specified, were secular priests: such as Dominic, Olier, Montfort, Liguori, Chaminade, Colin, Champagnat. And many others acquired their exceptional devotion to Mary as priests in the world. Other secular priests, in ever greater numbers and of intense Marian piety, entered later into the orders consecrated to Mary, drawn precisely by the great devotion to the Virgin with which they were animated even before crossing the threshold of the monastery.

It would probably be easy for each of us to recall some parish priest who was recognized for both his apostolic spirit and his profound piety toward Mary. Among the most remarkable of the 19th century were the Curé of Ars in France and Edouard Poppe in Belgium.

Msgr. Trochu, biographer of the Curé of Ars, wrote:

> He had loved Mary from his cradle. Having become a priest, he worked with all his strength to extend her cult. To be convinced of that, it was enough for the pilgrims to see the little statues of the Virgin at all the village doors. Under each roof there was a colored image of the Mother of God, a gift from the Curé bearing his signature. In 1844, Father Vianney set up a large statue of the Immaculate near the entrance to his

church. Eight years earlier, on May 1, 1836, he consecrated his parish to Mary conceived without sin. The tablet that perpetuated this consecration … is placed at the entrance to the chapel of the Blessed Virgin.

A short time later, he had a heart made of gilt bronze which is still suspended today from the neck of the "miraculous Virgin." The names of all the parishioners of Ars, written on a white silk ribbon, are enclosed in that heart. On the days which were feasts of Mary, "communions were always numerous and the church was always full." On the evenings of those feasts, the nave and the side chapels could barely contain the crowd because no one wanted to miss Father Vianney's homily in honor of the Blessed Virgin, so great was his fervor in extolling her holiness, her power, and her love.[114]

The saintly Father Poppe, {beatified in 1999}, marvelous apostle of Eucharistic devotion in Belgium, was also a great servant of Mary. He was so united to his Mother that, for some time,

---

114 F. Trochu, *Le Curé d'Ars, Saint Jean Marie Vianney*, Emmanuel Vitte, Lyon. [English tr.: *The Curé of Ars, St. Jean-Marie Vianney (1786-1859)*, Charlotte NC 2007]

his spiritual director thought he was exaggerating, elevating Mary to the place of Jesus. Poppe was obedient, but greatly distressed. Later, addressing himself to Mary when speaking of this period of his life, he said:

> You were banished from my sermons, from my confessional, from my altar, from my prayer. My children, who are also yours, scarcely heard any further discourses about their Mother. Did I no longer love you? Why, even among the sick and the dying, was my heart so void of tenderness? I spoke to them words I didn't mean, with tongue half-paralyzed.[115]

Later, his director understood him better and gave him the following advice: "Your union with Mary must become characteristic of your life."[116]

Apostle of the Eucharist, Poppe also became apostle of Mary through his sermons, his collaboration with *l'Etendard de Marie* {*The Standard of Mary*}, his guidance of souls, particularly of chosen souls. The first question addressed to a new penitent was:

115 Od. Jacobs and Ed. Ned, *Une Ame d'Apôtre, M. Edouard Poppe,* (*The Soul of an Apostle*, *Fr. Edward Poppe*), Lethielleux, Paris, p. 172.

116 *Une Ame d'Apôtre, M. Edouard Poppe*, p. 173.

"Is your heart afire with love for Jesus and Mary?" If the affirmative, he rejoiced, certain of obtaining consoling results. If negative, he neglected nothing to fire up a new hearth with love. "I lead them all to her," he said, "so that, in her, they may learn to find and to love the Christ."[117]

CHAPTER ELEVEN

Mary and the Apostolate of Catholic Action[118]

The clergy and religious are not the only members of the Church called to the apostolate. Every

---

[117] *Une Ame d'Apôtre, M. Edouard Poppe*, p. 184. See also Duperrey, *La Spiritualité du clergé diocésain et la Dévotion à Marie, (The Spirituality of the Diocesan Clergy and Devotion to Mary)* in *Maria. Etudes sur le Sainte Vierge*, vol. 3, pp. 659-695, especially 681-691; and E. Neubert, *Marie et notre Sacerdoce*, especially pp. 209-283. [English tr.: *Mary and the Priestly Ministry*, New Bedford MA 2009]

[118] See P. Richard, Archbishop of Bordeaux, *Marie et l'Action Catholique,* in *Maria. Etudes sur le Vierge Sainte*, vol. 1, pp. 903-915

Christian has an apostolic vocation because, first of all, every Christian should imitate Christ, the Apostle *par excellence*; and then, because the great commandment of Christ is to love God and to love neighbor as self. Now, the first good we must procure for ourselves is eternal life, for which we should be ready to sacrifice all the world's goods and even the life of the body. Therefore, we should also strive to procure eternal life for our neighbor.

Recent popes since Saint Pius X have recalled this duty to the Christians of our era and, in order to bring it to fruition, it has been organized under the name of Catholic Action, defined as "the participation of the laity in the apostolate of the hierarchy."

Now Mary, with and under Christ, should be the source of every apostolate, therefore of Catholic Action also. We shall see this later in the section on "theological precisions." But even simple Christians who have never been exposed to theology easily understand that the Mother of the Redeemer must have a role — and an important role to play — in the work of the conversion and sanctification of souls. It is evident to them that she must be interested in the salvation of those for whom her Son sacrificed His life, those who are her children, for whom she has suffered so much. It is also evident to them that, with the aid of the Distributrix of all graces, it will be easier for them to successfully carry out their task as members of Catholic Action.

Fervent Christians — and they are the ones mostly concerned with Catholic Action — will naturally give Mary a place in the apostolic activity. They have need of the Virgin for another reason, not the least being:

> When a priest or a layman explains the necessity and advantages of Catholic Action to certain categories of well-disposed believers, at first, a rather good proportion responds enthusiastically or is, at least, won over: "everything is new, everything is beautiful." But soon, that initial fervor cools. One can take it or leave it, all depending on the mood of the moment or the inconveniences which the action entails. Sometimes the leaders themselves throw in the towel, frustrated with their members, and perhaps more often with the hierarchy.

> This is because success in Catholic Action, a supernatural work, requires supernatural dispositions: a dedication geared to self-forgetfulness and self-sacrifice; to humility, obedience, interior spirit, prayer,

mortification. Therefore, we find all these dispositions, all these virtues, being practiced to the highest degree of perfection and in the most natural and captivating way in the different episodes of Mary's life.[119]

In some countries, Catholic Action is comprised of specialized divisions, particularly among the youth of France, with obvious advantages to group dynamics: people tend to fraternize more easily with others of the same age or culture, or with those having similar occupations or social standing. It is also easier to understand one another, to support one another, to find solutions together and to carry them out. Their focus is twofold — exterior: some reform, some social advantage to achieve; and interior: a common spirit to be developed and certain supernatural dispositions to be cultivated to energize exterior action.

In general, founders and spiritual counselors insist on this **soul** of the movement, without which the work loses it sense of direction and runs the risk of dying, like a body without a soul. In fact, there is danger that some members become too preoccupied with exterior achievements, since what is seen and

---

119 P. Richard, *Marie et l'Action Catholique*, in *Maria. Etudes sur le Vierge Sainte*, vol. 1, pp. 909-914

tangible is of more interest than what is spiritual and, consequently, invisible. That this should be quite natural among the simple faithful should not surprise us if we consider how easily the same temptation besets priests and religious, both men and women, because of our natural propensity!

From time to time, someone close to God shows up to warn us against "the heresy of works" and to remind us with authority that "the soul of every apostolate" is the interior life. We admit: "That is true!" But, in the whirlwind of exterior activities, we succumb anew. If this can happen to consecrated souls, how much more easily for the simple faithful, especially the young for whom exterior activity is a natural function. So it is that, at one time or another, we learn of a specialized movement "going through a crisis," perhaps quite prolonged or even fatal.

Experience shows us that those members who are especially devoted to the Blessed Virgin are much more likely than others to maintain the soul of a movement and to spread it to others. In certain cases, one of the two following solutions has taken place: 1) restructuring the leaders of specialized movement into a Marian movement; 2) infiltrating the specialized movements with members of a Marian movement.

1) Creating a Marian movement for the elite:

> Once a month, a certain pastor of a large city parish brings the leading militants and directors of the women's movements together in a Marian sodality: JECF, JICF, and JOCF,[120] guide and leaders. At the foot of the Virgin they renew themselves spiritually, becoming more aware of their close ties in the field of the parish apostolate, and supporting one another both practically and spiritually.

> A certain chaplain of Catholic Action was fortunate enough to offer the advantages of a Marian sodality to his national leaders of the JOC, JIC, and JAC.[121] Many of them were very happy to have the opportunity to deepen their spirituality, to love each other more, and to help each other under Mary's eye.

> Such Marian devotion cultivated among the leaders and militants of Catholic Action generally gives them a special physiognomy, with a greater interior spirit and, more specifically, the Marian

---

[120] {Early Catholic Action groups in France included the JECF Young Christian Students (feminine), JICF Young Christian Independents (feminine), JOCF Young Christian Workers (feminine).}

[121] {Respectfully, Young Christian Workers, Young Christian Independents, Young Christian Farmers.}

virtues of humility, gentleness, and psychological finesse, which give their apostolate greater influence and adaptability.[122]

2) Infiltration of specialized movements by members of a Marian movement:

Elsewhere, a different approach is taken. The members of a Marian movement (sodalities, Children of Mary, Legion of Mary) are the ones who enter into a specialized movement existing in their neighborhood. Priests and bishops have remarked that these specialized movements exercise a very good influence whenever the sodalities, Children of Mary, or Legionaries of Mary take part in them, and that this influence

---

122 *Maria. Etudes sur le Vierge Sainte*, vol. 3, pp. 684ff. Joseph Leo Cardijn, founder of the JOC has often insisted on the importance of devotion to Mary for the Jocistes. To the author of this present volume, who had sent him a copy of his book, *La Reine des Militants*, he wrote: "May your wish be realized and may the entire JOC become Marian; only then will it be truly militant." More recently, after receiving the biography of a young Marianist priest entitled *Apôtre de la Vierge et de la J.O.C., Père R. Mougel* (*Apostle of the Virgin and of the J.O.C., Père R. Moguel*), Cardijn wrote: What a beautiful title! How I wish that all the chaplains might deserve it by inculcating in all our militants this inseparable love of their Mother in Heaven and of their brothers and sisters here on earth! Only Mary can teach them how they should love them, and what they must offer in order to save them."

tends to dwindle with the disappearance of young apostles of the Virgin.

Marian Lay Associations

Apart from apostolic groups directly attached to the hierarchy, and the diverse movements of Catholic Action which, while being preoccupied with temporal activities, pursue a spiritual apostolate by participating in the hierarchical apostolate, there are a certain number of pious associations in existence, many of which also pursue an apostolic goal under the banner of Mary.

CHAPTER TWELVE

Marian Sodalities

The oldest of the Marian lay associations are the sodalities. Their history, from their beginnings until the 18th century, has been written by Father

Villaret, the man who is undoubtedly most competent in the matter. After having reviewed before our eyes all the works in defense of the Faith and of Christian morality undertaken by these associations of young Christians consecrated to Mary, we are tempted to ask ourselves whether there are many religious orders which have, to their credit, apostolic successes superior to, or even equaling, those of these lay associations. Without having proposed to themselves at the outset any great apostolic conquests, their belonging to Mary has quite naturally led them to enter the struggle in support of the Church and the salvation of souls.

It happened, however, with the suppression of the Society of Jesus and the Jansenistic and Voltairian influences that, in many cases, the Marian sodalities lost their apostolic ardor and became content with being associations of more-or-less formalistic piety.

Here and there, especially with the end of the French Revolution, there were signs that a new spirit was blowing among them. In Paris on February 2, 1801, Father Delpuits began the exercises of the sodality with six students. On exactly the same day in Bordeaux, a group of twelve young men gathered around Father Chaminade and solemnly committed themselves to the service of the Immaculate Virgin, Mother of Youth. On his return from Saragossa,

alive with the mission he had received from the
Virgin of the Pillar — by December 8, 1800, he had
already begun to recruit the first young men who
were to form the army of the Virgin.

A sodality of young women soon followed;
thereafter, one of married men and, then, another;
a fourth, of the Ladies of the Retreat. After a few
years, he had formed an army of 700 sodalists just
within the city of Bordeaux. Similar groups were
formed in different centers in the west of France.
By their Christian conduct, "without fear and
without shame," as well as by various works of zeal
and charity, they contributed greatly to the religious
renewal of Bordeaux and its surroundings.

This was because Chaminade, convinced of Mary's
apostolic mission in modern times, devoted himself
to making each sodalist an apostle of the Virgin. He
was criticized as an innovator by a number of priests
whose ideal of a sodality continued to be the type
they had seen functioning before the Revolution.
He defended himself, pointing out the need for new
sodalities adapted to the new conditions in which
the Church founded herself. He pointed out:

> In the former sodalities, it was almost entirely
> a question of supporting devoted Christians
> along paths of mutual edification. But in our

day, in the time of renewal in which we find ourselves, religion requires something other of its children. It wants all of them together to second the zeal of its ministers and, directed by their prudence, to work at restoring it. Such is the spirit inculcated in the new sodalities. Each director is a permanent missionary; each sodality is a perpetual mission.[123]

This is really what Pius XI said about Catholic Action in his letter to Cardinal Bertram a hundred years later:

In our day, the integrity of the faith and of morals experiences a greater threat each day; and priests, by reason of their small number, are absolutely unable to provide for all the needs of souls. This is the moment to call upon Catholic Action, which will help to close the gaps in the clergy's ranks by multiplying collaborators among the laity.

It is curious to note that, with regard to the various other slogans of Catholic Action: diversity and unity; union without confusion; elite and

---

123 *Esprit de notre Fondation*, vol. 3, p. 237. {These references can also be found in Fr. Neubert's *Ecrits*, where these and other texts may be found in their entirety.}

mass — Chaminade's directives were conformed in every way to those which Rome has given to Catholic Action.[124]

Another characteristic feature of the new sodalities which Chaminade pointed out to his critics was especially dear to his heart for, in his view, the *sine qua non* of success was this:

> In effect — and no doubt, we should have begun with this because, of all the means, it is the most powerful and most dear to us — the new sodalities are not only associations **to the honor of the Blessed Virgin**; they are a new militia which advances **in the name of Mary**, which truly wants to combat the forces of hell under the special direction of and obedience to the One who is to crush the head of the serpent.[125]

Chaminade's sodality, therefore, was already a "Catholic Action" — a Catholic Action under the leadership of Mary, *Maria duce*!

> As has been said, the victories carried out by Mary's army of apostles were marvelous! A great religious renewal took place in Bordeaux

---

124 *Esprit de notre Fondation*, vol. 3, pp. 120-140.
125 *Esprit de notre Fondation*, vol. 3, p. 238.

during the 19th century; even historians minimally favorable to the Church admit it. The sodality contributed in great part to this renewal. Cardinal Donnet concurred in 1869: "When we go back to the origins of all our works in Bordeaux, the name of Chaminade is inscribed at the head of every one of them."[126]

With regard to the creation of diverse religious institutions in that period, it can be said that, in general, "the sodality was not a stranger to any one of them; to many, it provided their entire membership." This was especially so with the two Marian institutes that came out of the sodality of Bordeaux: the Society of Mary and the Institute of the Daughters of Mary. Their first members were sodalists, elated to exchange their promises of fidelity to the Queen of the Apostles for the vows of the religious life.

We can include some precise numbers to this general overview. From the sodality of Bordeaux, one hundred priests and male religious came forth,

---

126 J. Simler, *Guillaume Joseph Chaminade, chanoine honoraire de Bordeaux, fondateur de la Société de Marie & de l'Institute des filles de Marie*, Paris 1901, p. 210. [English tr.: *William Joseph Chaminade: Founder of the Marianists*, Dayton OH 1986]

and as many women religious, six bishops, seven founders of religious societies, many missionaries (including a martyr), four "servants of God" whose causes for beatification were introduced to the Roman curia.

In a number of countries, various issues during the 19th and 20th centuries prevented the sodality from maintaining the commanding influence it first had: the discredit cast upon the sodality by the enemies of the Church under the Restoration, when the political underground maneuvers of a government association called "Society of the Cavaliers of the Faith,"[127] were attributed to the society; the passivity of many of the directors of sodalities whose associations were mere banal, pious gatherings; the creation of other associations, especially the specialized movements of Catholic Action which better answered the youths' need for hands on activity.

Efforts to restore them to their apostolic spirit of former times have been attempted in various places, with growing success. As has been previously said, the presence of sodalists in these modern groups

---

127 See thesis of Bertier de Sauvigny, on *Le comte Ferdinand de Bertier et l'Enigme de la Congrégatio* (*Count Ferdinand de Bertier and the Enigma of the Congregation*) Les Presses Continentales, Paris, 1948.

seems to be necessary to prevent them from losing their supernatural spirit and their apostolic effectiveness. Besides, Marian sodalities are spread throughout the world and they have not all encountered the obstacles which were problematic in France [and still are].

Pius XI, the Pope of Catholic Action, had ranked the Marian sodalities among the auxiliary works of Catholic Action because, by their example and prayer, they were of invaluable help to the various groups.

Pius XII, who had a profound knowledge of the sodalities of the Blessed Virgin through his personal experience of the older sodality and his historical study of the work, found that the sodalities had always carried on a very active apostolate and that they lacked none of the marks of Catholic Action. Consequently, by his Bull *Bis saeculari* of September 27, 1948, he declared that the Marian sodalities may, with every right, be called "Catholic Action undertaken under the inspiration and with the help of the most Blessed Virgin."[128]

---

128 *Acta Apostolicae Sedis*, (abbreviated hereafter AAS) 1948, pp. 393-402.

Not only did Pius XII attribute a precise, active apostolate to the Marian sodalities, but he recognized it as one of the first order.

> In our day these Marian phalanxes march in the glorious footsteps of their ancestors and are religiously faithful to their rules. Under the auspices and direction of the hierarchy, they strive to maintain first place in works to be undertaken, and to constantly uphold the greater glory of God and the well-being of souls. They should, therefore, be counted among the most spiritual and powerful forces in the defense and extension of the Catholic religion.

And this, for many reasons! The primary reason mentioned by the Pope was the astonishingly rapid multiplication of sodalities at that time. While "in the preceding centuries, the annual number of affiliations to the Prima Primaria never exceeded a dozen — since the beginning of the 20th century, it has easily reached one thousand."

CHAPTER THIRTEEN

The Children of Mary

The Marian associations of young girls — the "Children of Mary" — developed on a par with associations of young men. Among the Children of Mary, some are attached to the sodalities of the Jesuits. Others have their origin in the Blessed Virgin's request to Saint Catherine Labouré (Our Lady's messenger for the origin and diffusion of the Miraculous Medal) to have her confessor found the "Confraternity of the Children of Mary." They are under the guidance of the Sisters of Saint Vincent de Paul and of the Vincentians, and are the subject of our immediate topic.

Founded in 1837 and approved canonically by Pius IX in 1847, they experienced a rapid expansion. Thirty years after the birth of the Association, they had amassed 60,000 members throughout Europe, Africa, and the two Americas. They devoted themselves to piety and to the apostolate: religious instruction, seeking out non-baptized children or those who had not yet made First Holy Communion, diffusion of good books, working among the poor, etc.

Little by little, however, their former enthusiasm grew weaker through lack of adaptability and the negligence of their directors. They lost the interest of a great number of the faithful (the young in particular), and also of the clergy. Catholic Action, especially the specialized movements, attracted attention and responded better to the aspirations of the young for initiative and exterior activity, rather than associations which seemed to exist only for piety and simply required an attitude of obedience. Even within the associations, many lost confidence in the ***work***.

However, among the sons and daughters of Saint Vincent de Paul, there was a certain number who could not, and would not, believe that a work founded by Mary should be aborted. Among the prisoners detained in Germany at the beginning of World War II, there was a Vincentian priest who was deeply concerned with the decline in numbers of the Children of Mary. Against all odds, he was sent back to France because of a serious illness. In gratitude to the Blessed Virgin, he decided to use all his energies to revive the ***work***; and with the approval of the bishop of Lourdes, he decided to launch a "crusade" in favor of the Association of the Children of Mary.

Evidently, the spirit of these groups had to be renewed in keeping with the times by giving them an apostolic orientation. The priest was convinced that Mary is not only a "special vessel of devotion," but also the "Queen of Apostles." A book presenting apostolic filial piety according to the spirit of Father Chaminade found its way into his hands and gave him great satisfaction because it was a confirmation of his own views.

The "crusade" went forth from the Grotto of Lourdes in 1941 and quickly took on a triumphal momentum. Not only did a goodly number of languishing groups emerge with new life, but many new ones were formed. In January 1, 1941, there were 865 groups in France; by 1948, there were 1,400. In 1947, a pilgrimage of 500 Children of Mary went from Paris to Rome on the occasion of the canonization of their foundress, Saint Catherine Labouré. They were happy and proud to hear Pius XII declare their Association "sovereignly useful, even eminently necessary."

In 1948, an international congress in Paris brought the Children of Mary together from around the world—they numbered 12,000. For three days, they studied the essential orientation that had to be given to the *work* in keeping with the theme: Tradition and Renewal. Emphasis was placed on consecration to Mary, on a deeper understanding of Christian doctrine, on a solid supernatural formation, on a spirit of adaptation, and on the sense of personal responsibility.

Animated with this new spirit, in complete agreement with the aspirations of souls in the mid-20th century, the Children of Mary are ready to carry out their apostolic task. They do so in two ways: by "integrating their associations within the framework of both parish and diocese," and by their "collaboration with other works and movements." Since a pontifical decision of 1931, they are no longer a work reserved to the Daughters of Charity. They may, therefore, be "increasingly established in all the parishes and schools in keeping with the unanimous desires of pastors and bishops. The Children of Mary thus constitute an elite group of young women of the parish, under parochial direction, and specifically at the service of the parish. More and more, the Children of Mary at boarding schools are being formed to join the parochial elite upon graduation. Instead of fading into the background, the groups of the Children of Mary are being federated into diocesan units more and more."

By that very fact, establishing fraternal harmony with all the other works and movements becomes easier. In fact, the Children of Mary are practically all engaged in the apostolate. They are among the best militants and directors of our specialized Catholic Action movements. In any case, they are almost the only ones who stabilize the entire gamut of parish works.

In 1954 there were about 1,000 associations of the Children of Mary in France, and some 36,000 throughout the world (perhaps even more). But, more wonderful than the increase in numbers was the transformation of souls. Priests who saw the Children of Mary only a few years ago as merely pious and unproductive women, have marveled at their dynamic energy now. How many of the clergy presently {1955} see that, among the militants and directors of specialized movements, the most dedicated and most capable are generally the Children of Mary!

CHAPTER FOURTEEN

The Militia of Mary Immaculate

The Militia of Mary Immaculate owes its origin to {Saint} Maximilian Kolbe. One of his compatriots, Maria Winowska, popularized his life under the title of "Our Lady's Fool."[129]

Before Kolbe's mother ever considered marriage, she had thought of entering the religious life. Subsequently, however, she married a pious young man and five male children were born of this union. Two died at a young age; two became Cordeliers {Conventual Franciscans}; and the future Father Maximilian set his sights on becoming a merchant. When the family had grown, his mother revisited her ideal of days-gone-by and went on to become a Felician extern; his father entered the Franciscan Order and later left to join the Army during World War I. After capture in battle he was executed by Russian military. This struck young Kolbe like a

---

129 M. Winowska, *Le fou de Notre-Dame: le Père Maximilien Kolbe*, Paris, Editions du Cerf, 1949. [English tr.: *Our Lady's Fool. Fr. Maximilian Kolbe, Friar Minor Conventual*, Cork 1951]

thunder bolt, whereupon he also sought admittance to the Cordeliers.

Upon ordination to the priesthood, he discovered that six of the brethren shared his dream and, together, they founded the "Militia of the Immaculate." This was in October of 1917 — the year of Mary's apparitions at Fatima.

At another point in his life, doctors diagnosed him as terminally ill and he was sent to a sanitarium for the remainder of his time. But, one fine day, much to the consternation of his superiors, he returned to his convent in Krakow and proposed his desire to publish a Marian magazine. Treated as a fool, he was spared no insults! Stubborn, but likeable, he continued to pursue the challenge and finally obtained permission. However, his community did not provide a single penny for his undertaking; yet, funding arrived in a mysterious way! In 1922, he published *Mary's Knight*. He further hoped to purchase a printing press and a late-model Linotype. It was his dream to create a publication center on the outskirts of Krakow, and to furnish office space and work areas with state-of-the arts equipment.

His superiors always found his projects too extravagant; however, they allowed him to forge ahead because necessary help always arrived at the opportune time. Over 700 workers labored without pay as Father Kolbe always recruited lay brothers for Mary's work. This new city was named Niepokalanow (Mary's Garden). Publication of *Mary's Knight* increased with each edition: a few thousand copies at first; 400,000 in 1930; a million in 1939.

The whole world was about to be conquered for Christ under the auspices of Our Lady! Then came the day when the superiors were astonished to learn that the good priest was hoping to go to Japan to publish *Mary's Knight* in the Japanese language. After relentless supplications, he received permission from the bishop, and exactly one month later, he launched the first edition of *Mary's Knight* in Japanese. In December of the same year 25,000 copies were printed and distributed without charge.

Two years later, Kolbe left for India. His idea was that "a local Niepokalanow should be founded in each country from which the Immaculate could enlighten the entire region." Subsequently, he returned to Poland. To the weekly *Knight*, he added the *Little Newspaper*, which soon became the most popular newspaper in the country. At the same time, he published the *Miles Immaculatae* for priests, in order to reach beyond his own country to the entire world.

The spiritual doctrine that was the basis of this immense apostolic activity — belonging entirely to Mary Immaculate — also sustained his interior life and that of his co-workers. He would say to them: "It is Mary who should form us, raise us, sanctify us. ... Each day, we should become more the property of the Blessed Virgin, her knights-errant ... In the hands of Our Lady, we should be ... like a pen in the hand of a scribe, like a brush in the hand of a painter, like a chisel in the hand of a sculptor, that she might make of us whatever she wishes!"

The Militia of the Immaculate was marching onward from triumph to triumph when war broke out in 1939. Poland was the first to be attacked. From September 19th, Kolbe and his community were taken by trucks to Amfitz, a camp in Germany. He urged his confreres to rejoice because the Blessed Virgin had sent them *gratis* on a mission to Germany. "What a godsend this is," he said, and immediately set to work distributing — even to the Germans — the "miraculous medal," of which he always had a pocketful. On the feast of the Immaculate Conception, word came that they would be set free.

Kolbe had dreamed of martyrdom. In May of 1941, a packed truck took him to the extermination camp at Auschwitz. The following July, one prisoner disappeared from his cell block. In reprisal, ten men were chosen to die in the "starvation bunker." One of them cried out: "My poor wife, my poor children"! Kolbe broke ranks and offered himself to "Kraff the bloody," commandant of the camp, to die in the place of the unfortunate father of a family. Kraff, who had a deadly hatred for Kolbe because he was a priest, accepted the offer.

He and his companions were imprisoned in a death block. There would be nothing more to eat and, what is infinitely more torturous, nothing more to drink until death. Earlier, this bunker had resonated with the howling screams of the damned! But now, what a startling change! The SS could not understand it: the condemned men prayed and sang. Two weeks later, only Kolbe was still alive until a prison guard administered the lethal injection. His body was burned in the crematorium with all the others.

Then, prayers began to ascend to him from everywhere and numerous miraculous favors were being attributed to him; hence began his process for canonization.

And what of the work he accomplished? Did it die with him? Quite to the contrary! At the present time {mid 20th century}, the Militia continues its conquests in nearly all parts of the globe with centers in Poland, Italy, Spain, Holland, Belgium, Romania, and South Africa.

A perhaps more astonishing triumph was with his brethren who, having all been opposed to so many of his endeavors and seeing him only as a fool, all became infected with his folly. The general chapter of the Order decided on the establishment of the Militia in every friary, and the foundation of Niepokalanow branches in each country. The various Franciscan publications devote articles to the Militia and increasingly strive to place all their apostolate under the banner of Mary Immaculate. "Our Lady's fool" did not work or suffer or sacrifice his life in vain. Those who battle under the standard of the Immaculate are always victorious!

CHAPTER FIFTEEN

The Legion of Mary

The Legion of Mary was born in 1921, in Dublin, Ireland, on the first vespers of the Nativity of Mary.

Several people had arranged to meet in a building named Myra House. The group consisted of a priest {Fr. Michael Toher}; Frank Duff, an employee at the ministry of finances; and some fifteen women, almost all office workers or store employees. They wished to devote themselves to a distinctly spiritual apostolate, similar to that of the associates of the Saint Vincent de Paul Society. They assembled around a table on which a statue of the most Blessed Virgin had been placed.

After the recitation of the *Veni Sancte Spiritus* and the rosary, Duff spoke of the discovery he had just made of the *Treatise on True Devotion to the Blessed Virgin* by Grignion de Montfort, which he found offensive upon first reading it. The doctrine of the universal mediation of Mary, however, had struck him and he was convinced that this doctrine is the source of life. He was determined to draw apostolic consequences from it. With contagious ardor, he explained to those in attendance that a sincere devotion to Mary must be active: it compels us to work for Mary, to help her save the souls for whom she suffered so much.

It was decided that they would go two-by-two to visit the United Hospital of Dublin to give spiritual encouragement to the patients, and that they would return to the Myra House the following week to report on the results and to be assigned new tasks. Gradually, the group increased and became organized. It took on the name of Legion of Mary because it was organized like a Roman legion. In this way, it avoided giving the group an Irish identity since its intent was to extend to all the countries of the world.

The Legion has a central council or *concilium legionis*, a national council called a *senatus,* a canton council called a *curia*, and a local group called a *praesidium*. The praesidium is the strategic unit of the Legion, its center of apostolic influence. It is composed of the Legionaries of the parish and directed by a president, a vice-president, a treasurer, and a secretary. Whenever possible, a priest serves as spiritual director.

The praesidium meets every week and all Legionaries consider regular attendance at the meetings their first duty. It is there that they absorb the apostolic and Marian spirit of the Legion. It is there that they gather to give a report on the work accomplished and to receive assignments for the apostolate for the following week. In addition to active members, the Legion has auxiliaries who assist with the daily recitation of the rosary and other prayers contained in the *tessera* [certificate of membership].

The *Handbook* states that "the spirit of the Legion is the spirit of Mary herself." Three titles of Mary, above all, should capture the attention of the Legionary:

1) Her quality of Mediatrix of all graces –

"The Legion's trust in Mary is limitless, knowing that by the ordinance of God, her power is without limit" (*Handbook*, p. 19).

2) Her Immaculate Conception –

The Immaculate Conception is referred to by God in the same sentence in which Mary herself is first promised to us. ... "I will put enmity between you and the Woman, between your offspring and hers. She shall crush your head and you will lay in wait for her heel" (Gen 3:15).[130]

To these words, addressed to Satan by Almighty God, the Legion turns as the source of its confidence and strength in its warfare with sin. It aims with all its heart to become in fullness the seed, the children of Mary, for there is the pledge of victory. In the measure that it makes her more and more its mother, is the Legion's enmity with

---

130 {Vulgate version.}

the powers of evil intensified and victory made more complete (*Handbook*, p. 20).

3) Her spiritual maternity in our regard –

Truly her children, we must conduct ourselves as such, and indeed as very little children, utterly dependent upon her. We must look to her to feed us, to guide us, to teach us, to cure our ailments, to console us in our grief, to counsel us in our doubts, to recall us when we wander, so that wholly confided to her care, we may grow to resemble our elder brother, Jesus, and share in His mission of combating sin and conquering it (*Handbook*, p. 21).

The *Handbook* concludes:

Legionary devotion {is} the root of the Legionary apostolate. One of the dearest duties of the Legion shall be to show whole-hearted devotion to the Mother of God (*Handbook*, p. 22). ... Adequate devotion to her is only achieved through union with her. Union necessarily means community of life with her; and her life does not mainly consist in claiming admiration but in communicating grace (*Handbook*, p. 32). ... Our Lady might declare: 'I am the Apostolate,' almost as she said:

'I am the Immaculate Conception' (*Handbook*, p. 32).

It is to the Holy Spirit, the Spirit of the apostolate, to whom the Legionaries make their promises. But the Holy Spirit never acts without Mary and always acts through Mary. Here is part of the text of the promise:

Most Holy Spirit, I, … ,

> Desiring to be enrolled this day as a legionary of Mary,
>
> Yet knowing that, of myself, I cannot render worthy service,
>
> I do ask of you to come upon me and fill me with yourself
>
> So that my poor actions may be sustained by your power
>
> And become the instruments of your mighty designs.
>
> But I know that you, who have come to regenerate the world in Jesus Christ,
>
> Have not willed to do so except through Mary;
>
> That, without her, we can neither know nor love you,
>
> That it is through her that all your gifts, all your virtues, all your graces are distributed to whom

she pleases, whenever she pleases, and in the quantity and manner in which she pleases;

And I realize that the secret to perfectly fulfilling the service of a legionary consists in uniting myself entirely to her who is so completely united to you (*Handbook*, p. 98).

For this reason, taking in hand the legionary standard which presents all these truths before our eyes,

I stand before you as her soldier and her child,

And I therefore proclaim my entire dependence upon her.

She is the mother of my soul.

Her heart and mine are one;

And from the depths of her unique heart, her words echo as of old:

'Behold the servant of the Lord.'

And once again, you come through her to do great things (*Handbook*, p. 90).

Growth came slowly for the Legion. Five years after its foundation, it was still confined to the Archdiocese of Dublin. But, then, "behold, the blast of a tempest: in 1927, the Legion began to move into all the dioceses of Ireland; in 1928, it crossed the seas and took root in Scotland." Then, in 1929, England opened its gates to it. In 1931, it entered America; in 1932, Australia; in 1933, Africa; in 1937, Asia, through China; in 1940, the Philippines; in 1948, Japan.[131]

Now, there are millions of active and auxiliary members of the Legion. It is, in fact, difficult to give exact figures, for what is true today may be too little tomorrow. At the end of 1953, the *tessera* was being spoken in some seventy languages. A report from Dublin at the end of February 1956, noted:

> The Legion is working in more than 900 dioceses, with an increase of about two per week. On the average, a new *praesidium* is formed every day in the Belgian Congo, in the Philippines, and in Central America. Last year, 150 *praesidia* were founded in 150 days. Other locations also indicate increase in numbers.
>
> The only places where the Legion does not exist today are in the "russianized" {Communist} parts of the world, i.e., Russia itself and the adjacent countries behind the Iron Curtain. Of course, it is possible that the

---

131 Report of Bishop Suenens, in *Maria. Etudes sur le Sainte Vierge*, vol. 3, pp. 651-652 {later Archbishop and Cardinal}.

Legion secretly exists there, but we have no information on this point {as of mid 1950's}.

All the apostolic nuncios and delegates today are in favor of the Legion.

The Legion's apostolate is universal. It is obedient to Mary's word to the servants at Cana: "Do whatever he tells you," i.e., *He*, being the Christ, through the voice of His representatives, visiting the elderly, the sick, lepers, the poor, the imprisoned; teaching catechesis; taking of parish census; recruiting sodalities and other apostolic works; rescuing children, adults, and prostitutes from moral depravity; preparing candidates for First Holy Communion; re-validating marriages; caring for immigrants; giving retreats to military personnel and Protestants; providing the apostolate to itinerants; giving classes to North Africans; converting non-Catholics: Protestants (in great number), schismatics (work has begun), Muslims (with success on some points), Buddhists (numerous conversions), Communists (many have become dedicated apostles of Christ).

In the name of Mary, the Legion has accomplished marvels from its inception and continues to do so every day. This can easily be seen by reading the *Bulletins* and other Legion periodicals. The Chinese

Communists have learned, to their chagrin, and have taught the entire world of what caliber is the apostolic courage with which Mary arms her Legionaries.

At present {1950s} the Legion of Mary is the most spectacular proof of the apostolic mission of the Immaculate Virgin and of the effectiveness of an apostolate carried out in her name.

What is the secret of the Legion of Mary's great fruitfulness? It can be attributed to both natural and supernatural causes.

Natural Causes: both its suppleness and its rigidity –

Suppleness in its works: A specialized work, as are almost all apostolic works (preaching, teaching, Catholic Action movements, etc.), may not appeal to some parishes or dioceses. But a work which adapts itself to multiple and changing needs always finds a field of opportunity in any place and at any moment.

Besides, the abilities required in other works generally demand prolonged formation, studies, and a practical apprenticeship over many years. The Legionaries begin their apostolic work immediately upon entry into Mary's army. And, since they go on mission with a companion, they always have one another's joint support. At the weekly meeting, they relate their successes and difficulties, and all in attendance profit from their experiences.

Rigidity in its method: The Handbook insists on "the immutability of the Legionary system." This immutability, which might appear to some as a spirit of intolerance, is the condition for the very existence of the Legion. For, if each praesidium or curia could modify or suppress some bothersome item, the Legion would discontinue to be what it is, and would quickly cease to exist at all.

Supernatural Causes –

Much more, even, than these natural causes of success, the supernatural factors are accountable for it. In most other works, the perfection of natural means has an important role. The preacher, the educator, the conference presenter, the monitor of works, the missionary — all take care to use every natural means to assure success. They run the risk of preoccupying themselves with the natural means at the expense of the supernatural. And, when they do succeed, the temptation is great to attribute it to personal talent, eloquence, or knowledge.

The Legion only relies for help from on high. It asks for two hours of external work each week, but special prayers every day, the rosary in particular, which is the apostolic prayer *par excellence* according to the experience of all the great converters of souls. At the weekly meeting, the report of work accomplished and the distribution of new tasks take but a short period of time, and these are preceded and followed by the recitation of various prayers and a short spiritual presentation. Besides this, the active members are helped by the millions of auxiliary members, generally religious men and women and other pious persons, who are all happy to contribute to the success of Mary's army with their prayers and sacrifices.

But it is, above all else, a very special confidence in Mary that confers on the Legion's activity an effectiveness often touching on the miraculous. This was previously stated with reference to the Legion's devotion to the Immaculate Conception. But there is reason to further highlight it as the most important factor. The *Handbook* repeatedly refers to it:

> Inspired by this love and faith in Mary, her Legion undertakes any and every task and 'does not plead impossibility, because it reckons that everything is possible and can be

accomplished' (*Imitation of* Christ, book 3:5) (*Handbook*, p. 13).

Bearing her name with inexpressible pride, the Legion is founded with unbounded and childlike trust in this good Mother, solidified by profoundly implanting it in the heart of each individual, thereby possessing the members who work together in a perfect harmony of loyalty and discipline. For this reason, the Legion of Mary does not consider it presumption but, rather, a right degree of confidence to believe that its system forms, as it were, a powerful mechanism which only requires the docile response to Authority to embrace the entire world. Therefore, Mary will deign to employ her instrument to accomplish her maternal work for souls, and to carry on her perpetual mission of crushing the head of the serpent (*Handbook*, p. 24). Would we be wrong to expect it?

These exhortations to absolute confidence in Mary, because the Legion is doing Mary's work, are present in one form or another throughout the entire *Handbook,* which is both code and gospel of the Legionaries. They find their trust is nourished in daily prayers, the weekly meeting, reports on members' successes, accounts to the *Bulletin* and other legionary periodicals. They try, they succeed; their trust is strengthened!

If the contemporaries of Jesus had enough faith to obtain miracles — and they were not saints! — it was because they perceived, that in the multitude of miracles, it sufficed to ask with faith in order to obtain. A view of the apostolic marvels produced throughout the world by the Legionaries in the name of Mary, serves to confirm that she comes through for them and for others as well, provided they act in her name. As a soldier in an always-victorious army, one fights with confidence when an invincible leader is in command.

CHAPTER SIXTEEN

Miraculous Interventions of the Queen of Apostles

Tradition has provided us with an imposing mass of testimony in favor of Mary's apostolic mission. We have, of course, simply referred to those most important, to which we can only give a minimal outline. The 19th and 20th centuries are particularly rich in documentation, and amply prove the truth of the prophecies of Saint Louis-Marie de Montfort and {Blessed} William Joseph Chaminade relative to the triumphant action of the Immaculate Virgin in these new times.

But one might say that all these proofs, startling as they may be, were not enough for Mary. She wished to add a succession of direct, miraculous interventions to them, not as formerly made in favor of one or another of her servants for their consolation or their personal edification, or to confide the mission of founding a new religious society to a particular man of God, but to the mass of the faithful in view of their conversion and sanctification.

No matter how convinced, ardent, and active a new religious society or association may be, its foundation, its growth, its organization, and a clear consciousness of its own mission generally require a rather long time before it can truly radiate its Marian message all around. To move quickly from a very indifferent period, from a Marian point of view, to a Marian period *par excellence*, the Virgin had to intervene directly.

We will only consider here the apparitions for which the ecclesiastical authority, after a more or less lengthy investigation (always lasting for several years), has recognized that they may be considered authentic. Many works have published these events.[132] Here, we will only highlight their apostolic impact.

****

Apparitions of Mary to Saint Catherine Labouré The Miraculous Medal

In 1830, Catherine Labouré, a novice with the Daughters of Charity at rue du Bac, Paris, was favored with two apparitions of the Virgin.

In the first one, on July 18th, Mary gave Catherine some personal advice on how she was to conduct herself, and warned her that she would encounter many contradictions and would see many evils befalling France (alluding to the July Revolution of 1830 which would occur a few days later, and to the Paris Commune and the murder of the archbishop). Then she gave her a message for Father Aladel, her confessor, to work toward reforming the two

---

132 An excellent summary of these facts was published by J. Goubert and L. Cristiani: *Les Apparitions de la Sainte Vierge de 1830 à nos jours*, La Colombe.

communities: the Sisters and the Priests of Saint Vincent de Paul, who had fallen into great laxity and to whom she promised her assistance.

The more memorable second apparition, took place on November 27th. Mary appeared to the Novice in the form replicated on the popularly-named "Miraculous Medal." She said: "Have a medal cast according to this image. All those who wear it will receive great graces. The graces will be abundant, especially for persons who wear it with confidence."

Aladel, to whom Catherine first communicated this apparition, only viewed it as the over-active imagination of a young girl. He made no effort to carry out Mary's directive. It was only after two years, following repeated insistence in the name of Mary and some providential signs, that he spoke of it to the Archbishop of Paris. The prelate, seeing nothing in the project contrary to faith or morals, granted the desired approbation — but one that was essentially negative.

Several years later, however, he published a praiseworthy review on the medal. He did this because, after becoming available, the medal had spread with prodigious speed. News abounded from everywhere of the miraculous cures and conversions performed by Mary in favor of those who wore it.

Very soon, it became known as the "Miraculous Medal." It rapidly spread beyond the borders of France to all nations of the world. Millions of these medals have been cast, and its popularity continues to increase.

With regard to what concerns the apostolic import of these apparitions, we note:

1) the personal holiness of the visionary, canonized by Pius XII in 1947. Now, if "every soul that is lifted up, uplifts the world," what must the influence of a saint be?

2) the return to fervor of two important religious societies: the Vincentians or Priests of Saint Vincent de Paul, whose apostolate extends throughout the world; and the Daughters of Charity, the most numerous and certainly one of the most apostolic societies of women in all the world.

3) the influence of the Miraculous Medal: There have been stories of innumerable conversions, some of them truly unbelievable, "miraculous" in the words of its beneficiaries of which it was, and still is, the instrument. The medal exercises still another apostolate, doubtlessly no less profound and more extensive through the supernatural spirit it creates and intensifies in millions of believers. The

medal is the insignia, the image, of their heavenly Mother who helps them feel that, above this world of matter and sinfulness, there is something other of purity, love, and goodness. For how many individuals is Mary the point of contact between Heaven and earth? For how many does she make faith more natural, more real, and more active? One can certainly have great devotion to Mary without wearing her medal. But for multitudes of Christians, her medal brings her closer, makes her more real, and helps them to better appreciate the goodness and mercy of her Son!

4) We mentioned earlier that, after these apparitions, Catherine Labouré was Mary's instrument in the founding of the Children of Mary, an immense army of apostles in diverse places throughout the entire world.

****

Apparition of Mary to Alphonse Ratisbonne

The conversion of Alphonse Ratisbonne is no doubt one of the most striking examples of the marvels performed through the intervention of the Miraculous Medal. It is appropriate to treat it separately because it is connected to an apparition of the Virgin, and because it was to have a very special apostolic impact.

Alphonse was born in Strasbourg to a family of Jewish bankers. He had no particular faith, but nurtured a special hatred for the Catholic religion. This was so because his older brother had embraced Catholicism and even became a priest, to the great scandal and blistering irritation of the family.

Alphonse was engaged to a young Jewish girl, but before contracting the marriage, he had decided to take a trip to the East. The ship took him to Naples where he was to remain for a few days. His hatred for the Catholic faith continued to increase and, out of curiosity, Alphonse went to Rome where he met Mr. de Buissières, a former Protestant, his schoolmate from the Lycée of Strasbourg who, having recently converted to the Faith, was afire with the zeal of a neophyte. De Buissieres spoke of the greatness and benefits of Catholicism, to which Ratisbonne only responded with sarcasm.

> "Since you have a mind so keen and enlightened," de Buissières finally said to him, "do you have the courage to submit to a very simple test?"

> "What kind of a test?"

"That of wearing a medal of the Blessed Virgin on your person."

Ratisbonne shrugged his shoulders; De Buissières persisted! Finally, Ratisbonne agreed, saying to himself that the incident would provide an interesting chapter to his "Impressions of My Trip." He took the medal and suspended it from his neck.

He had to remain in Rome longer than planned and each time when he met up with his friend, he expressed the usual invectives against the Catholic religion.

On the eve of his departure for Naples, quite by chance he happened to meet the carriage of de Buissières who invited him to come aboard for a short trip and, in turn, he accepted. When they reached the small church of San Andrea delle Fratte, de Buissières alighted from the carriage and went to the sacristy to arrange for the funeral of one of his friends — a fervent Catholic to whose prayers he had strongly recommended the young Jew's conversion. De Buissieres asked his companion to wait for him in the carriage. A moment later, though, Ratisbonne decided to visit the church. It was there that Mary was awaiting him.

I was in the church only a moment when, all of a sudden, I was overcome by an inexpressible emotion. I raised my eyes; the entire building disappeared from view! A concentration of bright light, so to speak, inundated the sanctuary, and in the midst of this brilliance, the Virgin appeared on the altar — great, shining, full of majesty and kindness, just as she is on the Miraculous Medal. An irresistible force thrust me toward her! The Virgin made a sign with her hand that I should kneel down. She seemed to be saying to me: "That is good!"

De Buissières returned and found his friend on his knees, breaking into tears and kissing the medal of the Immaculate Virgin with great tenderness. He could not explain what had happened, saying only: "She said nothing to me, but I have understood all." Upon his request, de Buissières took him to a priest to whom Ratisbonne related what had occurred.

He asked for Baptism. He was given an explanation of the teachings of the Catholic faith. He understood everything immediately, and accepted all the mysteries without hesitation, in particular, that of the Real Presence. The Virgin had said nothing to him, but he had understood everything so well that, after a very short time, he received Baptism and took the name of Mary.

But it was not a mere personal favor that the Virgin wanted to grant him; it would serve to benefit others.

For one thing, it solemnly confirmed Mary's promise to the faithful who would wear her medal. News of the astonishing conversion obtained through Mary immediately spread about Rome and then quickly to the borders. The Breviary provides this account on the feast of the Miraculous Medal, November 27th.

This event was destined to give birth to an undertaking for the conversion of Jews. Ratisbonne understood that the Virgin had so favored him only in view of a mission to be carried out among his former co-religionists. He renounced the world and became a priest in 1847. Already in 1843, with his priest-brother, Marie Theodore Ratisbonne, he founded the Society of the Religious of Our Lady of Zion (women), established to foster the conversion of the Jews. In 1856, he established a monastery of that congregation in Palestine, at Ain-Karim, the "town of Judah in the high country" where Mary had gone to visit her cousin. There, eighteen hundred years earlier, under the inspiration of the Holy Spirit, the young Virgin had chanted:

> *He has helped Israel his servant, remembering*
>   *his mercy,*
> *according to his promise to our fathers,*
>   *to Abraham and to his descendants forever.*[133]

There, three months later, the voice of the old priest, Zachariah, also under the inspiration of the Holy Spirit, echoed Mary's voice:

> *Blessed be the Lord, the God of Israel, for he*
>   *has visited and brought redemption to his*
>   *people.*
> *He has raised up a horn for our salvation*
>   *Within the house of David his servant,*
> *even as he promised through the mouth of his*
>   *holy prophets from of old.*[134]

****

Apparition of Mary
to the Two Young Children of La Salette

Drawing the attention of his disciples at Corinth to the mystery of their election, Saint Paul tells them:

---

133 Lk 1:54-55.
134 Lk 1:68-70.

Consider your own calling, brothers. Not many of you were wise by human standards; not many were powerful; not many were of noble birth. Rather, God chose the foolish of the world to shame the wise, and God chose the weak of the world to shame the strong; and God chose the lowly and despised of the world, those who count for nothing, to reduce to nothing those who are something, so that no human being might boast before God.[135]

The apostle is only commenting on the Master's thought: "I give you praise, Father, Lord of heaven and earth, for although you have hidden these things from the wise and the learned, you have revealed them to the childlike."[136]

In her apparitions (particularly those of the 19th and 20th centuries) — except for the apparition to Ratisbonne — the Blessed Virgin applied herself to following God's identical rule. Hadn't she previously chanted: "My soul proclaims the greatness of the Lord; my spirit rejoices in God my Savior, for he has looked upon his handmaid's lowliness"?[137]

---

[135] I Cor 1:26-29.
[136] Lk 10:21.
[137] Lk 1:46-48.

Catherine Labouré had barely learned to read and, much later, to write (her spelling was atrocious!). At least, she had good common sense and deep piety. The two visionaries of La Salette were not only small for their age, but were of mediocre intelligence and piety. They were born at Corps, a village in the area of Grenoble.

Maximin Giraud was slightly over twelve years old. He hardly ever prayed, often missed Mass, and knew almost nothing of the good God. Melanie Calvat was almost fifteen, but seemed more like twelve. She was often moody, lazy, and quite timid. As for prayers, she only knew the Our Father, the Hail Mary, and the Creed. In regard to her morals, she had never been the object of suspicion. Neither one made any attempt to attract attention, and would have preferred obscurity to publicity. Their families were in dire need and both children guarded flocks for other families.

On September 19, 1846, the eve of the feast of Our Lady of Sorrows, Maximin and Melanie were guarding the cows on the hills of La Salette. They ate their lunch at noon and then fell asleep in the lower valley near a dried out stream bed.

Around 2:30 in the afternoon, Melanie awoke and called to Maximin. Where were their cows? They climbed to the plateau above and saw the cows lying down a short distance away. Descending again to the valley to retrieve their sacks, Melanie saw a blinding light at the base. "Maximin!" she cried out, "do you see that brilliant light down there?" At that moment, the light parted and, little by little, revealed a beautiful woman, surrounded in glory, but extremely sad. She was in a seated position, with her elbows on her knees and her face buried in her hands.

The children were frightened! But the beautiful woman got up, crossed her arms over her breast and said to them: "Come here, my children. Do not be afraid! I am here to tell you some great news." Reassured, the children drew very close to her. The beautiful woman was crowned with a rich diadem. She was carrying a crucifix on her breast and weeping copious tears. She said to the children:

> If my people do not submit, I will be forced to release my Son's arm. It is so very heavy and cumbersome that I can no longer restrain it. I have long been suffering for you! ... If I wish that my Son not abandon you, I am obliged to pray unceasingly. As for you, you don't even care! ... No matter how much you pray or do good, you will never sufficiently compensate for the pain I have endured for

you! … I have given you six days to work. The seventh, I have reserved for myself, but you do not wish to yield it to me. Those who drive the carts do not know how to swear without using the name of my Son. These are the two things that lay weight to his arm. If the harvest is spoiled, that means nothing to you.

She cited the harvesting of potatoes, of wheat, of vineyards, and of nuts as examples, and announced other chastisements of famines and epidemics.

Then she gave a special secret to each of the two visionaries, and asked them: "Do you pray well, my children?" "No, madam, not really." "Ah, my children, you should pray every morning and evening. If you cannot do better, at least recite one Our Father and one Hail Mary; and when you have the time, you should say more."

The Virgin ended by saying: "Well, my children, you must pass this on to all my people." Then, ascending toward the heavens, she disappeared.

Obviously, such reproaches and threats were not intended for the shepherds themselves, but for the populace: "You must pass this on to all my people."

Heading home that evening, the children related their marvelous adventure to their masters. Their story was soon heard in the village and surrounding countryside by both skeptics and admirers. The church authorities made a lengthy inquiry into the occurrence; and after only five years, the bishop of Grenoble published a favorable judgment. Blessed Pius IX accorded numerous privileges to the chapel which had been erected at the place of apparition. Leo XIII did as much; and Pius XII honored the Missionaries of La Salette with a letter on the occasion of the centenary of the apparition. Moreover, the calamities predicted by the beautiful Lady happened: the vineyards, the potatoes crops, and the nuts were all diseased; there were 150,000 victims of cholera in 1855; more than 150,000 people died from starvation, etc.

Does that mean that Mary's intervention was in vain? Not at all! It elicited an extensive return to God, especially in the region where the apparition had taken place: cessation of work on Sunday, attendance at Mass, frequent confessions and communions.[138] Crowds of pilgrims arrived; subsequently, group pilgrimages were organized. The first was comprised of residents from Corps. A second soon followed, with six other parishes joining

---

138 See Gaëtan Bernoville, *La Salette*, pp. 66-68ff.

the parish from Corps. Others then came from the entire region, from all of France, and then from other countries. Duly certified healings occurred; remarkable conversions took place; many others, no doubt, remain in the privacy of individual souls. In order to care for the spiritual needs of the pilgrims, a small oratory was first established. It gave rise to a great basilica through enormous efforts and great sacrifices from 1852 to 1864.

Resident missionaries were assigned to the sanctuary. After a few years, they established the religious Society of the Missionaries of La Salette. In 1946, centenary of the apparition, they numbered 730. They have spread to various countries in Europe, Africa, America, and Asia, seeking to carry the message of La Salette to the entire world, in keeping with the beautiful Lady's admonition to the little visionaries: "You must pass this on to all my people."

****

The Apparitions of Lourdes

The facts of the Lourdes account are well-known to readers; it will suffice to revisit them briefly.

The visionary, Bernadette Soubirous, was born of very poor parents. She was fourteen years old at the time of the apparitions. She had been raised by her wet-nurse in a hamlet near Lourdes and was occupied with tending a small flock. Prevented by her work from going to school, she received the basics of religious instruction every evening from her nurse, but her less-than-receptive mind had great difficulty understanding and retaining the lessons. She was frail and asthmatic.

On the other hand, she was kind, always smiling, of a very friendly nature; she loved the good God and the Virgin Mary. She had requested that her parents have her sent back to Lourdes to attend school and to make First Holy Communion. Only a few weeks after Bernadette's return to her family, the Blessed Virgin chose her as her messenger to the world.

The Mother of Jesus appeared to her eighteen times in 1858, between February 11th and July 16th. We will only touch upon the more outstanding apparitions here.

On February 11th, Mary showed herself as a young woman, exquisitely beautiful; she smiled at Bernadette and motioned her to draw closer, but spoke not a word.

In the third apparition, on February 18th, the Lady spoke to her for the first time: "Would you be kind enough to come here for the next fifteen days?" Bernadette responded, "I will come with the permission of my parents." The Lady said, "I do not promise to make you happy in this world, but in the next…"

On the 25th, the Virgin had Bernadette unearth the miraculous spring of water.

On the 26th, she spoke in a sorrowful tone: "Penance! Penance! Penance!" She recommended that Bernadette pray and do penance for sinners, to which Bernadette agreed. Then the Lady asked her whether kneeling and kissing the ground would cause her too much repugnance or stress. Responding in the negative, the Virgin then told her to kiss the ground for sinners.

On the 27th, a first miracle attributed to the spring water took place: the cure of a lesion in the right eye of a worker, result of an accident and declared incurable by the doctor.

On March 2nd, the Lady said: "You must go to the priests and have them build a chapel and come here in procession."

In a long exchange on the 4th, the Lady revealed three things to her, but forbade her to share them with anyone: "the secret of Bernadette."

After the fifteen days requested by the Lady, Bernadette stopped going to the grotto. The crowds, however, continued to go and pray there.

On March 25th, feast of the Annunciation, Bernadette felt a strong urge to return there around five o'clock in the morning. She had a great desire to ask the Lady her name. At her first request, the Lady bent her head, smiled, but said nothing. The young girl repeated her question, getting the same result. A third time, she asked the question more humbly but more insistently. The Lady assumed a grave and humble appearance. ... She parted her hands, extended her arms, raised them up, and placed them over her breast. She looked up to Heaven and, with trembling voice, said: "I am the Immaculate Conception."

On June 3rd, feast of Corpus Christi, Bernadette made her First Holy Communion. On July 16th, the feast of Our Lady of Mount Carmel, she again received Communion and returned to the place of the apparitions. Mary appeared to her for the 18th and last time. The happy child exclaimed: "I have never seen her so beautiful"!

These events naturally aroused much enthusiasm, many discussions, and considerable anger. There were investigations, medical examinations, threats, and prohibitions; and the crowds continued to increase and became more convinced.

The ecclesiastical authorities had a detailed study made of the reasons for and against authentication. After four years, the bishop of Tarbes declared that the apparition of the Immaculate Virgin Mary to Bernadette Soubirous "bears all the earmarks of truth and the faithful have grounds for believing it certain." In 1907, Saint Pius X extended to the universal Church the feast of the apparition of Mary Immaculate at Lourdes (February 11th).

As for the little messenger of the Immaculate Virgin, she was entrusted to the Sisters of Charity of Nevers who had a house at Lourdes. Six years later, she asked for admittance to their Congregation. Because of her delicate health, she had to wait two years before entry. After her profession, she became an assistant infirmarian, then a sacristan. She died in 1879, at the age of thirty-five, after a life of heroic humility and union with God. Pius XI canonized her December 8, 1933.

The essential message of the Virgin at Lourdes, as at La Salette, was a message of penance. "Penance! Penance! Penance!" she said to Bernadette in the apparition of February 26th, and she asked the young girl to do penance for sinners. But, undoubtedly, by the word "penance" she less meant acts of mortification than of repentance, conversion, according to the meaning of the word from the mouth of John the Baptist and of Jesus Himself when they asked those who came to them to do penance, to believe in the good news, and to be converted.[139]

Although, at La Salette, conversion consisted above all in forsaking grave sin and returning to the practice of God's law, at Lourdes it was manifested, before all else, by a more serious Christian life and greater union with God and the Virgin. At La Salette, Mary threatened, foretold punishments, and wept; at Lourdes she smiled and responded with graces and miracles. Judging from the facts, the grace of Lourdes consists primarily in a sudden deepening of faith, confidence, and love.

Deepening of Faith

At Lourdes, the supernatural becomes tangible. There, in the grotto, the Virgin permitted that she be seen as many as eighteen times, more than ever before, in all her heavenly beauty. Although she is no longer seen, her presence continues to be felt; she remains there as an invisible but palpable, always

---

139 Mt 3:1-6, 9:17; Mk 1:2-6; Lk 3:3-6.

active presence. The miraculous stream which she caused to spring up still flows! Miracles, even some more astonishing than most of the early ones, occur every day to reward the faith of the believers. A no less marvelous fact is that the sick, whose bodily infirmities are not cured, are completely happy. Their renewed faith leads them to adore, in heartfelt peace, the infinitely merciful designs of God who allows their physical sufferings to continue as a means of loving and being all the happier for all eternity.

At Lourdes, we are no longer in the 20th century, a century of doubt and unbelief: we often have the feeling of being transported into the "centuries of the faith" of our forefathers in the Middle Ages. We pray in public, sing canticles; we speak of God, of the Virgin, and of supernatural matters in a completely natural way. And this way of thinking and acting does not only pervade pilgrims on the esplanade of the basilica. Everyone has a sense of being seized by it from the moment they set foot on the pilgrimage train, provided they have boarded as pilgrims and not simply as tourists.

To the great majority, Lourdes provides a sudden increase of faith. For some who have come as skeptics, it is faith itself that is given or re-awakened. How many unbelievers (doctors, scientists, philosophers, artists) have been overwhelmed in witnessing with their own eyes, impossible miracles, which they are forced to admit, in spite of their rational prejudices. The case of Alex Carrel, recipient of the Nobel Prize for medicine and author of *Man, the Unknown*, who recounted his own conversion, is only one case among thousands.

A deepening of faith naturally leads to a deepening of confidence. Among Jesus' many contemporaries, there were those, no doubt, who did not follow Jesus to the end, but had nevertheless obtained miracles. Having been witness to so many miracles performed for all kinds of afflicted persons who came to Jesus, had given His followers enough confidence to obtain their own miracle.

At Lourdes, where the Virgin performs countless miracles, it is more natural to have confidence in her goodness and power. Many obtain miraculous healings; these, however, are lesser in number. Yet even those who return home without having been healed believe they have been heard, though in a different manner. They have come to understand the supernatural meaning of suffering and the loving designs of God who allows it for their greater good. They leave the Virgin of Lourdes, heart filled with supernatural peace and a greater trust in Mary.

Deeper faith and greater confidence naturally engender a greater love for God and for neighbor.

A greater love for God: For many heretics, the fact of Lourdes is one of the great scandals of the Catholic Church. There, especially, Mary has dethroned her Son: she is the one to whom people sing, who people acclaim, to whom they unceasingly repeat the same refrain: "Ave, Ave, Ave Maria!" It is from her that miracles are expected, and it is to her that thanks and ex-votos are offered.

Those who are scandalized at Lourdes appear to have seen only one or another compelling manifestation of the events. They have not seen the crowds thronging to the confessionals to be cleansed of offenses committed against God, promising henceforth to be more faithful to him. Nor have they seen the thousands of Communions distributed each day; nor the uninterrupted series of Masses attended by great numbers of the faithful; nor the crowds following the path of the fourteen enormous Stations of the Cross. They seem to know nothing of the procession of the Blessed Sacrament, when the Son of God comes to give a special blessing to each of the sick, and miracles take place.

If they would observe the facts with less prejudice, they would note that, at Lourdes, Mary carries on the same role she had at Nazareth and Bethlehem: that she is the one who presents Jesus to souls of good will, and that people return from her *chosen domain* with more affective and more effective love for her Son.

And, just as at Lourdes we can feel our love for God grow, so we can also feel our love for neighbor intensify. People come from different cities or villages, from different regions, from different countries and continents, yet they are not strangers to one another. They are interested in the welfare, sufferings, hopes, and joys of all those they encounter. Are they not all our brothers and sisters, having the same Mother in common? Whenever an invalid stands up cured, there is a general enthusiasm whether the person is from Spain, France, Germany, North Africa, Poland, America, or China.

Sometimes the love of neighbor is manifested in a truly touching way. Many of those who are ill initially set out for Lourdes with the hope of obtaining a cure. Having arrived at the Virgin's apparition site and seeing so many of her children in distress, they have rather asked her to heal someone whom they just met, and whose condition has touched them in a special way. At Lourdes, a great many souls have learned to love heroically!

All this deepening of faith, confidence, and love for God and for others, takes place in an especially joyful atmosphere. We are close to Mary! It is thanks to Mary that we have become more believing, more trusting, more pure, more generous toward Our Lady and toward our neighbor. Long before coming to Lourdes, we knew that Mary is our Mother. But here, we sense it to an incomparably greater degree; we see it in its effects. From that comes this expanding goodness which we experience in finding ourselves near to her as we begin to discover what she has been for us and what she must, henceforth, be in our lives.

It is with joy in our hearts that we leave Lourdes, often with the thought: "I shall return!" Many of those who say this will not be able to return. But, in the dark hours of their lives, it will be the remembrance of Lourdes that will lead some of them back to Mary and, through Mary, to God!

****

Our Lady of Pontmain[140]

The last of the great apparitions of Mary in the 19th century was at Pontmain, January 17, 1871, though

---

140 See M. Cellier (chaplain of Notre-Dame de Pontmain), *Récit de l'apparition de Notre-Dame de Pontmain*; P.

not as well-known as those preceding it. France had been invaded by German troops; the French troops were rendered powerless and retreated. The enemy was at the gates of Laval with orders to take the city; they were so sure of victory that they had already decided to impose an enormous tax of three million gold francs on the citizens.

At 5:30 on January 17, 1871, evening had fallen at Pontmain, a village of five hundred inhabitants, situated north of Laval. It was very cold and snow covered the ground. The night air was calm and fresh, and countless stars shimmered in all the beautiful clarity of a wintry night.

Two children, twelve year old Eugène Barbedette, and his ten year old brother, Joseph, were working in a barn with their father. They were grinding fruze[141] to feed the horses. A woman neighbor arrived, bringing news of an older brother being mobilized. Eugène poked his head out of the open door and looked up to the sky. Never had he seen so many stars! In one area of the sky, where there were fewer stars above a house across the way, he saw a beautiful lady with arms lowered and outstretched, smiling at him. She was wearing a long blue dress

---

Richaud (Bishop of Laval, Archbishop of Bordeaux), *Le Mystère de Pontmain*.

141 {Or gorse: a spiny bush with yellow flowers.}

studded with stars and a glittering golden crown on her head. He watched her for a quarter-of-an-hour.

The neighbor stepped outside and Eugène asked her whether she saw anything; she saw nothing; neither did his father. But Joseph saw her and described the apparition exactly as Eugène had. Their mother came; she saw nothing. Other children came, both boys and girls. They all saw the same exact apparition; meanwhile the adults, including the religious teaching-sister and the fervent pastor, saw nothing but three, large, very brilliant stars which had never before been seen nor have they ever again. Their formation was triangular and, according to the children's account, the Virgin was encased therein. The shoemaker's wife brought her two year old daughter, Augustina, who immediately began stammering: "Jesus, Jesus!" raising her little hands toward the apparition. Despite her mother's attempt to distract her, she continued to turn toward the same spot.

The pastor shouted: "Let us pray"! And all fell to their knees to recite the rosary. Then he asked the religious sister to intone the *Magnificat*. The first verse was not yet finished when the children announced that a long white streamer began to unroll below the apparition. Then, letters of gold slowly began to appear. At the end of the *Magnificat*, the little ones read: "But pray, my children." The pastor had them sing the Litany of the Blessed Virgin. New letters appeared, and the children spelled out: "God will answer your prayers soon." The people intoned the *Inviolata*. Letters appeared again and the children read: "My Son allows Himself to be swayed." After the recitation of evening prayer, the Virgin slowly disappeared. The phenomenon had lasted three hours.

At first glance, this apparition seemed to have nothing to do with the apostolate. It announced a seemingly human favor: the end of the war.

Yet that, of itself, had an apostolic import: France, despite its shortcomings, had always been and should remain the apostolic nation *par excellence.* Its liberation would again enable it to take up its providential mission in the world with renewed zeal.

However, the importance of Mary's apparition at Pontmain is of less importance in what she foretold than in what she recalled.

To begin with: a lesson on prayer, as at rue du Bac and at Lourdes. There, Mary insisted on the necessity for extraordinary prayer in times of extraordinary needs. The first words: "But pray, my children!" Note the "But" spoken at the very outset. It is as though Mary had been unhappy, almost impatient, with the failure of human beings to pray. But the parish, directed by a truly Marian and holy priest, was fervent. Prayers were recited regularly, and the morning and evening prayers were quite lengthy. However, Mary wanted extraordinary prayers in those times of extraordinary anguish. The Virgin had appeared to the children without telling them what she wanted. It was only on orders from the pastor that the people began to pray and her message appeared on the banner; and with each succeeding prayer, a new part of the message unfolded.

It should be noted that on the evening of January 17th, special prayers began not only at Pontmain but elsewhere in France as well. While prayers were being said in this small village, a promise was being made to the Blessed Virgin at the Shrine of Our Lady of Hope at Saint-Brieuc, at 5:30 on that evening. Prayers continued there until 9 p.m. On the same evening, the principal chaplain at Our Lady of Victories, was suddenly inspired at that very hour, to asked the crowd to offer a silver heart to the Blessed Virgin "which will recall to future generations that today, between 8–9 in the evening, a people prostrated at the feet of Our Lady of Victories and was saved through her."[142]

"But pray, my children! God will soon answer you." The people prayed! The next day, the Germans encamped around Laval and, instead of taking the city, withdrew twenty kilometers to the rear. On January 28th, the Armistice was signed.

Another lesson on prayer: we must leave it to God to determine the manner in which he will answer us, for he loves us and knows better than we do what is best for us. Under the pastor's direction, a hymn had been intoned:

> *Mother of Hope,*
> *Whose name is so sweet,*
> *Protect our France.*
> *Pray, pray for us.*

Toward the end of this canticle, when we beseech Mary:

> *Along the road to glory,*
> *Lead our soldiers;*
> *Grant them victory ...*

---

142 M. Cellier, *Récit de l'Apparition de Notre-Dame de Pontmain*, p. 42.

the Blessed Virgin did not leave the promise, "God will soon answer you," suspended in the heavens; the white banner disappeared.

There is another remarkable fact which undoubtedly also contains a lesson: only the children saw the Virgin and were able to read her message. The oldest of the visionaries was not yet thirteen years old. And we saw a little two year old girl tenaciously drawn toward the apparition, stammering "Jesus!" The little ones kept repeating that the Lady was smiling much, and that she laughed while observing them as they joyfully clapped their hands. Is this not a reminder of the lesson from Christ: "I give you praise, Father, Lord of heaven and earth, for although you have hidden these things from the wise and the learned you have revealed them to the childlike."[143]

Was this a reminder of the lesson already given to the disciples and, perhaps, also a preview of what He was to give on evangelical childhood some years later through His faithful Carmelite of Lisieux?[144]

---

143 Lk 10:21.
144 There are other lessons to be drawn from Pontmain. See P. Richard, *Le Mystère de Pontmain*.

****

Our Lady of Fatima

As with the apparitions of Mary at Lourdes, those at Fatima are known throughout the whole Church. A brief resume follows here. In order to appreciate their impact, it is important to know something of the conditions in Portugal at the time of the appearances.

Over the centuries, Portugal had distinguished itself by its zeal for the spread of the Christian faith. In the 18th century, the government was receptive to anti-religious ideas and, from that time, Freemasonry set about de-christianizing the country. At the beginning of the 20th century, the moral and religious conditions in Portugal were abysmal. In 1911, the separation of Church and State became official. Between the years of 1910–1913, terror reigned: priests and bishops were imprisoned or exiled; religious orders were suppressed; almost all the seminaries were closed and their goods confiscated; missions languished or were abandoned. Freemasonry was all-powerful. From 1910–1926, there had been sixteen revolutions with forty changes in government officials.

Then, on May 13, 1917, a shining Lady appeared to three little shepherds in the village of Fatima,

Portugal. They were seven year old Jacinta; her nine year old brother, Francisco; and their ten year old cousin, Lucia. The Lady encouraged them to pray the rosary and to offer acts of penance; then she asked them to return on the 13th of the next five months. The children were faithful in coming, except for the 13th of August, when they were imprisoned by the mayor, a Freemason. He had threatened to throw them into a caldron of boiling oil if they did not reveal the secret confided to them by the Lady.

At each meeting, the Lady revealed to them a little more of God's designs. She foretold future misfortunes which they were to keep secret for the time being, and which were only revealed in more recent times by Lucia, the sole survivor. They had to do with an even more terrible war than the one of 1914–1918. The Lady asked for the consecration of the world to her Immaculate Heart, for only through her could God's help come to the world. On the last apparition of October 13th, she promised a great miracle which everyone would be able to see.

Curiosity drew ever-larger numbers to accompany the little visionaries to each meeting: there were some 25,000–30,000 on September 13th; and between 50,000–70,000 on October 13th.

On the day when the great miracle promised by the Virgin was to take place, torrential rain poured down all morning. The crowds were soaking wet but at noon, the skies cleared. Mary appeared to the three shepherds and revealed her name: Lady of the Rosary. She asked that people be converted and pray. Then, in the sight of 70,000 spectators, the sun, which had just appeared through the clouds, began to rotate three times; each rotation lasted three or four minutes, illuminating the trees, the crowd, and the earth, with all the colors of a rainbow. Then it zigzagged in the sky and descended as though crashing onto the crowd. People fell to the ground crying for mercy! Then the sun returned to its natural orbit. The astonished spectators noticed that their clothes were completely dry!

News of this miracle, witnessed by 70,000 people (including a number hostile to religion), spread like wildfire throughout Portugal and made a tremendous impression. The physical miracle was but a sign of another miracle: the enlightenment of souls and the conversion of the country.

Less than two weeks after the last apparition, the first sign of a new attitude was manifested by the protest of a great anti-Christian newspaper against a sacrilegious attack by a group of sectarians at Fatima. In 1918, the bishops were recalled from exile and were able to hold a meeting at Lisbon. The military chaplaincy was reinstated and relations with the Holy See re-established. At that point, the Masonic lodges had the president of the Republic assassinated. They sought to restore control to the anti-clericals, but their efforts failed.

In 1926, the first national Council was held. In 1928, the famous Oliveira Salazar rose to power. He was a great Catholic and a great statesman, a man providential for the financial, civil, political, and religious restoration of Portugal.

Toward 1936, a new and imminent danger menaced the land. The Russian Bolshevists decided to establish atheistic Communism in Spain and Portugal in order to spread it more successfully in the East and West, throughout all of Christian Europe. We know of their success in Spain, and Portugal seemed unable to resist their movement, organized with satanic cleverness. To dispel the danger, the bishops saw salvation only in the Blessed Virgin. In 1936, they promised — by what was termed an anticommunist oath — that the entire nation would make a pilgrimage to Fatima if Portugal were preserved from the looming threat.

Meantime, on the other side of the frontier in Spain, the "Reds" were massacring, profaning, pillaging, and burning priests and men and women religious, churches and convents, trying to extirpate the last vestiges of Christianity, while Portugal enjoyed the most profound peace. And so, in 1938, an enormous pilgrimage of half-a-million faithful traveled to Fatima to thank the Virgin for her miraculous protection.

In 1940, Portugal signed with the Holy See the most perfect concordat ever signed in recent times, from the Christian point of view. The Faith was proclaimed throughout the entire country with pride; the sacraments were frequented, Catholic Action flourished, priestly vocations were numerous; in eight years, the number of religious had quadrupled. In keeping with the prediction of the Virgin at Fatima, the Second World War was much more horrible than the first. Yet, although most nations of the world were embroiled in unspeakable calamity and suffering, Portugal continued its tranquil life under the protection of Mary.

The ecclesiastical inquiry into the facts of Fatima was opened in November, 1917. However, because of a number of circumstances, a verdict was only rendered on October 13, 1930, thirteen years later. Meanwhile, pilgrims continued to arrive, always more numerous, and usually on the 13th of each month. Healings were taking place and, in 1926, a review board was established similar to the one at Lourdes. More than a thousand scientifically inexplicable cures were recorded {by the mid-1950s}.

On the occasion of the 25th anniversary of the apparitions at Fatima, the ecclesiastical authority judged the moment suitable for revealing, in part, what the Virgin had asked Lucia to keep secret in the meantime.

In his radio message of October 31, 1942, to the pilgrims gathered at Fatima, Pius XII consecrated the Church and the world to the Immaculate Heart of Mary. He renewed this consecration the following December 8th in Rome. The bishops of the whole world also made this consecration of their individual dioceses on March 28, 1943. We know that the Pope confided to Cardinal Tedeschini that he himself had seen the solar phenomenon on October 30 and 31, and on November 1 and 8, 1950, on the occasion of the definition of the dogma of the Assumption.

The message of Fatima was heard in Portugal, and Mary's goodness marvelously repaid it. Has it been heard throughout the rest of the world? Certainly not enough! Otherwise, wars among nations by armed forces, and "cold wars" and fratricides within countries, would have ended long ago.

However, not all turned a deaf ear. The message of Fatima was received, at least in part, by a great number of Christians. Devotion to the rosary gained favor and was extended in many countries. As has been said, all the dioceses of the world have been consecrated to the Immaculate Heart by the bishops. At the moment when the Pope saw the solar miracle again, a statue of Our Lady of Fatima left Rome on a world tour which would last fifteen months and would carry her to Australia, Burma, Malacca, etc. During that trip she was received with tremendous enthusiasm not only by the Catholic populations, but by Protestants and Muslims.

Other statues of the Virgin of Fatima have made similar voyages to various parts of the world — even to the very heart of Russia. It is clear that the message of Fatima has moved many Catholics and has contributed to making our era the age of Mary. Its final word has not been spoken. What that word will be depends on the cooperation the Virgin receives from us.

****

Apparitions of Mary at Beauraing

There are two other series of the Virgin's apparitions, more recent than those previously acknowledged by Church authority. Both of them favored Catholic Belgium at Beauraing and at Banneux.

At Beauraing, in the diocese of Namur, Mary appeared a number of times from November 29, 1932, to January of 1933, to five children: a boy of eleven, and four girls aged nine, thirteen, fourteen, and fifteen. The first three times, the children saw a very beautiful, shining Lady who stood above a bridge or near a bush. She smiled, but did not speak.

On the fourth day, the children posed the question: "Are you the Immaculate Virgin?" to which she nodded affirmatively and told them to be very wise.

On December 8th, she was exceptionally beautiful and brilliant, and remained there longer than usual.

On December 30th, she urged them: "Pray, pray very much!"

On January 3rd, she confided a secret to each one of them and then took leave of them.

To one of the girls, she said: "I shall convert sinners. Adieu!" To another: "I am the Mother of God, the Queen of heaven. Pray always! Adieu!" And to a third: "Do you love my Son?" "Yes." "Do you love me?" "Yes." "Then sacrifice yourself for my sake. Adieu!"

In 1934, a commission of inquiry was formed by the bishop. It was a detailed and lengthy undertaking. In 1942, the Holy Office in Rome authorized the bishop of Namur to pronounce the final verdict; and three years later, the bishop authorized public cult. Since then, pilgrimages have been especially favored with graces of conversions and other spiritual benefits.

****

Apparitions at Banneux

Twelve days after her last apparition at Beauraing, Mary appeared to Mariette Beco a young girl from Banneux, a village of some three hundred and fifty inhabitants at that time, and situated some twenty kilometers to the southeast of Liège. The small Bèco house was near a road flanked by a forest of fir trees, just a few minutes south of the village. The family was not affluent, and rarely practiced their religion.

Mariette was the oldest of seven children — the family would increase by four more. She was almost twelve years old, of an impulsive and stormy nature, abrupt and brutally outspoken. She was a poor student and negligent in learning the catechism. Scolded one day by the chaplain because she did not know her lessons, she complained to her father. "If the priests torment you," he told her, "don't go to catechism any more." From that time on, she abandoned classes and Sunday Mass, with the probability of not being allowed to make her First Communion.

However, she did pray at times. She found a rosary along the road and asked her grandmother how to use it. Each week, she recited a few decades of the Hail Mary.

On Sunday, January 15, 1933, the first apparition occurred. That morning, Mariette had not gone to Mass. During the evening, toward seven o'clock, she looked out of the kitchen window waiting for her brother's return from early morning. Suddenly, in the garden, some seven or eight meters away, she saw a white glow and then a beautiful Lady. She called her mother who responded sarcastically: "Perhaps it is the Blessed Virgin or a sorceress"! The Lady smiled at the little girl; then she took up her rosary and recited some Hail Mary's. The apparition motioned her to come closer. Mariette started to go out, but her mother closed the door and locked it, and dragged her away from the window. Mariette went back to the window, but the Lady had disappeared.

The next day, Mariette spoke of this to her father and to a little friend; both made fun of her. The friend told the chaplain who was as skeptical as the other two.

Tuesday morning, January 18th, Mariette attended Mass and catechism. The chaplain posed some questions and was amazed at the accuracy of her answers.

Around seven o'clock that evening, Mariette felt drawn to go to the spot of the apparition. Suddenly she fell to her knees and extended her arms. For more than half an hour, without seeming to feel the cold (10–15 degrees below zero), and without answering her father's questions, she remained as in ecstasy. The Virgin appeared very near to her, elevated above the ground on a grayish cloud, at the same height as on Sunday, but she did not speak.

Then suddenly, on a signal from Mary, the girl got up and followed the apparition as it withdrew, as though gliding on the cloud. The Virgin stopped;

the girl fell to her knees, recited several Hail Mary's, and got up again. A second and a third time, she knelt down, prayed, got up, and walked on. Suddenly, she crossed the road at a right angle toward the forest and prostrated herself near a small spring of water at the foot of the slope.

For the first time, Mary spoke: "Dip your hands into the water." Mariette plunged her hands and wrists to the bottom of the icy waters. She looked up to the Virgin who smiled at her and said: "This spring is reserved for me." As she disappeared, she said to her: "Good night. Goodbye."

On Thursday, January 19th, there was a new apparition at seven o'clock in the evening: Mariette asked the Lady why she had said: "This spring is reserved for me"? Mary answered, smiling: "This spring is reserved for all nations — to assuage those who are ill. — I will pray for you. Goodbye."

Friday, January 20th – another apparition: The young girl asked the Virgin: "Beautiful Lady, what do you want"? "I want a small chapel," she replied.

For three weeks, Mariette went to pray each day but the Virgin did not appear.

Saturday, February 11th: This was the 75th anniversary of the first appearance of Mary to

Bernadette, but Mariette knew nothing of it. At seven o'clock that evening, the Virgin appeared to Mariette again. The young girl followed her to the spring. "I come," Mary said, "to relieve suffering." "Thank you, thank you," the child responded. And the Virgin bid her "Goodbye."

Mariette asked the chaplain to allow her to make her First Communion. In view of her total change in behavior and her progress in catechism, she obtained his permission and received First Holy Communion the next day, Sunday, February 12th. The Virgin did not appear that day or the following two days.

Wednesday, February 15th – new apparition of the Virgin: Mariette said: "Blessed Virgin, the reverend chaplain told me to ask a sign from you." The Virgin answered: "Believe in me; I will believe in you." She added: "Pray much." Then she confided a secret to the young girl and bid her "Goodbye." The child wept.

Monday, February 20th – Mary came: The child followed her to the spring. Mary was grave and said: "My dear child, pray much! Goodbye."

Thursday, March 2nd: It was raining hard that afternoon. Around seven o'clock in the evening,

Mariette went outside and recited two rosaries in the rain. In the middle of the third one, the rain suddenly stopped. The Virgin — solemn, almost sad — appeared to the child. She said: "I am the Mother of the Lord, the Mother of God. Pray much! Goodbye." She put her hands on the child and blessed her with the Sign of the Cross, and then she disappeared. Mariette thrust herself toward her but fell back on her knees, sobbing.

Increasing numbers of the faithful came to pray at the place of the apparitions almost from the very beginning, and they continued to come even after the Virgin had stopped appearing to Mariette.

Soon, evident miraculous occurrences were taking place: instantaneous healing of illnesses judged incurable, both on the spot and even far away, thanks to water from the spring; conversions and spiritual advancements. This continued for twenty-three years,[145] and the more recent miracles were as striking as those in the first months.

Bishop Kerkhofs of Liège began an official inquiry that continued for almost four years. In 1959, with the approval of the Holy See, he declared that the faithful could trust in the authenticity of the apparitions.

---

145 {To mid 1950's.}

On August 15, 1933, the decision was reached to construct the small chapel requested by the Virgin. In 1948 the first stone was laid for the future basilica.

Import of the apparitions of Our Lady of Banneux is twofold: personal confidence, and growth in the love among nations.

The spiritual atmosphere of the pilgrimage of Banneux has something special and, to a certain extent, recalls that of Fatima. The Virgin of Banneux is the Virgin of the poor, the Virgin of the humble, the Virgin of those who suffer. She does not raise her eyes to Heaven, but bows her head toward those who are at her feet, those who are physically or morally ill. In this sense, her choice of a visionary is an unruly little girl of minimal piety who she converts and makes her messenger. A choice which might at first be somewhat shocking is most appropriate to help us understand her intentions. We feel very close and quite at ease with this Virgin. She seems to be so simple, so understanding, so kind, and so desirous of easing whatever misery is brought before her, no matter what it might be. From the very first moment, she captures us!

Just as she inspires the people's confidence in her, so she inspires them to love one another. The spring of water which she gave to the poor for those who suffer is "for all the nations." In fact, the pilgrimage spot of Banneux exercises a universal attraction on the faithful of all regions of the globe. Pilgrims are immediately captivated by the special charm of the Virgin of the Poor. And when they return to their homes, they speak of her to their neighbors who then come and, in their turn, recruit others. Each day, the little chapel and the spring see hundreds, thousands, of pilgrims. They not only arrive from Belgium, but from England, France, Italy, Germany, and from the most distant lands. In 1954, there were 150,000 from Germany alone; in 1955, the count increased to 200,000.

As with the grotto of Lourdes, small chapels of Banneux (approximately five hundred) have been erected throughout the world; innumerable statues of the Virgin of the Poor are everywhere.

Near the Virgin of the Poor, Mother of all those pilgrims — from wherever they come, they have a sense of being brothers and sisters. One is no longer Belgian, or English, or German, or Italian, or French; all are children of the same Mother. They love one another in this kind Virgin Mary who deigned to descend so often to a poor little girl in this corner of Belgium in order to draw all the poor of the universe to herself.

CHAPTER SEVENTEEN

The Witness of the Liturgy

We know that the liturgy has always held an uncontestable place among the proofs for the truth of a doctrine. The principle: *Lex supplicandi, lex credendi*, "as is the prayer, such is the faith," is attributed to Saint Celestine, a pope of the fifth century, who merely expressed in a formula a principle in use from the very beginnings. We have already seen that the liturgy affirms the faith of the Church in the apostolic mission of Mary in the ancient antiphon: "Rejoice, O Virgin Mary, for you alone have destroyed all heresies in the world."

The liturgy celebrates a number of feasts in commemoration of the victories achieved by the Church over the enemies of the Faith, thanks to the intervention of the Virgin Mary. Such is the feast of "Mary, Help of Christians" (May 24th), which commemorates the return of Pope Pius VII from captivity in France, and his restoration to the papal throne in Rome on May 24, 1814. The prayer for that feast says: "All-powerful and merciful God who, for the defense of the Christian people, have marvelously constituted a perpetual help for them in the Blessed Virgin Mary, grant, we beg you, that through her powerful help, we may, after the trials of this life, have victory over the enemy at our death." The same affirmation is voiced in the offertory prayer and in the post-communion prayer.

The feast of the Holy Name of Mary (September 12th) was extended to the universal Church to recall the victory over the Turks at the walls of Vienna (1683), through the protection of Mary. That of the Holy Rosary (October 7th) was in gratitude to God for the victory won, thanks to Mary's intercession, over the same enemy at Lepanto (1571) and at Peterwardein (1716). The feast of Our Lady of Mercy (September 24th), instituted to commemorate the foundation of the Order of that name, declared that the Blessed Virgin founded it "to free Christians from the power of the pagans."

In the 19th century, the Sacred Congregation of Rites approved a feast of Mary, Queen of Apostles, as principal feast of the Pious Society of the Catholic Apostolate (Pallottines). This feast has also been granted to the Society of Mary (Marianists). This is its prayer: "O God, who gave the Holy Spirit to the apostles praying with one heart with Mary, the Mother of Jesus, grant that, protected by her who is also our Mother and Queen of Apostles, we may serve your majesty faithfully and spread the glory of your name by word and example."

Several texts in the Queen of Apostles office of the Mass recall the presence of Mary in the cenacle with the apostles, awaiting the descent of the Holy Spirit. The offertory prayer cites the following text borrowed from the Book of Judges: "It is I; it is I who chant a canticle to the Lord, who will sing to the sound of the lute to the Lord, the God of Israel. The strong ones of Israel have lost courage; they have remained inactive, waiting for a woman to rise in Israel. The Savior has chosen a new kind of war (*nova bella elegit Dominus*) and has destroyed the power of our enemies." The communion antiphon applies to Mary, the praise given to Judith by the high priest: "You are the glory of Jerusalem, the joy of Israel, the honor of our people."

The power of Mary, Distributrix of all graces, is mentioned several times in the Queen of Apostles office. The vesper hymn comments on Mary's presence among the apostles who await, in prayer, the gifts of the Holy Spirit. "But Mary's prayer is more ardent, for she, mentioned last, becomes the first, richer than others in divine gifts. ... Forget not, apostle, to have recourse to Mary, full of grace, so that the streams of this great flood may flow over you. … She will offer you a helping hand to aid your brothers."

CHAPTER EIGHTEEN

Teachings of the Sovereign Pontiffs

Mary's apostolic mission has not been the object of any solemn definition by the supreme authority of the Church. But it is taught as admitted truth by a certain number of popes, especially in more recent times. It is of course a fact that, for centuries, the sovereign pontiffs have recommended recourse to Mary in all dangers that menace the faith or the purity of the life of the faithful, or the freedom of the Church.

Leo XIII is remarkable for the number of his encyclicals and other writings in which he unceasingly recommends the recitation of the apostolic prayer *par excellence*, the holy rosary, "so that, in our times of great trials and prolonged tempests, the Virgin, so often victorious over earthly enemies, may help us triumph over those that are infernal."[146] Already in his encyclical *Adjutricem populi* (1895), he had explained:

> It certainly does not seem exaggerated to affirm that it is especially under the leadership of the Blessed Virgin and through her help that gospel wisdom and law have, despite extreme difficulties, spread so rapidly throughout the world, bringing with them a new order of justice and peace.

Three years later, he wrote: "For a long time, we have wished to have the salvation of human society rest on the extension of the cult of the divine Mary as on an unassailable citadel."

Saint Pius X, proposing to "restore all things in Christ," indicated, from the very beginning of his pontificate, an increase of piety toward the Virgin as a great means for this restoration.

> Who does not hold as established truth that there can be no path more secure or more rapid than Mary for uniting human beings to Jesus Christ? ... From the moment that the Son of God is author and consummator of

---

146 Office of the Most Holy Rosary, Matins, sixth lesson {outdated reference}.

our faith, it is totally necessary that Mary be said to be a participant of the divine mysteries and, in some way, their guardian, and that on her, as on the most noble foundation after Jesus Christ, also reposes the faith of all the centuries. Since it has pleased the eternal Providence to give us the Man-God through the Virgin … what is more natural for us than to receive Jesus Christ from Mary's hands? … No one in the world has known Him as she has. It follows, therefore, that no one can better unite humans to Jesus.[147]

At the end of his exhortation to the Catholic clergy, August 4, 1908, he wrote:

The wishes we have for you, we desire to confide to the august Virgin Mary, Queen of Apostles, that she might bring them to a more complete fruition. In fact, she has shown, by her example to the apostles at the happy inauguration of the priesthood, how assiduous they should be in common prayer until they are vested with grace from on high. She certainly obtained this strength for them by her prayers in even greater abundance, at the same time that she developed and

---

[147] *Ad diem illum*, Feb. 2, 1904.

strengthened them by her counsels, for the greater fruitfulness of their works.

At the end of the encyclical *Pascendi*, he expressed the hope "that the Immaculate Virgin, destroyer of all heresies, will help you with her prayer!"

Benedict XV, on the occasion of the first centenary of the Society of Mary, wrote a letter to Very Rev. Father Hiss, Superior General of the Society, which is a kind of approbation of Father Chaminade's views on the Marian apostolate:

> It is not without divine guidance that the Reverend Chaminade went into exile to Saragossa. There, visiting the shrine of our august Sovereign, he understood the plan of divine mercy to lead his country back to Jesus through Mary. Sensing, without a shadow of doubt, that an important role had been reserved for him in this apostolate, he prepared himself for that mission by meditation and prayer at the feet of the august image. It is, in fact, not an empty praise that we give to Mary by this title of Queen of Apostles. Just as she helped the apostles, educators of the nascent Church, by her support and counsels, so we must also affirm that she assists at all times the heirs of the apostolic office who seek to either

prepare victories or to repair disasters in the adult Church.[148]

"From the very beginning of his pontificate," Pope Pius XI "turned his eyes and his heart toward the most tender Mother as toward the hope of universal salvation."[149] He not only took advantage of every occasion to witness to his devotion toward his heavenly Protectress, but strongly insisted on the apostolic role of the Virgin in two encyclicals (one on the missions; another on the unity of the Church), wherein he speaks of the apostolate. He concludes the first one with this prayer:

> May the smile and the favor of the most holy Queen of Apostles descend on all missionary endeavors. Her maternal heart, having received on Calvary the care of all humanity, encircles with her solicitude and her affection, those who do not know their ransom by Christ and the blessed benefactions of that Redemption.[150]

In his encyclical on the unity of the Church, after having expressed the hope of seeing all the separated

---

148 AAS, 1921, p. 173.
149 AAS, 1927, p. 410.
150 AAS, 1926, p. 83.

Christians returning to the bosom of the Catholic Church, he added:

> In a matter of such importance, we take, and we would have others take as advocate, the Blessed Virgin Mary, Mother of divine grace, destroyer of all heresies and help of Christians, that she might obtain for us very soon the arrival of this day so greatly desired, when all peoples will listen to the word of her Son calling them to a unity of spirit in the bonds of peace.[151]

In his letter to the Primate of Spain, on the occasion of the Marian Congress of Seville, he returned to the same thought, adding the affirmation "that in our times in particular, it is from Mary only that the Christian people should expect their salvation."[152]

As for Pius XII, it may well be asked whether the Church has ever had a pope as Marian as he. With regard to Mary's apostolic mission in particular, he affirmed it in almost every one of his writings and discourses having to do with the Virgin.

Sometimes it was in explicit terms. Before the 15,000 delegates of Marian sodalities of the entire

---

151 AAS, 1928, p. 16.
152 AAS, 1929, p. 625.

world meeting in a World Congress during the Marian year, he expressed this wish that: "the Queen of Apostles animate them all." More recently, the constitution, *Sedes Sapientiae,* on the formation of religious clergy, begins as follows:

> She is the Seat of Wisdom, this Mother of God, ruler of all the sciences and Queen of Apostles—Mary, this most holy Virgin to whose honor we have consecrated an entire year. We do not err when we consider her the Mother and Formatrix of all those who, in the "states of perfection," also engage in the apostolic service of Christ, Sovereign Priest. They should apply themselves in an effective way to forming in themselves a very great and elevated vocation, at once religious, priestly, and apostolic. They have, therefore, the greatest need of being guided and helped by her who has been constituted Mediatrix of all the graces of sanctification, and who is rightly called Mother and Queen of the Priesthood and of Catholic Action. We therefore implore her favor: as she has obtained for us light from on high to formulate these rules, may she assist, with her help and her patronage,

those on whom falls the burden of assuring their execution.[153]

In a general way, Pius XII affirms this mission, pointing out that it is exercised by the Virgin. He did so in a solemn fashion in his radio prayer message to Portugal on the occasion of the twenty-fifth anniversary of the appearances of the Virgin at Fatima, November 1, 1942, and on the following December 8th, when consecrating the world to the Immaculate Heart of Mary. That prayer begins with the words:

> Queen of the most Holy Rosary, Help of Christians, Refuge of the human race, one who triumphs in all the battles of God, we prostrate ourselves prayerfully before your throne, confident that we will obtain mercy and find grace and timely aid in these present perils.

Then he begged the Virgin to send to the human race "the graces which can, in a moment, convert human hearts;" to make "the Son of justice enlighten ... unbelievers and all those who are still seated in the darkness of death"; to "lead anew to the unique flock of Christ ... peoples separated by error or strife"; to "obtain peace and complete freedom for

---

153 May 31, 1956.

the Church of God"; to "arrest the devastating flood of neo-paganism"; and to "augment the love of purity in the faithful, the practice of the Christian life, and apostolic zeal, so that the number of those who serve God may increase in merit and in number."

He ended with an act of faith in the victory of the reign of God through the intervention of Mary:

> May your love and your patronage hasten the triumph of the reign of God, and may all human generations, at peace among themselves and with God, proclaim you blessed, and together with you intone, from one pole of the world to the other, the eternal *Magnificat* of glory, honor, and thankfulness to the Sacred Heart of Jesus, in whom alone can truth, life, and peace be found.

He did the same in a great number of his writings: when prescribing recourse to Mary in all dangers menacing faith, or religion, or Christian morals; when expressing his confidence in the effects he anticipated from the glorification of Mary on the occasion of the definition of the Assumption; on the announcement of the Holy Year; on the institution of the feast of the Queenship of Mary.

Pius XII was not satisfied with merely stating Mary's apostolic mission; he provided the proofs. This was not in a systematic thesis after the manner of theologians, but on the occasions of different circumstances which led him to speak of it.

In an encyclical letter on the Mystical Body of Christ, he showed how Mary contributed to the building up of this Body,

– by "accepting, in the name of the entire human race, that a spiritual marriage should unite the Son of God and human nature";

– by "miraculously giving birth to Christ, source of true heavenly life";

– by " first presenting Him among the Jews and the pagans";

– by "strengthening the faith of the disciples through her intervention at Cana";

– by "presenting to the eternal Father her Son on Golgotha";

– by adding to it "the holocaust of her rights and of her motherly love";

– by "thus becoming the spiritual Mother of all the members of Christ";

– by "obtaining, through her most powerful prayers, a great effusion of the graces of the Holy Spirit onto the Church which had just been born";

– by "carrying her immense sorrows with a heart full of courage and confidence, true Queen of Martyrs, completing what was lacking to the sufferings of Christ for His body, the Church;"

– by encircling the young Church with her maternal vigilance and, through her constant insistence with her Son in Heaven, "promoting the descent of endless streams of grace upon all the members of the Mystical Body."

It is, therefore, her functions as Mother of Christ, as Co-redemptrix, as Distributrix of all graces, and as Mother of the members of the Mystical Body of Christ that are the foundations of Mary's apostolic mission.

In his constitution, *Sedes Sapientiae*, he mentions in particular her function as "Mediatrix of all the graces of sanctification."

In the encyclical *Ad caeli Reginam* {1954}, on the Queenship of Mary and the institution of its feast, he again pointed out her Queenship as being fundamental: "The Blessed Virgin shares in some way in the action by which, we rightly say, her

Son reigns over the minds and wills of humans."[154]
Now, for her as for Jesus to reign over the minds of
humans means to have them accept the teachings of
the Faith; and to reign over their wills means to have
them practice these teachings — two eminently
apostolic activities.

Pius XII also indicated the various means by which
Mary now exercises her apostolic mission. The
usual way is by obtaining graces of conversion and
sanctification for people, in virtue of her mission to
distribute all graces. But there are others. Sometimes
there is a direct intervention, such as at Fatima. In
his message addressed to the cardinals, bishops, and
faithful assembled at Fatima for the solemn closing
of the Marian Year, he spoke of the triumphant
journey of the statue of Our Lady of Fatima
through various countries of the world. Everywhere,
at her passage, "blessings poured down and marvels
of grace were so multiplied that we could scarcely
believe what our eyes beheld." The Pope underlined
the apostolic teachings which Mary gives to the
world:

> When, with special insistence, she inculcates
> the practice of the family rosary, she seems
> to be saying to us that the secret for peace

---

154 {Denziger-Schönmetzer, n. 3917}

in the domestic hearth is found in the Holy Family. When she exhorts us to be concerned for our neighbor as for ourselves to the point of praying and sanctifying ourselves for the neighbor's spiritual and temporal well-being, she indicates to us the truly effective way of restoring concord among social classes. When, in a particularly troubled and touching maternal manner, she asks for a general and sincere return to a truly Christian way of life, does she not remind us that it is only in peace with God and in respect for justice and eternal law that it is possible to securely build the edifice of world peace? For, after all, if God does not build, it is in vain that the builders labor.

The Virgin makes use of yet another means: believers gathered together under her banner to do apostolic work. Among such groups, this Pope particularly singles out the sodalities and the Children of Mary, as was said above.

From the beginning, Mary has carried out an apostolic mission in the Church. It is the Pope's conviction that this mission should shine in a very special way in our modern world. Is it not because of his conviction that, as he said in the bull of the definition of the Assumption, he consecrated the whole human race to her Immaculate Heart, declaring that she alone can save us? Is this not why he defined the dogma of the Assumption, decreed the Marian Year, and instituted the feast of Mary, Queen of the World?

In addition, he vividly expressed this conviction in his conversation with the General Director of the Marian sodalities:

> Can we differently label these times, this period in which we live, other than the times and period of the Virgin, Our Lady? Do you not see in the whole world the beautiful lesson of love, of extraordinary fervor — might I call it a holy folly for the Mother of God, the Mediatrix of all graces, the Coredemptrix of the human race, the divine Governess of heaven? What has always been the truth, what has always been a Catholic dogma, is now seen more clearly than ever before. It is the heartbeat of millions and millions of children of the Virgin Mary who love her, who venerate her. It is the triumph of Our Lady of Fatima in all nations, which you experienced not so long ago, and of which it is now my turn to animate in the various regions of Europe. It is the reign of Our Lady of Fatima … and Our Lady of Guadalupe,

and Our Lady of Lourdes, and Our Lady of the Pillar; it is the Virgin Mary, it is the Mother of God — under whatever name she is invoked. It is she who loves Christians, to whom Catholics recommend themselves, whom the multitudes of Christians in the entire world deliriously acclaim! It is the age of the Virgin Mary. Above all, it is the era, the times, the epoch of the sodalities of the Virgin Mary.[155]

More recently, noting with anguish that the present world is "marching on the roads which lead souls and bodies, the good and the wicked, civilizations and peoples into the abyss," Pius XII launched his first cry of alarm on February 10, 1952, which initiated the Movement for a Better World. This was a move to revolutionize the world by constructing a new world, a world "having Jesus Christ for basis and foundation." He explained why he chose this date of February 10th to launch this immense apostolic movement:

> If we have chosen tomorrow's feast of the Virgin of Lourdes [February 11th], to confide to you this anxiety of our heart, it

---

[155] Quoted in the periodical *Marie*, May-April, 1950, pp. 58ff.

is because it commemorates the tremendous apparitions which, some one hundred years ago, in a century of unchained rationalism and increasing religious weakening, were the merciful response of God and of his heavenly Mother to the rebellion of humans. The apparitions were an irresistible call to the supernatural, the first step toward a religious renewal ...

Having recourse once again, then, to the goodness of God and to Mary's mercy, each believer, each person of good will, should examine anew, with a determination worthy of the great movements in human history, what contribution to bring to the saving work of God to help save a world that is heading toward destruction, as is the case today.[156]

It is, therefore, permissible to affirm, as a doctrine based on Scripture, spoken of and, above all, lived throughout the whole of Tradition and taught by the ordinary Magisterium of the Church, that belief in Mary's apostolic mission forms part of the deposit of the Catholic faith.

---

156 Exhortation of Pius XII to the people of Rome, Feb. 10, 1952.

DOCTRINAL PRECISIONS

We must now lend precision to the true notion of Mary's apostolic mission, establishing its foundations, indicating its relationships with the Virgin's other functions, and distinguishing it from that of Christ and from that of the rest of Christians.

****

CHAPTER NINETEEN

Foundation of Mary's Apostolic Mission

At the beginning of this study, we saw that an apostolic mission presupposes the fact of having been sent by God to draw human beings from sin and to have them live a life in Christ and, that, by the total dedication of oneself to this purpose.

The sending of Mary by God to the work of Redemption and sanctification of the human race was included in her predestination as Mother of the Savior and, therefore, in the decree of the Incarnation.

This mission was announced to Mary by the archangel Gabriel: "The angel Gabriel was sent by

God."[157] That mission was accepted by her when she responded: "Behold, I am the handmaid of the Lord. May it be done to me according to your word."[158]

It was in a very conscious and voluntary manner that she pronounced this *fiat*. She did not become Mother of the Savior of the world as Rachel had become mother of the savior of Egypt. She knew through Gabriel that the infant she was to bear was the Messiah, the Savior. "You shall name him Jesus," which means "God saves." She also knew, through Isaiah and through David, that this Messiah would be a man of sorrows, a worm and no man, an opprobrium among men and a rejection by the people, whose hands and feet would be pierced.[159]

But she desired the coming of this Messiah and Savior of the world with all the strength of her will, whatever it might cost her! So it was that she pronounced her *fiat* with the most apostolic enthusiasm that had ever risen from a human heart. This apostolic determination, far from diminishing with the passage of time or with the incredible deepening of trials, became ever more intense,

---

157 Lk 1:26.
158 Lk 1:38.
159 See Isaiah, chaps. 52-53; Ps 21.

especially at the very moment of those trials. And it continues in Heaven, as do all our supernatural dispositions, but incomparably more perfect than here on earth, immutable in its orientation and constantly changing in its initiatives.

From this *fiat* depended the Incarnation of the Son of God and His condition as apostle, and the apostolate of the Twelve, and that of an unbroken series of popes, bishops, priests, religious men and women, and lay apostles until the end of time, as well as innumerable myriads of the blessed in the presence of God for all eternity.

A study of the relationships between Mary's apostolic mission and her diverse other functions will show how Mary carries out this mission.

RELATIONSHIPS BETWEEN MARY'S FUNCTIONS AND HER APOSTOLIC MISSION

From the point of view we are taking, we can divide Mary's various functions into those which call forth this mission and those which, in some way, are identified with it, being practical applications of it.

****

CHAPTER TWENTY

Functions of Mary Which Call For Her Apostolic Mission

Her Maternity with Respect to Jesus

Called by God to give Jesus to all of us in the mystery of the Incarnation, she is called to give Him to each one of us: an apostolic work.

"The gifts and the call of God are irrevocable," says St. Paul.[160] People change their collaborators because they come to regret having chosen them, through ignorance, though unsuited to their purpose. But God, who knows all the aptitudes and all the deficiencies of individuals, knows in advance

---

160 Rom 11:29.

whom he wishes to choose and does not change
his instruments. His choices are without recall.
Those whom he has chosen, he confirms in their
mission unless they themselves, through obstinate
abuse of grace, refuse their cooperation. He rejected
Judas — or, rather, Judas rejected himself by his
obstinacy and despair. He did not reject Peter who
denied him three times. On the contrary, after his
fall and his repentance, Jesus confirmed him three
times in his mission as first pope.[161]

Now, it was Mary's mission to give Christ to the
human race; it will always be her mission to give
Him to us. "Since it has pleased eternal Providence
that the Man-God be given to us through Mary,"
said Saint Pius X, "and since she, having had Him
through the fruitful power of the divine Spirit, truly
bore Him in her womb, what else can there be than
for us to receive Jesus from the hands of Mary?"[162]
Now, to "give Jesus" means to cause someone to live
the life of Jesus: the most eminent apostolic work.

Her mission as Coredemptrix:

Christ continues His redemptive mission until the
end of the world through His apostolic mission,

---

161 Jn 21:15-17.
162 *Ad diem illum,* in *Maria. Etudes sur le Sainte Vierge,*
vol. 3, p. 767.

for the apostolate is the redemption applied and continued.

As Redeemer on Calvary, He merited for us the grace of deliverance from the demon and from sin and, in principle, merited the divine filiation for all of us. In the work of the apostolate, He applies this grace to each one of us in particular. Of what good would it be for us if Christ had shed His blood to merit this grace for us, had it not applied to us? That is why He continues His redemptive mission through His apostolic mission.

For that apostolic mission, He makes use of collaborators: priests, religious, all true Christians. But it is He who, through them, frees souls from the dominion of Satan and leads them to the Father. When a priest baptizes, or absolves, or distributes Communion, it is Christ who baptizes, who absolves, who nourishes souls with His Body and His Blood. His redemptive function necessarily requires His apostolic function.

However, at the side of Christ, the Redeemer, is Mary, Coredemptrix: Coredemptrix under Him and through Him, but truly Coredemptrix. Her function as Coredemptrix also necessarily calls for her apostolic function. The grace of redemption and of divine filiation which she has merited, under and with Christ, for all of us in principle, needs to be applied to each soul until the consummation of ages, therefore requiring of her an apostolic mission which will not end until the end of time.

The Association of Mary with Jesus

Christian sentiment has always understood that the Son of God made-man should share His prerogatives with His Mother to the extent that she, mere creature, was able to share as such. This has been formulated in the following principle: "To the various privileges of the humanity of Jesus correspond analogous privileges in Mary, in keeping with the manner and extent required by the difference between her condition and that of her Son."[163]

Certainly, the true Apostle of humanity is Christ. Now, if Mary shares in the different functions of her Son, she must also share in His apostolic mission. Her Son must have shared with her — to the extent she was capable of receiving it — His mission of apostle, which will continue as long as there are souls to be saved and sanctified.

---

163 See E. Neubert, *De la Découverte progressive des grandeurs de Marie* (*On the Progressive Discovery of the Grandeurs of Mary*), Ed. Spes, p. 56.

CHAPTER TWENTY-ONE

Mary's Functions Pertaining to Her Apostolic Mission

The Distribution of All Graces through Mary and her Apostolic Mission

The doctrine of the distribution of all graces through Mary is very old in the Church. Recent popes have taught it repeatedly. It is, as these popes have said, a natural consequence of Mary's coredemptive mission. By that mission, the Virgin contributed with Christ in the acquisition of all graces. It is natural, then, that she should contribute with Him in their distribution.[164] Beyond doubt, God has willed that we receive all graces through Mary so as to oblige us, in a way, to turn toward her and to allow her to more easily fulfill her function as Mother in our regard.

If, then, we consider more closely the apostolic function, we note that it depends absolutely on grace. Snatching souls from Satan can be done only through grace; helping a soul to live the life of Jesus

---

164 See E. Neubert, *Marie dans le Dogme*, 3rd ed., p. 156-180. [English tr.: *Mary in Doctrine*]

Christ absolutely requires the help of grace. The one who evangelizes and the one being evangelized both need the help of grace along every step of the way. The evangelizer needs grace to desire to be an apostle — a grace, or rather an infinite series of graces to be prepared for the apostolic mission: graces of enlightenment, graces to touch others, graces to obtain conversions, graces to assure perseverance. The one being evangelized needs the grace to meet an apostle, and the additional graces of light, graces of strength, graces of docility, graces of perseverance.

And it is Mary who obtains all these graces for both of them. Without her help, no sinner could pass from spiritual death to divine life; no justified person could, even with heroic effort, move a single step closer to holiness. No missionary, however eloquent, learned, or competent, would succeed in convincing a pagan to embrace the law of Christ. Any authentic apostolate is the work of grace; and every grace presupposes the intervention of Mary.

Since the day of her Assumption, all souls who have been converted or sanctified — or who will be until the end of the world — by the twelve apostles and their collaborators and by the innumerable line of bishops, priests, religious; by lay members of Catholic Action and of all others societies; and by heretical ministers who have never called upon Mary and who might even have spoken against her intercession, but who have done so in good faith, and have in fact truly loved Christ, but imperfectly — all these multitudes without number, of all nations, tribes, peoples, and tongues who will stand before the throne and the Lamb, dressed in white robes and with palms in hand, and chanting with powerful voice: "Salvation comes from our God, who is seated on the throne, and from the Lamb forever and ever"[165] — all of them, without exception, will owe their glory and their beatitude to the Mediatrix of all graces.

Mary's Spiritual Maternity and Her Apostolic Mission

Mother of Christ, Mary is also Mother of all the members of the Mystical Body of Christ.[166] God did not first decide on the maternity of Mary relative to his Son, and then her maternity relative to us. From all eternity, he decreed the Incarnation of his Son as Head of his Mystical Body; that is, Mary's maternity relative to "the whole Christ."

---

165 Rev 7:9-10.
166 E. Neubert, *Marie dans le Dogma*, pp. 105-107.

Every mother is the first apostle of her children; she has as mission to preserve the little ones from sin, and to help them live the supernatural life. If she confides them to other educators, these others are only her helpers; she remains the first one responsible for this mission.

With even more reason, Mary is the first apostle of her children. And that, for two reasons: first of all, because she is the most perfect of mothers; then, and above all, because she is their supernatural Mother. An ordinary mother who neglects the soul of her child would be a bad mother, but she would nevertheless still be mother because of the physical life she has given to her infant. But Mary's case is quite different; her maternity consists completely in giving supernatural life. In her, maternity and apostolic action merge: all her maternity is exercised through her apostolic action, and all her apostolic action flows from her maternity.

What, in fact, does she do as Mother? She calls us to the life of Christ; she brings us forth to that life. She preserves it, sustains it; she helps us grow in it until we will have attained the stature of her First-born, Christ. Are not these precisely the various acts of the apostolate? Mary is, therefore, essentially apostle because she is essentially Mother. We must either attribute to her a supremely apostolic mission, or deny her spiritual maternity.

To be Mother — Mother of Jesus and our Mother — is the whole reason for Mary's being. It is also the whole reason for the being of her other functions. She is not Mother because she was called to be Coredemptrix and Distributrix of all graces; she is Coredemptrix and Distributrix of all graces because she was called to be Mother.

It can also be shown how Mary's royalty and her quality as Mother and Associate of Christ-Priest presumes in her an apostolic mission. Her royalty[167] allows her to reign over the minds and wills of humans in order to subject them to her Son. She subjects minds to Jesus by getting them to understand, love, and profess His teachings. She subjects their wills to Him by leading them gently and maternally, but very effectively, to the practice of His Commandments, even the most difficult ones, such as purity and pardon of injuries. Her royalty is also a royalty of victory; she wants to transform the enemies of her Son into obedient and loving subjects. All of these actions comprise the apostolate.

---

167 E. Neubert, *Marie dans le Dogma*, pp. 233-238.

Her Quality as Mother and Associate of Christ-Priest

Among persons called to the apostolate, the priest occupies a special role. Mary is not a priest; but from a sacerdotal point of view, she occupies a very special place. She is the Mother and Associate of Christ-Priest. All ministerial priests, even the Sovereign Pontiff, are simply ministers of Christ. All these reasons show the reality, the grandeur, and the supremacy of Mary's apostolic mission.

CHAPTER TWENTY-TWO

The Apostolic Mission of Jesus, That of Mary, That of Other Apostles

We have just looked at the solid foundation of Mary's apostolic mission. In addition, we saw at the beginning of this study that Christ is the true and only Apostle and, that, before ascending to Heaven, He transmitted to His disciples the mission received from His Father. What relationship is there among the apostolic missions of Jesus and those of Mary and of other apostles?

The Apostolic Mission of Mary and that of Jesus

Like her Son, Mary received her apostolic mission directly from God. "The angel Gabriel was **sent by God** ... to a virgin, and the virgin's name was Mary."[168] He asked her, in the name of the Most High, to contribute to the salvation of the world by giving it a Savior. Mary's *fiat* was an essentially apostolic *fiat*.

Presupposing the divine decision to save the world by means of the Incarnation, the apostolate of Jesus was necessary of itself to work out the salvation of the world. Only an action of infinite value could produce such a result.

Mary's apostolate is not necessary of itself. It is necessary by God's decision to associate the Mother's action to that of her Son.

The apostolate of Jesus was sufficient of itself to achieve the conversion and sanctification of all humans. That of Mary has value only through its

---

168 Lk 2:26.

union with that of Jesus, from which it draws its entire efficacy.

However, the extent of this action is the same for both the Mother and the Son. There is not a domain reserved to Jesus and another, lesser, reserved to Mary. The whole Christian apostolate is carried out by both Jesus and Mary. Here, as with her other functions, Mary is the "Associate of Christ," participating in His action in keeping with her condition as Woman and Mother, and drawing all the efficacy of her action from that of her Son.[169]

Of what use, then, is this participation in Christ's action since His is fully sufficient?

First of all, it was an unutterable satisfaction for the filial piety of Jesus to associate His Mother in the work for which He was incarnated in her. Then, for Mary, it was an unutterable satisfaction for her to be able to help her Son in His divine work, and to contribute to the sanctification and salvation of all her children.

---

169 It is clear that the relationship of Jesus' apostolic mission and that of Mary are the same as the relationship of Jesus' mediation function and that of Mary. This is normal, since their apostolic function is only a continuation and application of their mediation function.

For us, too, there is immense joy and a most powerful motive for courage and confidence in knowing that our Mother is so concerned in sanctifying and saving us, and so powerful in succeeding. If devotion to Mary has proved itself to have such marvelous efficacy for the preservation of purity, for progress in virtue, and for leading people to sanctity, is it not because we know that her Son had confided to her the mission of helping us in all these pursuits? What a difference between the behavior of Christians who include Mary in their spiritual work, and of those who ignore her!

The Apostolic Mission of Mary and that of the Other Apostles

The other apostles: the Twelve, the members of the hierarchy, the religious, and the simple faithful — unlike Jesus and Mary who received their apostolic mission directly from the Father or from the Most Holy Trinity — have received or presently receive their apostolic mission from the Son of God made-man. Their apostolic activity perpetuates that of Christ's and depends on His. It also continues Mary's apostolic activity and depends on hers as we have indicated in the preceding chapter, and as we shall see in greater detail in the second part of this study.

As to their sphere of activity, it is not universal in time or in space as is that of Jesus and Mary, but more or less restricted to a given period of history and to a limited part of the universe, depending on other circumstances.

Here, once again, as with her other functions and prerogatives, we note that Mary's place is to be sought closer to the side of her Son than to the side of other humans.

CHAPTER TWENTY-THREE

Role of the Holy Spirit in the Apostolic Mission of Jesus, of Mary, and of Ours

The mystery of Pentecost does not allow us to doubt that the Holy Spirit had, and still has, a role to play in the Catholic apostolate. Our Lord Himself had chosen twelve men whom He named "apostles." But these twelve scarcely exercised any apostolate during the lifetime of Jesus on earth, apart from the few days when He had sent forth the seventy disciples. They allowed Jesus to evangelize alone, and to save Himself from the numerous traps which the Pharisees and the Sadducees repeatedly set for Him. Their Master was imprisoned; they fled and hid behind locked doors for fear of the Jews. They were still in hiding in the cenacle in the early hours of Pentecost.

Suddenly, the Holy Spirit shook the house as would a hurricane! He appeared in their midst in the form of tongues of fire which divided themselves and rested upon each of their heads. Behold, they began to talk in various tongues as the Holy Spirit moved them. Crowds gathered and heard them speak, each in his or her own language. They were amazed, not knowing what to think! Peter, with the other apostles, bravely presented himself before the multitude. He declared that they had put the Messiah to death, crucifying Him at the hands of unbelievers; that God had raised Him up and that He had just sent the Holy Spirit to them according to His promise. "Let the whole house of Israel know with certainty: God had made Him Lord and Messiah, this Jesus whom you have crucified."

No eloquent oration; just simple facts, a reference to Joel and two Psalms, a two-fold repetition of the crucifixion of the Lord. But the Holy Spirit spoke through his mouth and, behold, that very day, some 3,000 people joined them.[170] Had the Master ever been so successful in any of His preaching?

Shortly after that, having cured the lame man at the gate of the temple, Peter gave a second discourse to the people. This brought the number of the believers (counting men only) to about 5,000.[171] Several more times, the author of *Acts* makes the comment: "The number of believers increased considerably in Jerusalem, and a multitude of the priests rendered obedience to the faith. The Church, like a building, grew under the consoling support of the Holy Spirit."[172] Soon the disciples spread out into Samaria, Antioch, Damascus, into all the regions of the Orient, and even to Rome. The apostles dispersed and carried the Faith of Christ to all corners of the known world.

Wouldn't we be inclined to say that the true founder of the Catholic apostolate was not Christ, but the Holy Spirit? No! Christ's role was to found the apostolate; the role of the Holy Spirit is to bring it to its fullness. Within the Divinity, the person of the Holy Spirit is the one who completes the Most

---

170 Acts 2:41

171 Acts 4:3.

172 Acts 6:7; see Acts 9:31; 12:24; 16:5.

Holy Trinity and who completes it in love; for he is the substantial love of the Father and the Son. Apart from the Divinity, his role is equally one of achievement, of perfection — of perfection in love.

In the apostles, he completed the work begun by Jesus.

He completed the enlightenment of their intelligence. How many times did the Master complain: "Do you not yet understand?"[173] He taught them in public, and again in private. But at the moment when He is about to leave this world, their intelligence is still closed to many truths.

The Holy Spirit opened it for them in an instant. "I have much to tell you," Jesus confided to them in His farewell address after the Supper, "but you cannot bear it now. But when he comes, the Spirit of truth, will guide you in all truth. He will not speak on his own, but he will instruct you in all that he has heard, and will declare to you the things that are to come. He will glorify Me because he will take from what is Mine and declare it to you."[174]

Up to the moment of His Ascension, the apostles were still deluded by the dream of reestablishing the

173 Mk 8:14-21.
174 Jn 16:12-14.

temporal kingdom of Israel. With the coming of the Holy Spirit, the issue was settled. They understood that the true kingdom of Israel is the Church.

The repeated mention of the Passion remained shrouded in mystery for them. Their leader dared to protest to the Master: "No such thing shall ever happen to you!" And Jesus replied: "Get behind me, Satan! You are not thinking as God does, but as humans do."[175] When that event took place, they were utterly confused and did not understand it. But, once the Holy Spirit had come upon them, they preached the mysteries of the Passion, of the Resurrection, and of the Triumph.

The Holy Spirit brought the dispositions of their hearts to perfection. Until that moment, their egotistical passions were manifested in quarrels of jealousy and ambition. Afterwards, all that mattered was the glory of Christ! They were exceedingly happy to have been scourged for the name of Jesus.[176]

The Holy Spirit strengthened their courage. Those who fled on the night when Jesus was taken prisoner were now preaching the name of Jesus openly. When threatened, they continued with even greater fervor. Peter, who had denied his Master with a curse at the

---

175 See Mt 16:21-27; Mk 8:31-33.
176 Acts 5:40-42.

voice of a servant girl and the question of a ruffian, dared to defy the high priest and all the Sanhedrin. "Filled with the Holy Spirit," he reproached them for killing Jesus, proclaimed His Resurrection and, when ordered to stop preaching about Jesus, he replied that it was better to obey God rather than men. He was cast into prison a second time and accused before the high priest. Once again, he proclaimed the crime of the Jews, the Resurrection of Jesus, and His excellence as Head and Savior. He added: "We are witnesses of these things, as is the Holy Spirit, given by God to those who obey him."[177]

The Holy Spirit made them "powerful in words and in works." Jesus had foretold this:

> When they take you before synagogues, and before rulers and authorities, do not worry about how or what your defense will be or what you are to say. For the Holy Spirit will teach you at that moment what you should say.[178]

These were unlettered men. During the lifetime of Jesus, they did not preach; they were embarrassed

---

[177] See Acts 5:17-32.
[178] Lk 12:11-12; Mk 13:11; Mt 10:19-20

when the Pharisees posed objections to them.[179] But when the Holy Spirit spoke through their mouths, no one could resist their eloquence. At the time of Peter's first arrest, the chiefs, the elders, the scribes, as well as Annas, with Caiaphas the high priest, and John Alexander, all the members of the pontifical family assembled to judge him. Peter opened his mouth and all the chiefs and doctors were unable to respond; they could only dismiss him with threats. On his second arrest, the high priest and those of his party arrived and convoked the Sanhedrin and the whole senate. Peter spoke again, and the entire cohort was unable to refute his words, other than to bring a judgment of death against the apostle.[180]

After some time, they turned their attention to Stephen, the deacon. The members of five synagogues engaged him in discussion, but "they could not withstand the wisdom and the spirit with which he spoke." They dragged him before the synagogue. There, he discoursed at length, reproaching them for resisting the Holy Spirit. They were furious with him and gnashed their teeth! But, filled with the Holy Spirit, Stephen, eyes raised to heaven, saw the glory of God and Jesus standing at the right of God. His adversaries rushed upon him

---

179 Mt 15:12
180 See Acts 5:17-32.

and stoned him to death! He prayed for them and
for Saul, the future Paul, who was guarding their
garments.[181]

The Holy Spirit rendered them especially
powerful in works. Those works were, above all,
the conversions that followed one after another
throughout the known world. These works also
included the miracles effecting those conversions.
Jesus foretold the apostles that they would do
the same works as He did, and even greater ones.
During His lifetime, the apostles enjoyed the power
of performing miracles only when on mission.
Afterwards, miracles abounded under their hands!
Formerly, a woman with a hemorrhage had been
cured when touching the hem of Jesus' mantle.[182]
Subsequently, the mere shadow of Peter was enough
to produce equally startling effects.

> They even carried the sick out into the streets
> and laid them on cots and mats so that when
> Peter came by, at least his shadow might fall
> on one or another of them. A large number
> of people from the towns in the vicinity of
> Jerusalem also gathered, bringing the sick and

---

181 See Acts 6:6; 7:69
182 Lk 8:40-42.

those tormented by impure spirits, and they were all cured.[183]

The Holy Spirit worked marvels not only in the apostles and deacons, but also in the simple faithful. At the moment when the apostles laid hands on the newly baptized to confirm them, the Holy Spirit descended upon the neophytes and manifested his presence by all sorts of extraordinary gifts, the *charisms*, of which Saint Paul speaks on various occasions.[184]

But, what was even more excellent than these charisms was the union and fraternal charity established by the Holy Spirit within the Christian communities. Of these, Jerusalem was the model.[185] All had only one heart and one soul because the Spirit of love made them aware that they were all well-beloved children of the same heavenly Father, brothers and sisters in Jesus.

In view of these marvels attributable to the action of the Holy Spirit, who would be surprised that devotion to the divine Spirit should be so popular

---

183 Acts 5:15-16.

184 For example, I Cor chaps. 12-14. See also the case of Simon the Magician who wanted to purchase with silver the marvelous power of bestowing the Holy Spirit – Acts 8:9-24.

185 Acts 4:32-37.

in the early Church? Nowadays, for the majority of Christians, the Holy Spirit is the "Great Unknown." That is because charismatic prodigies ended a long time ago. Saint Paul gives us the reason for their disappearance. "Tongues are a sign for unbelievers — not for those who believe."[186] Those charisms were very useful for converting Jews and pagans to the truth of the new religion. Such demonstrations would not be useful in a Christian environment.

However, it would be wrong to neglect devotion to the Holy Spirit. Are the interior effects of his action — sanctification of souls, apostolic successes — any less needed now than at the time of the apostles?

One might excuse this negligence, it would seem, on the basis of a principal of Trinitarian theology, i.e., that every activity of God *ad extra* (outside of himself) is common to the Three Divine Persons. Therefore, the special graces of light, strength, piety, etc., which are called the "gifts of the Holy Spirit," are given to us by the Father and the Son and the Holy Spirit at the same time and in the same manner by each of the Three. It is only by "appropriation," as the theologians put it, that we

---

186 I Cor 14:22.

attribute certain effects of the divine action to one or the other Person; the effects remind us in some way of the "properties" of the Persons. So to the Father, the principle of the Son and of the Spirit, we attribute creation; to the Son, redemption; to the Holy Spirit, sanctification.

But it would be a mistake to conclude from this principle that it is a matter of indifference whether we hold to the veneration or the invocation of a specific Person to whom we experience a greater attraction. All Three Persons are equally great, powerful, and loving, and all Three merit a special cult. Since God has revealed to us the trinity of Persons in the unity of the divine nature, it is obviously so that we might render a cult to each of the Three Persons. We would displease God and obtain less grace by practically ignoring one of the Persons.

For the relationship we should have with each of the Three Divine Persons, we should follow the indications God furnished to us in Scripture and the example of the Church, especially in its liturgy. Could it perhaps be due to a failure to follow these indications that, some Christians, called to holiness, but forgetting the Holy Spirit, do not make greater progress in perfection or do not enjoy greater success in the apostolate?

Just as Mary is associated with the mission of Jesus, she is also associated with that of the Holy Spirit, although in a different way.

Apostolic union between Mary and the divine Spirit dates far back. Predestined to be the Mother of Christ the Apostle, the Virgin had to be totally pure. From the first moment of her existence, the sanctifying Spirit overshadowed her, preserved her from all stain, and filled her with a plenitude of grace above that of all the other saints. From that moment on, the Spirit constantly worked in her in preparation for her mission.

The moment for the Incarnation had arrived. As soon as she pronounced her *fiat*, the Spirit came to her for a new work: together, she and he — she, by him — gave existence to the One who would be the great, the only Apostle, the One from whom all other apostles would receive their mission. Without this common working of Mary and the Holy Spirit, there would have been no Christ-apostle; there would have been no apostle; there would have been no apostolate — at least not in the present economy of salvation. In making the Virgin to be the Mother of Christ, the Holy Spirit also made her the Associate in Christ's apostolate and in that of the Twelve, and of all clerical and lay persons who are concerned with sanctifying and saving the world.

Before sending the disciples the Paraclete, who would instantaneously grant them the understanding of all that he had taught them, and would bestow on them strength from on high which nothing could resist, Jesus had commanded them to assemble in the upper room and there await the divine Spirit. They prepared themselves there and, all of one heart, "persevered in prayer with ... Mary, the Mother of Jesus."[187] There can be no doubt that Mary's prayer greatly helped the apostles to receive this fullness of apostolic power which was to astound the world and increase conversions with amazing speed.

Now, the vocations and the gifts of God are without recall. What Mary did for the first apostles, she is called to do for all their successors until the end of the world. She will always help apostolic messengers in their work with souls to give that undertaking its full fruitfulness. That is a strong motive for them to have recourse to her to obtain the special assistance of the Holy Spirit in their labors.

There is a second motive: all graces come to us through Mary including, therefore, those which are specifically attributed to the Holy Spirit. Ignoring Mary while having recourse to the divine Spirit would be as unacceptable as ignoring her when

---

[187] Acts 1:14.

wishing to go to Jesus. Let humans not separate what God had joined!

Moreover, in keeping with the remark of Saint Louis-Marie de Montfort (and he certainly knew what he was talking about):

> When the Holy Spirit finds Mary in a soul, he flies there; he enters there fully; he communicates himself abundantly to that soul, to the extent that it is open to his Spouse. One of the main reasons the Holy Spirit does not cause great marvels in souls now is that he does not find a sufficiently great union there with his faithful and inseparable Spouse. I say **inseparable** Spouse for, since this substantial love of the Father and the Son espoused Mary to produce Jesus Christ, the Head of the elect, and Jesus Christ in the elect, he never repudiated her, for she has always been faithful and fruitful.[188]

---

188 *Traité de la Vraie Dévotion à la Sainte Vierge*, no. 36. [English tr.: *True Devotion to Mary*]

Part Two

OUR PARTICIPATION IN MARY'S APOSTOLIC MISSION

CHAPTER TWENTY-FOUR

Jesus Wishes Us to Be Aware
of Mary's Mission

Given that Mary's apostolic mission is a mission subordinated to that of Jesus and drawing its efficacy from His and that, on the other hand, it is exercised at the same time as that of her Son even if we do not advert to it — is that reason for us not to be concerned for it in the practical order?

Analogously, given that the mission of the Mediatrix of all graces is subordinated to that of Christ from which it draws all its efficacy, and that it is exercised at the same time as that of her Son, even if we do not advert to it — is there no profit in our being engaged in it in the practical order, i.e., that we should call upon Mary? Catholics are unanimous in their response and do not desist from addressing their requests to her.

In this case, as in all our conduct, we should follow the indications of God's will as manifested through the conduct of the Church. For many long centuries, apostolic souls have been instinctively concerned to associate Mary with their endeavors for the conversion and sanctification of souls. That fact is especially striking since the beginning of the 19th century and particularly in our present age, the "age of Mary," foretold by voices which we may certainly consider inspired. It is also true that numerous and surprising facts have proved the efficacy of such conduct.

Why should such a comment surprise us? God asked Mary for her cooperation in the work of Redemption — her cooperation in a total life of sufferings, anxieties, fully accepted, freely willed, out of love for her Son and love for us. Is it strange that, after having required of her so burdensome a cooperation in our salvation, he should now wish to give her the joy of cooperating openly in the application of the graces of salvation, and also wish to call her children to help her in this task? If he has made her so pure, so beautiful, so perfect, so great and, at the same time, so humble, so kind, so merciful — in a word, so motherly — was it not precisely in order to allow her to more easily exercise this apostolic influence which attracts the just and the sinner to her?

Wouldn't the desire to ignore God's intentions and to bypass Mary's help in our activity in favor of others, be a manifestation of pride? Wouldn't this condemn our work to sterility? On the other hand, wouldn't including the Virgin in our apostolic contacts as much as possible, assure them of ultimate fruitfulness? The success of the Legion of Mary is evidence of it.

CHAPTER TWENTY-FIVE

Mary Desires Our Cooperation in Her Apostolic Mission

It is not difficult to understand Mary's desire to have us cooperate in her mission. There are several reasons of great importance for her to have such a desire.

She has need of us:

Christ Himself has need of us for the success of His mission. That is what Pope Pius XII affirmed in his encyclical on the Mystical Body of Christ. In fact, this is what he wrote:

> We must maintain, though this seems truly astounding, that Christ has need of help from His members. He wishes to receive help from His Mystical Body in order to accomplish the work of Redemption.
>
> However, that is not because of any indigence or weakness on His part but, rather, that He has assumed this disposition for the greater glory of His Spouse without stain. Though, when dying on the Cross, He communicated the limitless treasure of the Redemption to His Church without any collaboration on her part — when it is question of distributing this treasure, He shares with His Immaculate Spouse the work of the sanctification of souls...
>
> A redoubtable mystery, certainly, which can never be meditated upon enough: the salvation of a great number of souls depends on the prayers and mortifications, assumed

for this purpose, of the members of the
Mystical Body of Jesus Christ.

Like her Son, Mary has need of us. This is because
God wills that we cooperate with her and with
Jesus, not only for our own salvation, but also for
the salvation of others. It is an infinite honor for us
to be the collaborators, the *necessary* collaborators,
of the Redeemer and of the Coredemptrix. But
it is also a redoubtable responsibility which we
can never meditate upon enough: the salvation
of a more or less great number of souls depends
on our faithfulness in providing Mary with the
collaboration she expects of us.

So, then, if Mary needs our cooperation to carry
out the functions which God has confided to her, it
is clear that she should desire this cooperation with
the full ardor of her being.

The glory and the love of God:

Mary's mission is to snatch souls from Satan so
that she might make of God's enemies who are
ready to fall into hell, his friends, his well-beloved
children, who will praise him eternally in heaven.
The glory of God and his love for his poor creatures
are therefore also at stake. But since she has need of
us, Mary cannot achieve these results without our

help. Let us imagine, if we can, how close to her heart the glory of the Most Blessed Trinity and the love of the heavenly Father for his children on earth must be. We might then grasp how much she must desire this help.

The love of Jesus for His Father and for us:

No one else can understand, as does Mary, Jesus' love for His Father and for human beings. Jesus came upon earth; He accepted a life of humiliation and torments, even going to the extreme limits of His capacity to suffer in order to restore His Father's glory. Now, His Father is glorified in this, that His enemies become His friends, His children, who will love and praise Him in Heaven eternally.

How greatly Mary must desire to help Him in this glorification of His Father! But she can only do so with our help.

Christ also came into the world for love of us. He became one of us; He became our Brother. He wanted to help us live of His life so that, one day, we might enjoy His happiness. At times, He has let us see the excess of His devotedness in saving us — in saving even the worst sinner. He is the Good Shepherd who leaves the ninety-nine faithful sheep in the desert to seek out the one who abandoned

Him. With what tenderness He takes it upon His shoulders! With what exuberance He calls to His friends and invites them to rejoice with Him![189] He arrives, exhausted, at the gates of Sychar and seats Himself at Jacob's well to wait there and to converse (with great finesse) with a sinful woman.[190] He sheds His Blood, even to the last drop, for the conversion of sinners.

How could Mary not share in His sentiments? How could she remain indifferent to the conversion of these people for whom Jesus submitted to such horrible torments? But for her to do so effectively, she needs our help!

Her spiritual Maternity:

Mary is our Mother. Every Christian mother desires the sanctification and salvation of her child. When that salvation is endangered, great anguish fills her heart! For many years, Monica shed tears over her son, Augustine, who was headed to perdition; she sought to save him by all the means she could conceive. There was no joy for this poor mother as long as he was obstinate in his wandering. How many pious mothers experience the same anguish

---

189 Lk 15:4-7.
190 Jn 4:7-30.

today? They ask themselves how they could ever be happy in Heaven if their son were eternally damned. Let God send them whatever trials he might choose as long as their son is saved!

But what common measure could there be between the desire of a Christian mother, even if a saint, and that of our heavenly Mother? She is incomparably more perfect than any other mother and, therefore, incomparably more loving and infinitely more desirous to preserve her child from eternal damnation. And, she realizes infinitely better than any Christian mother, the horror of that damnation.

Besides, as we have already pointed out,[191] every other mother is still truly a mother even if she does not help her child live supernaturally. Mary's maternity, on the contrary, consists entirely in the fact of helping a human being to live of that divine life. If she is not successful, she cannot carry out the function for which God made her Mother of His Son. She wants to make another Jesus of that human being, but it remains a spiritual cadaver to be cast into the fires of hell. For her to be truly its Mother and to render it participation in the life of her First-born Son, she needs our help. She is ardently desirous of it!

---

191 Part One, Chap. 21, above.

Witness of history:

Furthermore, the life of the Church furnishes us with facts that prove Mary's desire to have us assist in her apostolic mission.

In Part One of this work, we pointed out that all the great converters, at least since the late Middle Ages, were all quite remarkable for their devotion to Mary. It is a fact of history that it was Mary who led them to the apostolate, or the apostolate that led them to Mary. But, behind the obvious causes, the work of grace implements our ideas and inclinations to realize its purposes. Now, every grace comes to us through Mary. If apostles feel drawn toward the Virgin, or devotees of the Virgin toward the apostolate, it is she who, even without their knowing it, has prepared valiant collaborators for her mission.

In more recent times, especially from the beginning of the 19th century, we have seen innumerable founders of new apostolic societies put their enterprises under the banner of the Queen of Apostles. If, as in the case of Venerable Libermann, they did not initially see the relationship between their enterprise and devotion to the Virgin, it was the Virgin herself who compelled them to consecrate themselves to her.

Saint Louis-Marie de Montfort, Venerable Libermann, {Blessed} Father Chaminade and others clearly saw that they carried out their apostolate in the name of Mary. There are others who view this with less clarity and may be content to sense the existence of a relationship between their devotion to Mary and their apostolic activity. But Mary, for her part, knows full well that it was to her — Coredemptrix, universal Distributrix of grace, Mother and Queen of the universe — that the universal mission of giving Christ to the world was first confided, after her Son. She knows that all other apostolic workers, whether they know it or not, are and only can be her subordinates, her helpers in this mission; and it is in this capacity that she called or calls them to the apostolate.

CHAPTER TWENTY-SIX

Our Obligation to Assist Mary in Her Apostolic Mission

When speaking of an *obligation* to assist Mary, it is not a matter of some duty imposed under pain of sin, some duty that would consist in having the Blessed Virgin intervene directly in our apostolate. It is, rather, a matter of an exhortation, as emphatic as possible, and based on the love of our Lord, of Mary, and of souls — an exhortation to give our apostolate the maximum efficacy by carrying it out under the name, according to the intentions, and with the help of Mary.

Such an obligation is based on the quality of our children of Mary. It is an obligation of filial piety for every child to assist its mother if she happens to be in need. And in her apostolic mission, Mary has need of us. She needs us in order to carry out her task as Associate of Christ the Redeemer; she needs us in order to save her children from eternal damnation.

Besides this fundamental reason, there are certain other reasons that lead us to fulfill our apostolic task in union with Mary. This union enables us to give maximum return to our apostolate.

Every Christian has an apostolic duty.[192] Now, by exercising our apostolate with Mary, according to her intentions and with her help, we assure its greatest possible efficacy because we conform ourselves perfectly to the intentions of God himself. He has given Mary this apostolic mission and has given us to her as her children.

Consequently, union with Mary in our apostolate makes us more capable:

– of glorifying the Most Holy Trinity, being entirely conformed to its intentions;

– of leading to the Father the greatest possible number of submissive and loving children;

– of assuring the fruitfulness of the Passion of Christ and of gaining a multitude of brothers and sisters for Him;

– of facilitating our Mother's task, and multiplying her children and her collaborators;

---

192 See Chap. 11, Part One, above.

– of assuring the triumph of the Church in the midst of the incessant struggles which her numerous and hateful enemies wage against her;

– of saving the multitudes of souls who were headed for hell;

– of assuring for ourselves a powerful means of sanctification and a very great joy; and of giving joy to Jesus, to Mary, and to others here on earth during the brief years of our life and for all eternity in Heaven;

– of helping to revive the reign of the Spirit of the early Church.

All these motives do not create an obligation to assist in the strict sense of justice, i.e., an obligation of commutative justice. But, for a loving and generous soul, they do form the even greater obligations of equity, love, and gratitude.

It must also be acknowledged that there are various degrees of obligation to assist Mary in her apostolic mission. They are dependent on multiple factors and on our awareness of this obligation. A law obliges only if it is known. There are many Christians, even very devoted to Mary, who have no idea of the obligation to assist her in a mission of which they may even be ignorant. In terms of

Marian assistance, they only know of the one they expect from her, not of the one she expects of them.

However, many of them, without ever having heard of Mary's apostolic mission, sometimes have the feeling that, in a given circumstance or in a certain need, the Blessed Virgin desires their supplications to intervene and to provide some help.

This obligation also depends on the possibilities at one's disposal. Lay Christians who have to struggle all day long with material difficulties may not have the same obligation to help the Virgin as do priests or religious men and women.

This obligation also depends on the commitment they have made to Mary's service. Members of a Marian association, especially those of a religious society officially placed under the patronage of the Virgin, are naturally more strictly obliged to be concerned with her interests than are Christians not tied to her service by a special commitment. And among such Christians are those whose Marian commitment has, as direct object, the assistance of Mary in her apostolic mission, and who are evidently more strictly held to give themselves to it than those who propose to only honor a special virtue or mystery of Mary.

Finally, this obligation depends on the personal vocation and abilities of each one. What is important is that each soul be faithful to its Marian grace and "to *all* its Marian grace"!

DISPOSITIONS REQUIRED
OF THE VIRGIN'S APOSTLE

CHAPTER TWENTY-SEVEN

The Spirit of Faith

We shall now turn our attention to some of the dispositions required of any apostle of the Virgin. The spirit of faith is its foundation. Faith, according to the Council of Trent, is "the foundation and root of all justification."[193] It is the *sine qua non* condition of all the other dispositions.

---

193 Denzinger, no. 801 {DS 1532}.

To work in the apostolate means to lead people to accept and to live the truths of the Faith. But we can teach only what we know and, when it is a matter of faith, we can teach only what we live. Theoretical faith is not sufficient; what is needed is a practical faith, the spirit of faith which is the "habit" of practical faith.

To believe is to think the thoughts of Jesus about the things of this life and of the next. His thoughts are revealed to us in His gospel, in particular in the "Sermon on the Mount." He has also revealed them even more clearly by His life. In what has to do with the values of this life and those of the next life, with riches and poverty, with pleasure and renunciation, in relations with neighbors, friends, and enemies, we must ask: what did Jesus think? What did He say? What did He do? As for me — what do I think? What do I do? With regard to judgments and reflections heard or read, or with regard to events that happen to us or to others, we should ask ourselves what the thoughts and teachings of Christ are on these matters.

Ask yourself, too, what the Blessed Virgin thinks of it, or ask her directly. The Holy Spirit proclaimed her "blessed for having believed."[194] Mary is the

---

194 Lk 1:45.

great Model of our faith; our Lord could not be such insofar as He did not live by faith but by vision. Mary enjoys a special charism to teach us to think the thoughts of Jesus. She renders them particularly clear and attractive for us.

In the following chapters, we shall explore the special means for acquiring and perfecting this spirit of faith.

CHAPTER TWENTY-EIGHT

The Interior Spirit

It is with reason that the interior spirit has been termed "the soul of the apostolate."[195] Blessed William Joseph Chaminade, who believed he had been called by Mary to found an "Order that was essentially apostolic in the universality of its members," explained to his first followers the spirit proper to the new foundation:

---

[195] Title of a well-known work by Dom Chautard, Abbot of Seven-Fountains.

God, who has chosen us for this work, gives us, children of Mary, the spirit proper to us; that spirit is the interior spirit.

The religious makes of his soul a temple of the Lord ... He never loses sight of the presence of God; he converses calmly and familiarly with God because God has taken up residence within him. He also makes of his heart a sanctuary for Mary, from which fervent prayers are addressed to her.

Who is the model of this spirit for us? It is the august Mary who lived only for God and who always carried God within herself through perfect submission of her will. The spirit of the Institute is the spirit of Mary; that explains everything! If you are children of Mary, imitate Mary.

The essential, therefore, is to form the interior spirit within ourselves.[196]

It is not difficult to see reasons for the importance of the interior spirit for the apostle.

---

196 *Espirt de notre Fondation*, vol. 1, nos. 232ff.

First of all, without an interior spirit, there is no holiness; and, without holiness, there is no apostolic fruitfulness.

In addition, without an interior spirit, we would operate only according to our natural lights or, even often, only according to our feelings or a momentary whim. We would not be guided by the Holy Spirit nor accomplish any supernatural good, even though others might admire our eloquence or cleverness.

Without an interior spirit, there would be no supernatural confidence, nor true giving of ourselves to others, nor any perseverance amidst difficulties. Quite simply, without an interior spirit, we would not succeed in truly having any of the dispositions required for an apostolate toward others.

How is this spirit acquired and conserved? {Blessed} Father Chaminade says: "Imitate Mary!" This instruction is applicable in all circumstances. It is, indeed, quite easy in any situation to ask ourselves how Mary would act, or to discover how to remain recollected, whether alone or in contact with others. We need only envision her in Nazareth, at Aïn Karim, in Jerusalem, in Egypt, or at the foot of the Cross.

It is good, meanwhile, to directly apply ourselves for a certain length of time to acquiring this spirit. This means, first of all, to avoid whatever might disrupt our effort to remain in the presence of God. We must practice exterior and interior silence which prevents us from leaving our sanctuary, as well as custody of the eyes which keeps the outside from entering in.

We must also make positive efforts to enter into, and to renew, our contact with God. We must, therefore, pray regularly and develop the habit of ejaculatory prayers. Once or twice a day, at fixed moments, we should have a time for conversation with Jesus and Mary so as to learn to think the thoughts of Jesus and so, to live of the life of Jesus.

It is above all in such moments of conversation that we should appeal to the Holy Spirit. Without him, we run the risk of rendering beautiful considerations sterile. With the Holy Spirit, everything changes. Through his special graces, he helps us grasp the profound and vital sense of the truth, not by reasoning but by intuition. As a consequence, the truth impresses us as though we had just discovered it, and its importance strikes us never before. He leads us to taste and love this truth which, heretofore, had perhaps left us cold.

The Holy Spirit can show us how to live our truth in daily practice despite the obstacles that may surround us. He introduces us into a life of intimacy with God and fills us with truly filial dispositions toward him. It is he who teaches us how to really pray, for "we do not know how to pray as we ought." The Spirit himself intercedes for us with inexpressible groaning; and he who searches the heart recognizes the desires of the Spirit. He knows it is according to God's will that he intercedes in favor of the holy ones.[197]

Just as we go to Jesus with Mary, so we also go with Mary to the Holy Spirit. We experience, thanks to her, how union with the Holy Spirit becomes easier, more intimate, more fruitful, and more transforming.

---

197 Rom 1:26ff.

CHAPTER TWENTY-NINE

Holiness

Venerable Francis Mary Paul (Jacob) Libermann used to say to his disciples: "Note well that the great rule of the whole apostolic life is holiness. … To begin with: personal holiness; next, personal holiness; always, personal holiness."

Another priest, Father Edward Poppe, a great apostle, made the comment: "It is said there are not enough priests. No, there are enough priests; but there are not enough saintly priests."

A hundred years before him, {Blessed} Father Chaminade had said the same thing: "With saintly people, we can do much; with mediocre religious, we can do almost nothing."

The same truth is affirmed for us by another personage who is not usually cited as a witness in matters of spirituality and of apostolate: it is the "father of lies." Yet even the demon slips into giving witness to the truth at times. One day he said to the Curé of Ars: "If there were three like you, it would be the end of my dominion over humans."

We may affirm that there is a vast difference between the action of a very fervent person, but one who seeks self from time to time, and that of a saint who always and everywhere practices the total gift of self to God. There is, indeed, a difference between one who gives ninety percent, and another who gives one hundred percent. The latter does not exercise ten percent more influence than the former but, rather, infinitely more! For the influence of the first, though great, is limited, while that of the second is without limit.

A saintly person places no boundaries on generosity; that is why God places no boundaries on his liberality. The saint poses no obstacle to God's action and, God, in keeping with his infinite mercy and love, gives freely through that saint. And so, while the radiation from ordinary apostles remains circumscribed in space and time, that of saintly apostles expands throughout the centuries, perhaps even to the end of time; it extends itself little by little, at least indirectly, to an infinite number of persons.

The saintly person is another Jesus Christ. To the extent that we are holy, we are Jesus. And Jesus is the Apostle *par excellence.*

For transformation of the Christian into Jesus, Mary is the shortest road. We may remember the words of Saint Pius X cited earlier: "Who does not hold as established truth that there can be no path more secure or more rapid than Mary for uniting human beings to Jesus Christ and for obtaining, through Jesus Christ, that perfect adoption as sons and daughters which renders us holy and without stain before God?"

We have explained elsewhere, with theological and even psychological rationale, why union with Mary is such a perfect and quick road for leading a generous soul to sanctity.[198]

Besides, we may say that Mary desires infinitely more to make saints of her apostles than they do themselves. It is because, the more they are holy, the more effectively can they help her to save her children.

---

198 E. Neubert, *La Dévotion à Marie*, Centre de Documentation scolaire, 38, rue du Dragon, Paris, pp. 38-52 [English tr.: *Devotion to Mary*].

CHAPTER THIRTY

Participation in Mary's Love For Souls

The apostolic spirit or zeal for the salvation of souls is a necessary consequence of the supernatural love we have for them. Our apostolate is a participation in Mary's apostolate. Our apostolic zeal is the necessary consequence of our participation in Mary's love for souls.

In order to fully understand this love, we would have to have an immaculate heart and one as perfect as hers; or, rather, we would have to have *her* Immaculate Heart. We can, however, make an effort to form some ideal of the reasons which lead Mary to love humans, all humans. She loves them for what they are to God, to her Son, and to herself.

What they are for God:

God loves all his creatures just as human beings love what they have made, especially if they have produced a masterpiece. God has made all his works with perfection. But the most perfect among them — at least in this world — is the human being, animated with a free and rational soul — a spiritual soul, like God. He has so loved this creature that he wanted to render it a participant in his divinity.

But, by a folly of ambition, the first human being substituted a plan suggested by Satan for the plan of God. That first man lost the right to divine life for himself and for his entire race. Yet, God, in his infinite love, wished to return humans to their sublime vocation. He decreed that his only Son should become human so that humans might again be children of God. His First-born Son would form a single body with them, a body of which the Son would be the Head and the others His members. He would produce this marvel, thanks to Mary, who would be the Mother of his First-born and the Mother of all His members.

Mary, therefore, sees in each human being a child of God, loved with an infinite love, called to be her child in Jesus, destined to live the same life of Jesus — the divine life.

What they are to Jesus:

According to the plan of the Most Holy Trinity, humans would therefore be brothers and sisters of Jesus having again become, through Him, participants in His divinity; like Him — children of the same Father, destined to live just as He does, the blessed vision of God for all eternity. Jesus loves these brothers and sisters in the heavenly Father and in Mary with such love that He was willing to suffer the most atrocious torments for their sake, even death, in order to merit eternal life for them.

What they are to Mary:

It is with this love of the Father and this love of the Son for mankind, that Mary loves us. She would love us with this two-fold love, surpassing all understanding, even if we were strangers to her. But we are not strangers. We are infinitely loved children, for she had engendered us through torments, and to a life infinitely superior to the physical life to which our mothers engendered us according to nature. For this reason alone, her love for us incomparably exceeds the love of the most perfect mothers for the most perfect of their children.

Mary, then, sees in each of us the chosen child of the heavenly Father, the brother or sister of Jesus, loved by Him even to the sacrifice of His life. She sees her own child who she, in principle, engendered on Calvary and who she, in fact, is to engender to the life of her Son. In keeping with her apostolic mission, she is to form that child in the most perfect resemblance possible to Jesus.

Our apostolic mission is a participation in hers. We must, then, enter into her soul and allow her incomparable love for the children of her heart to transfer into ours. We must see humans through Mary's eyes and love them with Mary's heart.

Yet, humans are so often undeserving of love. They are so egotistical, so cowardly, so inconstant; sometimes deceptive, perverse, rebellious! This being perfectly obvious to us, must we be blind in order to love them? Not at all! Our Mother sees all the faults and all the sins we see in them, and many more. She sees everything and yet, she loves them so much; it is precisely because of this that she loves them so much. She sees, better than we can, the risks they run; she knows better than we know, how horrible eternal damnation is! It is for this reason that she desires, infinitely more than we do, to preserve them from it.

Did Monica's love for her son, Augustine, blind her to his behavior? Did she not find in it a reason to dedicate herself to him even more? Seeing human beings through Mary's eyes means seeing their sins and their vices as she does; but also seeing the love which their Father, their Brother, their Mother have for them. It also means seeing her desire to make loving children of them for the Father, other selves for Jesus, other well-beloved children for herself.

At first glance, the Virgin's apostle will not succeed in seeing the persons to be evangelized in this light. We must constantly make the effort to see them as God, as Christ, as Mary see them. Before any apostolic gesture, we must cultivate the habit of saying to Mary: "My Mother, this is your child (or your children). Help me to see with your eyes and to love with your heart!"

CHAPTER THIRTY-ONE

Awareness of Our Apostolic Responsibility

Sensitivity to our apostolic responsibility must be added to the love for souls so as not to allow our zeal to languish or our love to lose its ardor. To make us aware of this responsibility, it would be well to reread the words of Pope Pius XII, cited above, on the need Christ has for us:

> It should not be thought that Christ, being the Head and occupying such an exalted

position, does not require the help of His body. ... We must maintain, though this seems truly astounding, that Christ has need of the help of His members. He wishes to receive help from His Mystical Body in order to accomplish the work of Redemption.

However, that is not because of any indigence or weakness on His part, but rather that He has assumed this disposition for the greater glory of His spouse without stain. Though, when dying on the Cross, He communicated to His Church the limitless treasure of the Redemption with no collaboration on her part, when it is question of distributing this treasure, He shares the work of the sanctification of souls with His immaculate Spouse...

The Holy Father adds:

Certainly, an awesome mystery upon which we can never meditate enough: the salvation of a great number of souls depends on the prayers and mortifications assumed for this purpose by the members of the Mystical Body of Jesus Christ.[199]

Let us, then, meditate on this mystery which he terms "awesome" and in regard to which he complains we do not meditate upon enough. Permit me, at this point, to quote several pages which I have published elsewhere.

In speaking of the conversion of pagans, Saint Paul quotes the prophet Joel: 'And it shall come to pass that all who call upon the name of the Lord shall be delivered.'[200] And he then remarks: 'But how are they to call upon him in whom they have not believed? And how can they believe in him of whom they have not heard? And how can they hear without someone to preach? And how can people preach unless they are sent?'[201]

Without doubt, 'God desires all to be saved.'[202] He offers every soul sufficient grace to attain eternal life. 'Many will come from East and West and sit at table with

---

199 Encyclical on the Mystical Body of Christ {*Mystici Corporis*, 1943}.

200 Joel 2:32.

201 Rom. 10:13-15.

202 I Tim 2:4.

Abraham, Isaac, and Jacob.'[203] God will not damn anyone because of some fault on the part of an unfaithful apostle. Those who are lost are lost through their own fault. Yet, it is also true that some would have received much more help for attaining heaven if the apostle God called to assist them had been more faithful to the mission. ...

There is still another point of view to be considered in the responsibilities of chosen souls. We, who are lacking in faith and love, are especially struck by the eternal sufferings of hell to which souls are exposed. But what should be even closer to our hearts is the glory of God, the love of our Lord. For a holy soul gives incomparably more glory to God, satisfies much better the desires of his heart, and also contributes immensely more to the salvation of the world than a thousand mediocre souls, though in the state of grace. It depends on those called to the apostolate that not only sinners would be saved, but also that faithful souls achieve holiness.

Whenever a chosen soul has accomplished its mission of coredemption, it has succeeded

---

203 Mt 8:11.

in converting or sanctifying countless multitudes. Who can say how many more blessed there are in heaven, or who love God with an incomparably more perfect love for all eternity because of Saint Francis of Assisi, or Saint Dominic, or Saint Theresa, or many others? Certainly, millions — perhaps billions — since we must consider not only the souls directly affected by the action of these Saints but also the long line of natural or spiritual descendants of those souls, even to the end of time. …

On the Cross, Christ destroyed, in principle, all of the demon's power. 'Now is the time of judgment on this world; now the ruler of this world will be driven out.'[204] 'Take courage, I have conquered the world.'[205] How is it, then, that the cause of Christ among the masses is vanquished? How is it that our mother, the Church, has to weep over the desertion of so many of her children, and that so many of them who call themselves Christians are in fact pagans in their thought and in their conduct? Is it not because, apart from a certain number of apostles (happily

---

204 Jn 12:31; 14:30.
205 Jn 16:33.

on the increase) who devote themselves to the task without reserve, there are many others who carry on their mission without conviction and without zeal? …

Christ and Mary have called me to the apostolate. In God's plan, a certain number of souls are to be saved through me. How many? Perhaps a very large number, though I know nothing of that. Suppose that, as a result of my lack of zeal, a single soul would have to be plunged into the most atrocious despair throughout all eternity, cursing God and the Virgin and me — me, the one who could have saved it! Could I bear such a thought? … Yet, I am no doubt called to save more than a single soul, perhaps even a great number, perhaps thousands. Paul, Francis of Assisi, Ignatius, Francis Xavier, Canisius, Vincent de Paul, Teresa of Avila, and others, have contributed to the holiness and salvation of millions. 'But they are saints!' But they did not begin by being saints. …

Mary has called me to help her in her apostolic mission. If I am faithful to being used or allowing her to direct me, I can be assured of saving and sanctifying all those souls whose salvation or sanctification depends on me. O Mother, may an obsession to save souls for you and through you be mine day and night, so that not one of those you have confided to me be lost through my fault!

CHAPTER THIRTY-TWO

The Total Gift of Self to Others

The apostle, as such, lives only for God and for souls. An apostle is not an end, but a means. The function of apostles is to serve, and they are apostles only if they spend themselves in service. Their ideal is the ideal of the man who, among all the apostles, has been simply called "the apostle." He wrote to the Corinthians: "I want not what is yours, but you. … I will most gladly spend and be utterly spent for your sakes."[206] Or, rather, their ideal is that of the One whom the Father himself sent into the world and from whom all other apostles draw their

---

206 II Cor 12:14-15.

apostolic mission. He Himself said to His apostles: "The Son of Man did not come to be served, but to serve."[207]

True apostles have understood Him. "The priest — and, therefore, the apostle — exists to be consumed," said Father Chevrier. Perhaps inspired by those very words, Blessed Columba Marmion wrote: "Every day at the altar, I partake of Jesus Christ immolated, so that I may have the grace of allowing myself to also be consumed every day by souls."[208]

A sincere apostle of even an unworthy human cause knows that he or she must be ready to suffer for it. We might think of some apostles of Socialism or Communism who have bravely faced persecution and imprisonment to spread their doctrines of death. Should apostles of life be less generous than they? The vocation of the apostolate is a vocation of martyrdom. That is true not only because of the dedication of every instant and of every sacrifice which natural reason requires but also, and above

---

207 Mt 20:28.

208 R. Thibaut, *Dom Columba Marmion: Abbé de Maredsous (1858-1923); un maitre de la vie spirituelle*, Paris 1953, p. 392. [English tr.: *Abbot Columba Marmion, a Master of the Spiritual Life, (1858-1923)*, London 1923]

all, for the supernatural reason that souls to be saved must be *ransomed*.

A certain degree of apostolic devotedness is easy, especially for the young; it satisfies a need for activity and brings with it the joy of exercising influence over others. But we are concerned with **total** devotedness, with the sacrifice of all that one has and all that one is and all that one does: work, time, pleasure, rest, life itself, and even reputation. It is a devotedness that has no other bounds than those of the possible. And the possibilities are expansive, allowing their stretching according to the power of love. Let us think of the devotedness of a Francis Xavier, of a Curé of Ars, and of so many others who, in more obscure circumstances, have immolated themselves during their entire life in the service of others.

The gift is not total unless it is free of any ulterior motive for reward or compensation. We might think ourselves generous because we give with our right hand, but then take the equivalent or even more with our left. Nature is so clever in seeking compensation for the sacrifices it agrees to make, and in justifying these same compensations on equally clever pretexts. Saint Paul, in fact, felt obligated to voice a negative remark with regard to the evangelical workers of his day: "They all seek their own interests, not those of Jesus Christ."[209]

Such compensations are of various kinds:

– seeking material advantages: money, gifts, conveniences of a bourgeois life;[210]

– seeking more or less worldly satisfactions: occasions to show off or to escape the hardships of a rule, or to take pleasant trips, or to participate in festive parties.

There are exigencies of the heart: zeal — this is love. No one loves as much as the apostle of Christ and of His Mother. And it is natural to expect some return of love from those to whom we give ourselves. But there is danger that this return might be desired for self and not for the good of souls.

We have worked for people who have shown no signs of affection or even gratitude. "Is it worth the trouble to spend ourselves for those who do not even say 'thank you'?" So we drop them. Was it for their

---

209 Phil 2:21.
210 On the spirit of poverty of a priest, see E. Neubert, *Marie et notre Sacerdoce*, pp. 123-136. [English tr.: *Mary and the Priestly Ministry*]

"thank you," or for their salvation, that we were working? If Jesus had wished to shed His Blood only for grateful persons, would we be numbered among those saved?

Others truly respond with love to the love of those who are devoted to them. But if your affection for any of them becomes disturbing, obsessive, or troubling — watch out! It is no longer their spiritual good that is being sought but, rather, personal satisfaction. Do not become a satan to the souls for whom you pretended to be the savior.

There exist such things as vain ambitions of the will. The apostle exercises a spiritual paternity over those being evangelized. Paternity brings with it a certain right of dominion. Dominating characters, under the guise of doing good to souls, run the risk of drawing satisfaction from the position of superiority given by their role, and of treating souls as their property. But souls do not belong to us; they belong to God. And God respects the freedom and personality of each human being with infinite delicacy.

It is important to know exactly the different sentiments which we experience in the exercise of the apostolate. For this purpose, it is good to expose them in all simplicity to her, in whose name we devote ourselves to others. "Is it because of you, my Mother, and of Jesus, or of myself, that I feel happy, enthusiastic, unhappy, depressed, or uneasy?"

Look at Jesus: there is never a self-centered satisfaction. This was evident to the point that Saint Paul could make a statement concurred by all: "Christ did not please himself. *Christus non sibi placuit.*"[211]

Look at Mary; there is never any self-seeking. Her happiness was to do the will of the Father: "Behold, I am the handmaid of the Lord. May it be done to me according to your word,"[212] and to share in the redemptive work of her Son.

Look at the souls you are destined to save. Would you wish, for your own satisfaction, to let ten be lost, or perhaps a hundred, or maybe a thousand, or even a single one, for all eternity?

Long live Jesus and Mary; long live souls, whatever the cost to me!

---

211 Rom 15:3.
212 Lk 1:38.

CHAPTER THIRTY-THREE

Humility

For the apostle, the most important form of self-forgetfulness is humility. It was a searching for their own glory that precipitated into the depths of hell a third of the pure spirits that God had created so perfectly. And this is what would have cast our first parents and their descendants into unspeakable and unending misery—except for Mary. And this is also at the heart of the failure of a great number of apostolic enterprises and the loss of numberless souls.

The tendency to seek one's own glory in apostolic work is so subtle and perfidious! An apostle might take satisfaction in success, not because it is the success of Christ and His Mother, but because it is his or her own success. They might desire and expect praise. Do they do it because of Jesus and Mary and souls, or because of themselves? Perhaps they might believe they are rendering to God all the glory of their success. But why, then, are they unhappy when others do not praise them?

One may be humble in the presence of praise, but why, then, this irritation in the presence of criticism? Sometimes, when criticism causes harm to the souls being drawn to Christ, it is legitimate, even necessary, to defend the rights of truth. But then, it should be done with calm. Loss of peace of soul, even in the most sacred causes, is sign of a secret self-seeking.

It may be that an apostle tends to criticize predecessors, or to experience joy at hearing them criticized. Let the apostle be humble and charitable to merit the grace of doing good in circumstances which prevented others from doing it. Do not believe that you bring to the world the definitive formula for liberation!

Others might consent to provide their cooperation in some work. But, behold: those in charge choose not to follow their suggestions or to assign them to the roles they sought. Consequently, they abandon the work! Was it in order to achieve a success for the cause of Christ that they offered their help, or for their own personal ambition?

Some learn that other militants in the same cause have more success and, so, they become envious. They might even be inclined to criticize, or to even place obstacles in their path. Are they envious of the success of the cause of Jesus and Mary? Are they placing obstacles to the cause of Jesus and Mary?

Or, perhaps, they learn that others have failed, or even that some scandal has erupted among them. Those who are envious experience great satisfaction, and not always secretly. Are they happy that the interests of Jesus and Mary have experienced failure, or that Christ has been offended instead of being glorified?

Others may devote themselves entirely to their own kind of apostolate. They ignore the others, even though they may not disdain them. The souls that the others save, the concerns of Jesus and Mary that others succeed in promoting, count as nothing in the eyes of the envious!

Those who are called to exercise authority are exposed to certain temptations: they run the risk of confusing their personal glory with the glory of God whose representatives they are. They tend to listen willingly to the approval of flatterers, at least to those who know how to give praise without seeming to; they remain cold, if not hostile, toward others who simply do their work or do not practice the art of adulation, or merely offer some remarks for the common good. Is it solely concern for the greater glory of God and the Queen of Apostles or for the good of souls that inspires such conduct?

The more you cultivate humility, the more you assure the success of your apostolate. Every time you seek your own glory in your apostolate, you sabotage it!

If you are praised, remember that it is Jesus and Mary who have succeeded through you, and think of the even greater success that They would have had, had you been more faithful to "all your grace." Others may praise you for having made a hundred converts. As for you, think of the nine hundred others you might have converted if, on many occasions, you had not been so careless or so vain.

If you are criticized, remind yourself that unjust accusations are part of the redemptive work of Christ. Instead of concentrating your attention on the exaggerated side of the criticism, look to see whether it might suggest something that needs correction in your method or in your behavior.

Have a heart sufficiently "Catholic" to enable you to rejoice at the good done by others and to offer your help even if no glory comes to you. Is it not enough for you that Jesus and Mary be glorified?

Do not be preoccupied with pleasing and do not fear to displease. To seek your own popularity is to seek failure because it means seeking yourself instead of Jesus and Mary and souls.

In your apostolate, every time you find yourself moody, hurried, upset, jealous, tell yourself that you are in the process of demolishing your work. Examine yourself: what matters are souls, the interests of the most Blessed Virgin, and the glory of Christ — not you!

Contemplate often, at length, and lovingly, Mary's humility in the exercise of her apostolic mission: at Nazareth with Gabriel; with Elizabeth, when singing her *Magnificat*; during Joseph's uncertainty; at the birth in the stable; at the presentation in the temple; at the flight into Egypt; before the teachers admiring her Son; in the obscurity of the hidden life; during the public life; her absence from the enthusiastic crowds; her presence at the foot of the Cross, in the Cenacle, and in the silence of her passing from view in the Assumption.

In all these circumstances we see her as very simple, completely docile to the will of God. It is clear that she thinks of herself as nothing and that all she has is a gratuitous gift from the infinite love of the Most

High; all she has to do is submit herself to God's desires. She is not surprised at the infinite greatness to which he calls her through his angel; it is almost as though she is not even aware of it. Yet, a few days later, she proclaims that all generations will call her blessed. But this is the work of God alone.

Before Paul, she had understood that "God chose those who count for nothing to reduce to nothing those who are something, so that no human being might boast before God."[213] The Omnipotent had cast his eyes upon her because of her lowliness for he always uses his power in favor of those who are nothing, and casts down the powerful from their thrones. That is the ideal attitude of apostolic humility: to know that one is nothing of oneself, yet to be at the disposal of the will of God. It means not to refuse, out of false humility, the responsibilities that God confides, but to accept them with simplicity, counting on the infinite power and goodness of the one who imposes them. It means not to exalt oneself in the sight of success entirely due to the action of God. Christian humility does not engender cowardice, but audacity.[214]

---

213 I Cor 1:28-29.

214 See the remarkable chap. 6 of L. J. Suenens, *Théologie de l'Apostolat de la Légion de Marie*, Paris 1951: "*Humilité et audace apostolique,*" pp. 121-137 [English tr.: *Theology of the Apostolate of the Legion of*

CHAPTER THIRTY-FOUR

Marian Prudence

All apostles know, at least in theory, that zeal must be accompanied by prudence. The young tend to have more zeal than prudence; the older, more prudence than zeal. Both are mistaken because their zeal or their prudence is too much in the natural order. The zeal of the former may be only the need for activity or a burst of energy; the prudence of the latter, a concealed laziness.

Here, we are in the supernatural order and we are concerned with supernatural prudence. In human enterprises, prudence leads us to carefully examine the advantages and the disadvantages, the chances of success and the danger of failure, in order to weigh them all before making a decision. Despite all these suppositions and confrontations, the result is often quite different from what we had foreseen, for "human reason always falls short to some degree." In supernatural works, it is simply a

---

Mary]; E. Neubert, *Marie dans le Dogme*, 3rd ed., pp. 360-362 [English tr.: *Mary in Doctrine*]; E. Neubert, *Marie et notre Sacerdoce*, pp. 112-122 [English tr.: *Mary and the Priestly Ministry*].

matter of discovering the will of God — that settles everything!

The most important decision a human being ever had to make — that on which the eternal happiness or eternal misery of the whole human race depended and, even more, the accomplishment of God's will with regard to the mysteries of the Incarnation and Redemption — was Mary's response to the proposal of Gabriel. The angel announced that she was to be the Mother of the Messiah. The Jews of her time expected a purely human Messiah. Mary had made a vow of virginity, because she knew with certainty this was God's will for her. God does not contradict himself. He could not, therefore, want her to become a mother in the usual human way. What should she do to comply with the will of God?

"How can that be," she asked, "since I am a virgin." The Angel explained to her that the Holy Spirit would make her a mother in a miraculous way. Some authors, to dramatize the story, place a pause at this point: Mary reflected on the advantages and disadvantages of the proposal. This is not at all probable! As soon as she knew God's desire, she did not hesitate for an instant. She simply answered: "Behold, I am the handmaid of the Lord. May it be done to me according to your word." She had no need to weigh the advantages and disadvantages; God would take care of this.

Supernatural prudence, then, consists in discovering the will of God and, once that will is known, following it in the face of, or in spite of, everything. Thus, far from dispensing us from any effort, it presses us into action, sustains our courage, and accomplishes marvels. The will of God may have reference to either the choice of action or the means of carrying it out.

In the first case, we should place ourselves in a holy indifference to everything. The fact that some work is attractive is not necessarily a sign of God's will. Such attraction might well come from a more or less egoistical, natural tendency which would find its satisfaction in that particular work. Conversely, a fear of or aversion to some work would not be proof that it should be set aside. It could be that nature recoils faced with whatever sacrifices the work might demand. We must not consider whether an enterprise pleases or displeases us, but whether it pleases God.

Such indifference is easier for apostles who have consecrated themselves completely to Mary and who are resolved to live their consecration. If I have truly given her all and, therefore, my will along with all the rest, I can no longer have any desire other than hers; and her will always coincides with the will of God. So, "whatever she wishes, because she wishes it, no matter the cost to me!"

What, then, is the will of God in a given situation? What does Mary ask of me? What will do the greatest good to this or that person? Would it be this approach, or that one? Should I consult this person or another? Mother of Good Counsel, enlighten me! It concerns your Son's interests — the interests of your children. Come, Spirit of wisdom and of understanding; come Spirit of counsel and of knowledge. Is there some indication of God's will? The more an enterprise is fraught with consequences, the more there is need to reflect, to pray, to consult and, generally, to wait for some indication of God's will.

Usually, the choice of an apostolic work has already been indicated by a superior, by some duty of state, or by circumstances. But it is in its execution that recourse to Mary becomes necessary. This is because it is a matter of having each action produce the maximum of supernatural returns. The same gesture, the same advice, may accomplish a hundred times greater good for a person, depending on the dispositions of the one from whom they originate. Here again, there is need to reflect, to pray, to profit from the experience of others, and, above all, to be guided by the Holy Spirit and the Mother of Good Counsel.

When, profiting from experience, a person has acquired a certain ability to manage personnel, there is always danger that the supernatural returns are inverse to natural ability. A person thinks he or she knows how to approach the matter and runs the risk of doing only a human thing. From the point of view of profound influence on souls, it is always possible to further progress; therefore, before every action, it is advisable to collaborate with Mary on how to best accomplish the greatest good for souls.[215]

---

215 On consulting Mary in the apostolate, I might refer to my own work on *La Vie d'union à Marie*, pp. 81-93, 224-226 [English tr.: *Life of Union with Mary*, Milwaukee 1959].

CHAPTER THIRTY-FIVE

Apostolic Confidence

The question of confidence in apostolic work is of capital importance. Sanctifying and saving souls is a supernatural work; it is, therefore, a work of grace. Grace is received through prayer, but in proportion to the confidence of the petitioner.

"Let it be done for you according to your faith," Jesus said to those who asked Him for cures.[216]

He promised the most extraordinary miracles to those of true faith: "Amen, I say to you, if you have faith the size of a mustard seed, you will say to this mountain, 'Move from here to there, and it will move.'"[217]

Now, to convert some souls, there are mountains of sins, bad habits, and all kinds of obstacles to overcome. It is, therefore, necessary for the apostle to attain the greatest possible confidence — a confidence in miracles! The sanctification and salvation of many souls come at this price. If I have

---

216 Mt 9:29.
217 Mt 17:19.

great enough confidence, such as a Francis Xavier, a Curé of Ars — rather than saving a hundred souls, I might perhaps save ten thousand or even a hundred thousand or more.

God gives us all his graces through Mary — apostolic workers know that. They instinctively turn to her to obtain God's blessing on their work. Is there a single supernatural work, especially in our day, which is not placed under the patronage of Our Lady?

Moreover, confidence in Mary's help is easy. First of all, the voice of the whole Church teaches us of the Virgin's liberality toward those who invoke her help. Has not the *Memorare* elevated this belief, so to speak, to an article of faith? Then, who does not understand that Mary, as Mother of God, is powerful enough to obtain all graces from her Son; and, as Mother of humans, that she is good enough to procure them? With regard to apostolic workers, she must be especially liberal because there is question here, not of personal favors, but of the sanctification and salvation of souls.

Yet, in working with souls, it is not enough to have an ordinary confidence, or even fairly great, or even very great, confidence. There is need for absolute confidence, unlimited confidence, confidence worthy of miracles in order to succeed, in consideration of all the souls who must be sanctified or saved through us, according to God's designs. Not a single one must be lost insofar as it depends on us.

Indeed, our status as apostles of Mary allows us such a confidence. Ordinarily, when invoking Mary, we ask her to help *us* in *our* work, in *our* natural or supernatural interests. But, in an apostolate undertaken in the name of Mary, it is the reverse: it is a question of us helping *her*, in *her* work, in *her* interests.

In fact, we have already seen above that the Virgin has received the mission of participating in the apostolate of her Son in view of the conquest of souls, and that she is like the generalissimo in charge of this holy war, at all times and in all places. We are only her soldiers or her officers, fighting under her and for her in a sphere limited to time and place. The interests at stake, therefore, are all hers, and not ours. Those involved are her children, not ours, to be preserved from hell and led to Heaven.

Her love for the heavenly Father who sent his Son into the world to save humans; her love for Jesus who sacrificed His life to preserve us from eternal death; her love for these souls to whom she became Mother at Nazareth and on Calvary, at the price of so much anguish, at the price of her First-born — all these loves have filled her heart with an infinite desire, so to speak, to save souls. But to do so, she needs our cooperation. We have given ourselves to her as guarantee of our cooperation. If, in fact, we comply with her, wouldn't she wish to save these souls? We would have to be out of our mind or to understand nothing of the mystery of our salvation to even raise such a question!

Would it, then, not be enough for us to ask her to save all the souls who, in the designs of God, are destined to be saved thanks to us, so that, by the very fact, all would be saved?

Normally, that would be enough, although a soul might obstinately oppose the solicitations of grace, as was the case with Judas. Yes, that would be enough, but on condition that, at the same time, we give her as much help as she expects from us. And that help includes several things:

–   First, an habitual awareness that we act in her name and not in ours; that it is a matter of her interests and not ours; that what we seek, or should seek, is her affair and not ours. We have to devote ourselves to repeating this truth in whatever we do — before, during, after — until we have acquired, in practice, the first principle which guides all our ways of thinking, feeling, judging, willing, and doing. Always and everywhere: "This is her affair and not mine."

- It also includes a habit of consulting on the action to be taken and on the manner of carrying it out according to the indications given above. Mary will give infallible success to what we do if only we act according to her ideas and not our own.

- It further includes the use of the apostolic means which will be considered in the following chapters: apostolic prayer, an edifying life, sacrifices, direct action, preaching about Mary.

It should be clear that this reversal of points of view — it being no longer for our interests that we ask Mary's help, but for Mary's interests for which she expects our help — should give us a solid sense of confidence. For Mary's intentions are always conformed to God's intentions. And, for those intentions to be actualized, it is necessary and sufficient to provide her with the cooperation she expects from us. The Virgin's apostles, habitually seeing their activity in this light, find themselves animated, in fact, with a confidence in Mary that stops at nothing. The results correspond to their confidence.

We have seen the Legion of Mary proclaiming that "under the inspiration of the love and faith of Mary, it undertakes any action whatsoever, without ever claiming impossibility." {Blessed} Father Chaminade proclaimed the same thing: "*Maria duce* is our battle cry. ... We always go to combat under the banner of the august Mother of God. ... We must have confidence in order to convert the whole world under Mary's protection."

**THE WEAPONS OF THE
MARIAN APOSTOLATE**

CHAPTER THIRTY-SIX

The Witness of Life

An edifying life is a sermon preached in a language universally understood. Without it, any other sermon, eloquent as it may be, runs the risk of remaining sterile. Sometimes it even does evil since, as has been said, "nothing is more damaging than good counsel, followed by bad example." What one *is*, is much more persuasive than what one says. Our Lord practiced at the same time as He taught; that is why His doctrine was so well received, and that of the Pharisees so poorly received.

All the saints followed the example of our Lord and it is their behavior, in great part, which explains their influence. For some among them, scarcely had they spoken a word, when their listeners were won over; yet, they spoke simply and often fell short of the rule of human eloquence. It was much more by their life than by their words that the Christians of the first three centuries converted the pagan world. With regard to Saint Francis Xavier, the comment has been made by Bellesort that, much more than his miracles, it was the spectacle of his mortified life and especially of his unstinted dedication that converted the throngs.

What, in fact, are the factors of this apostolate of life? This depends in great measure on the personality of each apostle. It seems that we might name three in particular: self-possession in God, sincerity, and charity.

Self-possession: This reveals itself in a modesty and recollection that are without rancor or affectation, and that exhibit comfortable yet dignified manners — and all this, whether with strangers or friends, with superiors or inferiors, in health or in sickness. At the origin of this perfect self-possession, we find an interior principle of strength and rectitude; this interior principle has to be God.

Sincerity: This is a virtue practiced by Jesus as even admitted by His adversaries. The disciples of the Pharisees and of the Herodians who were sent to set a trap for Him, began by saying: "Teacher, we know that you are a truthful man and that you teach the way of God in accordance with the truth ... for you do not regard a person's status."[218] He exacted the same sincerity of His disciples: "Let your 'yes' mean 'yes,' and your 'no' mean 'no.'"[219]

The sincere man expresses his thoughts with simplicity. His "yes" or "no" inspires more confidence than the protestations of those who, on every occasion, "swear" that something is "such or such." Saint James says, "Let your 'yes' mean 'yes,' and your 'no' mean 'no.'"[220] If you do not always say what you think, always think what you say. Do not praise people in their presence and criticize them as soon as their back is turned. Your principles may not please everyone, but even those who criticize them will be convinced that you believe what you

---

218 Mt 22:15-16.
219 Mt 5:37.
220 James 5:12; See also Paul, II Cor 1:17-20.

say and practice what you preach — and they will respect you.

Like your words, so should your conduct be sincere. Others can then depend on you. You carry out the task assigned to you, and you do it well.

Charity: The apostle is kindly toward all, not out of worldly or business considerations, but out of concern for the neighbor. You should love to give pleasure and to render service, even at some inconvenience to yourself, and not only to friends but to strangers, and even to those who may have harmed you. You should respect the reputation of those who are absent and pardon everyone from the depths of your heart. Be fair-minded in the judgments you bring to bear on your adversaries, recognizing the good in them; not taking advantage of their misfortunes, but reaching out to help them in their need. In short, forget yourself and become all things to all.

These qualities of self-possession, of sincerity, and of charity, work in favor of the disciples of Christ even when they are not preaching. A life of union with Mary produces these qualities quite naturally. It adds to them the indefinable nuances of kindness, simplicity, surety, and uprightness which flow from an ongoing relationship with the most perfect of mothers.

CHAPTER THIRTY-SEVEN

Apostolic Prayer

Should we ask people involved in the apostolate what the first means for success is, almost all would certainly answer "prayer." Are all convinced of this? How is it that so many do not find time for prayer, or fulfill their obligatory prayers like forced labor, reciting the formulas almost without honestly trying to enter into contact with God for half-an-hour?

It is not difficult to understand the exceptional importance of prayer in the apostolate: converting and sanctifying others is a supernatural work. The supernatural is accomplished through grace; and grace is obtained through prayer.

Our Lord spent thirty years of His life, hidden in work and prayer. And, during the two or three years of His public ministry, He always remained united to His Father in intimate prayer, often passing the nights in prayer. The Queen of Apostles did not preach. She did not perform miracles, but she prayed throughout her entire life. Like the Virgin, Saint Joseph — named "cooperator in our salvation"[221] in the liturgy — offered his prayers and his sufferings for the ransom of the world. The apostles instituted the diaconate to free themselves from every non-apostolic activity, saying: "We shall devote ourselves to prayer and to the ministry of the word."[222]

Even as a very young girl, Saint Therese of the Child Jesus was aflame with a great desire to save souls. At first, she dreamed of entering an active religious order. Then, understanding supernatural values more deeply, she chose to become a Carmelite. It was as a Carmelite that Pope Pius XII named her as principal patroness of missionaries, on a par with Saint Francis Xavier.

It is also to be noted that it was the two great Popes of Catholic Action who most forcefully promoted the apostolate of prayer. Pius XI proclaimed: "Prayer

---

221 *Te Sator rerum ... dedit ministrum esse salutis* (office of the Solemnity of Saint Joseph, hymn at Laudes: {The shaper of the world chose you to be minister of salvation}). The replacement of this office by that of Saint Joseph the Worker, does not disavow the doctrine of the earlier feast.

222 Acts 6:4.

is really the most effective, the most powerful and, at the same time, the easiest of apostolates. It is the means of means taught by our Lord for obtaining everything." Pius XII attributed the meager progress in converting pagans, to the lack of apostolic prayer on the part of the faithful. In his encyclical on the Mystical Body of Christ, he wrote: "If many pagans, alas, still wander far from Catholic truth and refuse to submit to the divine Spirit, the reason is that not only they, but Christians as well, do not address more fervent prayers to God to this effect."

The mere recitation of prayer formulas is not a sacrament. It does not produce its effect *ex opera operato*, as theologians put it, i.e., automatically by the very fact that the prayers are said. Our Lord condemned the prayers of pagans who constantly repeated the formulas thinking, that by a mere repetition of words, they would be heard.[223] He censured the lengthy prayers of the Pharisees in the synagogues and on street corners.[224] Are there not many Christians who expect special favors from the recitation of a certain number of rosaries, or of some other formula, without really making an effort to think of God or the Virgin?

---

223 See Mt 6:7.
224 See Mt 6:5.

To be effective, prayer demands certain interior dispositions. The two essentials are humility and confidence.

Humility in prayer is the sentiment of our helplessness in producing any supernatural effect by ourselves alone. In the work of the apostolate, we cannot do any real good for souls with whatever natural qualities we might possess, for we cannot do anything supernatural with only natural means. Therefore, aren't the people who engage in apostolic works somewhat inclined to be lacking in humility? They are aware of the successes which their knowledge, their eloquence, and their ingenuity produce. Yet, if they lack humility, such successes must really be due to the prayers and sacrifices of others.

Let us suppose these apostles were the occasion for the conversion of ten thousand sinners. On the Day of Judgment, God will say to those eloquent preachers: "You have had your reward on earth. I give the eternal reward to the humble, the lowly, the sick, upon whom you never looked, but whose supplications and sacrifices brought these ten thousand souls to me." The more one seems to have success, the more important it is to dedicate oneself to the practice of the apostolic prayer which we spoke of in the previous chapter and, in particular, to often contemplate with love, the humility of Mary in the exercise of her apostolate.

Confidence must be added to humility. For the apostle, everything consists in a profound conviction of personal powerlessness without God, and all-powerfulness with God.

It is a matter of applying the theme of our absolute confidence in Mary to the particular situation in which we find ourselves, as explained above.[225] The souls which obedience or circumstance (i.e., Divine Providence), have put in our path in the interest of their spiritual well-being, are all children of the Virgin: very poor children, perhaps careless of their own eternal future, egotistical, impure, deceitful, having a taste for only the things of the world. They are, nonetheless, her children over whom she has shed tears, for whom she sacrificed her Son — children whom she wishes to save and can save, through us.

God wills the salvation of all and as long as humans are alive, the grace of salvation is offered to them. We have to look at them with the eyes of Mary so as to love them with Mary's heart. We have to consult Mary as to what we should do for them and, then, faithfully carry out whatever she suggests to

---

225 Part Two, Chapter Twelve.

us: prayers, sacrifices, approaches. How and when will their conversion take place? That is not our affair! Ours is to beg Mary to realize her maternal intentions for these souls, and to add to our prayers the cooperation of our sufferings and our direct action, and to do this with a firm conviction that Mary's intentions will be realized.

They will certainly be realized unless these souls obstinately refuse. In that case, they will be realized for other souls who Mary judges more worthy of being helped and who, no doubt, will only be known to us in Heaven. For we well know that Mary's intentions are more weighty than ours and, before all else, we wish that our cooperation may serve her according to *her* views. Therefore, provided that the assistance we bring to Mary's work conforms to her desires, we always find success. We go from one victory to another, even though these victories will not be known to us until we are near to our Mother in the realm of eternal triumph.

We must add perseverance to humility and confidence. Our Lord insisted on this in the parables about the man who went to his friend at night to ask for bread,[226] and the widow who importuned the

---

226 See Lk 11:5-8.

unjust judge.[227] At closer consideration, it is clear that perseverance is only a special case and a kind of test of confidence. It may be a case of giving up on praying to Mary, or caring little for the favor asked, or scarcely believing in Mary's goodness or power. We have to merit, by our confidence, the favor we desire. Perseverance increases the merit accorded to prayer. Oftentimes, when God wishes to grant a special gift, he will delay granting it so as to oblige us to pray for a longer period of time and to make more meritorious acts of faith.

If God had granted Monica's prayer for her son sooner, Augustine would have had himself baptized and would have contracted a lawful marriage in keeping with his mother's desires (like so many other Christians of his time). God wanted to grant her infinitely more: that her son become a great saint and one of the most brilliant luminaries of Catholic doctrine until the end of time, and that she, herself, become a saint.

As to temporal favors, God may judge it more beneficial not to grant them; therefore, we might reasonably stop praying for them. But when it is question of the salvation of a soul, the case is different: we know from Scripture that "God does

---

227 See Lk 18:1-8.

not wish that any should perish but that all should come to repentance."[228] We may, then, continue to pray for others until the moment they appear before God.[229]

As for "apostolic" prayers, every prayer can have this quality. It suffices to make it in view of an apostolic end and especially in an apostolic spirit: for the full realization of Mary's intentions for a certain person or work; with an awareness of our complete personal helplessness and our complete power through Mary's help. Morning prayers or evening prayers, prayers of the rule among religious or the breviary among priests — all can be used for apostolic purposes. It is generally not good to burden ourselves with an abundance of supererogatory prayers, especially if we have many occupations imposed by our duties of state. However, such prayers have their usefulness by the fact that they require a special effort and draw more attention to the favor being solicited. But we should also give apostolic intentions to our ordinary prayers.

---

[228] 2 Pt 3:9.

[229] See, for example, St. Therese of the Child Jesus who apparently obtained the repentance of an assassin at the moment when he was about to mount the scaffold, as well as that of the ex-priest, Hyacinthe Loison, on his deathbed.

Among prayers that are particularly efficacious in our work for souls there is, first of all, holy Mass. It renews the Sacrifice of the Cross offered by Christ for sinners, with the special character that the Mass is the particular application of the graces of conversion and sanctification merited on Calvary for all people in general. Assistance at the Holy Sacrifice and, with even more reason, its oblation in view of a certain apostolic work, is certainly of great efficacy. Each day, we may also offer all the Masses that are being celebrated throughout the whole world, for the success of our apostolic labors of that day. It is also good during Mass to offer to our heavenly Father, through Mary's hands, the other Masses being celebrated at that same moment. At Holy Communion, we can recommend in a special way our various apostolic plans for that day to our Lord through Mary.

After the Mass, the specifically apostolic prayer is the rosary. We know that this prayer has been recommended for apostolic intentions by the Sovereign Pontiffs since Leo XIII, and by Mary herself at Lourdes and at Fatima. We also have the prayer "O Mary, conceived without sin, pray for us who have recourse to thee," with the wearing of the Miraculous Medal whose very name connotes a particular efficacy for the conversion of sinners.

A glance toward Mary, a word: "My Mother," or "Mary, this is your business! This is about your child!" — can be very efficacious, apostolic invocations. Such short practices have the advantage of being inserted into our actual occupation at any moment, and of keeping us aware that we are working in her name, not ours.

To these personal prayers, we should try to enjoin the prayers of the greater number of pious souls, those of religious, especially of contemplatives, as well as those of children, of the elderly, and of the sick. The more we lean on these auxiliaries and the more we develop dispositions of humility and apostolic confidence within ourselves, the more we help Mary in her mission of snatching souls from Satan, to lead them to Jesus, their Brother, and to the heavenly Father.

CHAPTER THIRTY-EIGHT

Redemptive Suffering

Whoever believes in God easily believes that prayer fosters success in apostolic works; but the attitude changes when it is a question of suffering when working for others. All Christians admit that Christ saved us through the Cross. They also acknowledge that souls of a very special kind enclose themselves in cloisters to pray and suffer. However, what numerous Christians desiring to work for others do not understand is that they are not only called to work and pray, but also to suffer. We know that activity enlivens, and suffering debilitates and paralyzes. Nonetheless, it is Catholic doctrine that action, and even prayer, must be complemented with suffering. That is because, as participants in the apostolic mission of Christ, we must also participate in the suffering whereby He redeemed the world. All true apostles have understood this.

In his letter to the Colossians, after having congratulated the new converts on their faith in Jesus Christ and on their charity toward all the believers, Saint Paul wrote a text which must have been quite a shock to more than one of his readers or, at least, a cause of some astonishment! He said:

> Now I rejoice in my sufferings for your sake, and in my flesh I am filling up what is lacking in the afflictions of Christ on behalf of his body, which is the church.[230]

What is lacking in the afflictions of Christ? Were they not sufficient for the redemption of millions of worlds? Of course! But Paul remarked that what was lacking in these sufferings of the Man-God was a lack of suffering in his (Paul's) own flesh. "Paul, apostle of Christ by the will of God," needed, because an apostle of Christ, to add his sufferings to those of the Master in order to apply the grace of Christ to His Mystical Body. In his encyclical on the Mystical Body of Christ, Pope Pius XII commented on this word of Paul:

> Our Lord, through his cruel torments and horrible death, merited for his Church a treasury of absolutely infinite graces. Yet, by the design of Divine Providence, these graces are communicated to us only by degrees. Their abundance more or less greatly depends on our good actions which spontaneously obtain for humans the shower of heavenly

---

230 Col 1:24.

favors from God. Now, this rain of heavenly graces will surely be most abundant if, not content with offering God ardent prayers (especially in participating fervently, even daily, at the Eucharistic sacrifice) and not content with striving, by works of Christian charity, to lessen the misfortunes of so many needy people, we would prefer imperishable ones to all the passing goods of this earth. We should master our mortal body by voluntary penance, depriving it of forbidden pleasures and even treating it with severity and austerity. We should also humbly accept the burdens and sufferings of this present life as coming from the hand of God. Thus, according to the apostle, we would complete in our flesh what is lacking in the sufferings of Christ for his body which is the Church.[231]

Though suffering for the sake of suffering is stupidity or pride, suffering for the sake of love and redemption is a work of divine value.

The cross to be borne in following the Master is not the same for all apostles. Our Lord shapes it according to the strength and condition of each one. The cross takes many forms. There is, first of all,

---

231 AAS vol. 35, p. 245.

the constant, exhausting, often monotonous labor of the daily tasks, therefore, at the cost of becoming all to all, belonging to everyone except oneself. Ardent souls must sometimes be reminded that they do not have the right to expend their strength prematurely, through excessive zeal. They not only owe themselves to the souls in their presence at a given moment, but also to those whom God wishes to send them in the future. Their martyrdom is to be one of slow fire and not by the stroke of a sword. But there are others, more numerous, who must be urged not to fear disturbing their complacent self-esteem. They have to understand that part of the program of an apostle is to "overcome self" and "allow oneself to be devoured."

There are also all kinds of obstacles which harm or hamper the work undertaken, such as sickness, lack of resources, mishaps. There is the lukewarmness of some people, the criticisms of opponents, the defections of collaborators. There are hidden rivalries, overt or hypocritical oppositions, and the awkwardness and failings of the apostles themselves which compromise their work. There are the misunderstandings, sometimes the jealousies of those who should be giving encouragement, or the disapproval of those in charge.

All this is bearable if there is victory in the end. But what if the beautiful dreams of the apostolate, the constant and often heroic efforts, and the countless sacrifices lead to what is an immense failure in the eyes of others?

Christ himself had known all these trials. They constituted the sacrifice by which He redeemed us. They also constitute the cross by which His disciples are to ransom souls. And to these accepted sufferings, they add others, directly chosen. What supernatural apostle has not understood that certain graces of conversion are not obtained by prayer alone, but by prayer and fasting;[232] i.e., by voluntary mortification? Let us read, for example, of the extreme fasting which merited the Curé of Ars the transformation of a village into a fervent parish (where, previously, all the commands of God and of the Church were openly violated), similar to the first community of Jerusalem.[233]

It is important to constantly remind ourselves of the meaning of apostolic suffering. In itself, the cross is only a gibbet, suited for provoking rebellion, blasphemy, despair. Only the Cross bearing Jesus is redemptive. Our crosses are fruitful only to the

---

232 See Mt 17:20.
233 F. Trochu, *Le Curé d'Ars,* pp. 17-23. [English tr.: *The Curé of Ars*]

extent that we are united to Jesus crucified, united less by the similarity in suffering than by the identity of dispositions. The apostle must often contemplate Christ on the Cross in order to be one with Him.

To the contemplation of Christ crucified, the apostle will love to enjoin the contemplation of the Mother of Sorrows. Mary did not have to suffer to expiate personal sins as we must. Like her Son, she suffered only to glorify the Father and to save souls. The view of her suffering will encourage the apostle to be a resolute victim for souls. Such contemplation will be especially dear to someone who is consecrated to the Virgin and who has understood that every apostolate is a participation in the apostolate of Mary, Queen of Apostles because Queen of Martyrs.

Once we have set ourselves to meditating on the mystery of apostolic responsibility, we are struck by this truth: there are souls who will go to Heaven or to hell, depending on my generosity or my indifference. Once the thought of these souls has become like an obsession, we feel ready to cheerfully accept all the trials of the apostolate. "Would you not find the courage, Consummata (Marie-Antoinette de Geuser) asks a friend, "to think that a certain prayer, or sacrifice, or effort might decide the salvation of a person presently suspended between God and the demon?"[234]

An apostle who has truly understood the fruitfulness of the cross would not be content to accept it with resignation, but would rather rejoice in tribulations and thank God for such choice graces. Saint Therese of the Child Jesus merely expressed what all the great apostles experienced when she wrote: "Jesus has helped me understand that He would give me souls through the cross. So, the more I meet the cross, the more my attraction for suffering increases."

CHAPTER THIRTY-NINE

The Direct Apostolate

With regard to a "direct apostolate" — whether by oral or written word, by teaching or by

---

[234]   R. Plus & Marie-Antoinette de Geuser, *"Consummata": Vie et notes spirituelles de Marie-Antoinette de Geuser*, Toulouse 1946, p. 87. [English tr.: *Consummata; Marie-Antoinette de Geuser, Her Life and Letters*, London 1931]

works — there are two opposed ideas, both of them faulty. For many, and perhaps the majority, a direct apostolate is the best means for doing good to others. In theory, they admit the primacy of prayer and suffering, but they act as if nine-tenths of the success depends on an activity that can be seen and heard. That is what Cardinal Mermillod called "the heresy of works."

We also find, among so-called "pious" souls (but never among the saints), the opposite error, a sort of quietistic heresy which minimizes the importance of exterior action. They regularly and routinely acquit themselves of their small functions and think it sufficient to faithfully perform their exercises of piety; grace will do the rest. And if it does not do the rest, they will blame the sterility of the soil on which the divine seed has fallen. Could it be that they did not spade it well, fertilize it, and work to prepare it to receive the seed?

Some Christians are inclined to demote nature, thinking they thus exalt divine grace all the more. In reality, they deprive God of half of his domain as if, like the Manicheans, they think nature proceeds from some principle other than God. Is God not the author of nature as much as he is of grace? Apart from those Christians for whom direct action is impossible, God wishes the concourse of our natural and supernatural activity in our apostolate, just as he similarly wishes both matter and form in the confection of the Sacraments.

Since faith comes "from hearing,"[235] he wishes us to use every means to hear it well. In keeping with the expression of Saint Ignatius, we must use all the natural means as though everything depended on us alone, and all the supernatural means as though everything depended on God alone. To behave otherwise and still expect success is to tempt God; it is to ask miracles of him to make up for our inactivity.

That is why the great apostles, while much more supernatural than other people — depending above all on prayer and suffering — have also been persons of great initiative more than others. Let us look particularly at the founders of apostolic orders. They were faced with new needs, and they invented new means of success. And those who seem to have exercised the greatest influence in the Church are precisely those who have best understood the needs of their times and have invented the most suitable means for responding to them. Saint Ignatius took the most innovative initiatives. They astounded and

---

235 Rom 8:17.

even shocked many of his contemporaries, some of whom held high places in the Church hierarchy.

Those who burn with zeal to extend the kingdom of Christ under the auspices of Mary, will strive, therefore, to become well aware of the particular needs of those who come within their range of activity, and of the best means for responding to them. By exchanging ideas with other apostles, by studying the methods used elsewhere (even in enemy camps), together with their causes of success or failure, they can manage to perfect their own methodology. In addition, they will realize that there is no "unchangeable" method, because human conditions are in continuous flux. It goes without saying that they will consult, more than with humans, the One in whose name they struggle, following the directives given above.

Situations will arise, where it appears "there is nothing more to be done." Let us then heed the words of Cardinal Amette when he was given responsibility for the immense diocese of Paris: "When there is nothing more to be done, there is still one thing to do: become a saint." Saints succeed where others fail. For the predecessors of the Curé of Ars, there was nothing more to be done. But John Vianney was a saint who transformed his parish!

Francis de Sales, as a young priest, burned to convert the 80,000 Protestants of Chablais. Every morning, at the cost of unbelievable difficulties, risking his life at times, he set out to preach in their midst. It was useless; the heretics would not even come to his instructions. Some well-intentioned folks and clergymen told him that he was wasting his time and his efforts, as "there is nothing to be done in Chablais, and nothing will ever be done in Chablais." After eight months, he had succeeded in converting only one Protestant. But, three years later, almost all the lost sheep had returned to the bosom of the Catholic Church!

No matter how zealous and competent apostles may be, their direct action is necessarily very limited. Twenty centuries after the death of Christ, the number of Catholics is scarcely twenty percent of the world's population; and of this twenty percent, what proportion really lives out their Christianity? The word of Jesus remains true: "The harvest is great, but the laborers are few."[236]

We must not only multiply Christians; we must, above all, multiply apostles!

We must impress upon the faithful who come under our influence that every Christian has an apostolic

---

[236] Mt 9:37.

mission (as was said above) as imitator of Christ, as observer of the great commandment of charity. Our first obligation is to be concerned with the souls of our neighbors as with our own, as children of Mary, Queen of Apostles, who needs our help.

It is especially on educators that the duty rests for communicating an apostolic sense to the youth confided to them. They will have done only half of their task if they have simply taught their students to observe the Commandments of God and of the Church, and to frequent the Sacraments. When explaining to his disciples their apostolic mission as a consequence of their consecration to the Queen of Apostles, {Blessed} Father Chaminade insisted on the obligation of not only making Christians of their students, but of "multiplying Christians" through them. In fact, it is clear that they succeeded in making of formerly undisciplined pupils "apostles of their parents."[237]

The members of pious associations, especially those whose associations are placed more specifically under the patronage of Mary, should be led to understand that Mary not only awaits prayers and canticles from them, but their cooperation in the

---

237 J. Simler, *Guillaume Joseph Chaminade*, Paris 1901), pp. 80 ff. [English tr.: *William Joseph Chaminade: Founder of the Marianists*, Dayton OH 1986]

apostolic mission which God confided to her. They are to aid her in bringing back to God all of his children, so many of whom know neither their heavenly Father nor their heavenly Mother.

We should especially encourage entrance into the Marian associations that are more consciously apostolic: militant Marian Sodalities, the Children of Mary, and the Legion of Mary.

And, finally, Christians who have received a special apostolic vocation from God (priests, religious men and women, members of secular institutes of perfection) must understand the help that the Queen of Apostles awaits from them, and the help she wishes to give to them. It is especially for them that this book has been written.

CHAPTER FORTY

Revealing Mary:
Making Her Better Known

The final means of apostolate, the great means, is not only to preach *in the name* of Mary, but to preach *the name* of Mary, i.e., to reveal Mary to those whom we wish to convert or sanctify. Reveal? Yes! One only needs to conduct a small survey to note with astonishment the ignorance or false ideas about Mary that are prevalent among a high percentage of the faithful, even among those who belong to a Marian association. As to those who have studied her grandeurs, there is always need to learn more of the marvels about her for whom "he who is mighty has done great things"; he alone can know them all.

Revealing Mary is, in fact, the great means of the apostolate. Our Christian life consists in knowing and reproducing the life of Jesus. But Mary is the direct road which leads to the knowledge and imitation of her Son. Let us recall the words of Saint Pius X: "Who does not hold as established truth that there can be no path more secure or more rapid than Mary for uniting human beings to Jesus

Christ, and for obtaining, by means of Jesus Christ, that perfect adoption of sons and daughters which makes us holy and without stain in the presence of God?"

We have explained elsewhere the supernatural and natural reasons for this marvelously effective devotion to Mary.

The supernatural reasons:

– Mary, Dispensatrix of all graces; the love of Jesus for Mary and His desire to communicate His filial love for His Mother to all His brothers and sisters; the love of Jesus for us, wishing to save us by drawing us to His Mother.

The natural reasons:

– Devotion to Mary encourages efforts through love, intensification of desire, confidence, and imitation.[238]

These reasons are good for all times. But are they not especially good for the new age into which we have now entered? Our times, from the beginning of the 19th century, but more clearly from the

---

[238] See E. Neubert, *La Dévotion à Marie*, Centre de Documentation scolaire, 23, rue du Dragon, Paris, pp. 38ff. [English tr: *Devotion to Mary*, New Bedford MA 2010]

beginning of the 20th, are "the time, the epoch, of the Virgin, Our Lady," as stated by Pope Pius XII. It is, therefore, a providential indication of the will of God that Mary be honored and invoked with more confidence and more love than ever before.

In following the inspirations of Providence, we are assured of a plenitude of graces, just as ignoring God's will places obstacles to his liberality. What priest in this century can be deluded into thinking he can attract the blessings of God upon his pastoral work if he fails to invite souls to receive our Lord in Holy Communion more frequently than was customary in the Middle Ages? What priest of our century can count on solid and enduring results in his work with souls if he neglects to lead them to Mary?

Obviously, the devotion to Mary that we seek to inculcate must be authentic. There should be nothing of the faddish, or the childish, or sham, or merely external and sentimental, or anything solely based on legend. Nor must there be any devotion which places Mary in the position of Jesus; nor dispenses us from effort; nor reassures sinners, while allowing them to continue offending God since, at the end, Mary would intervene to obtain pardon for her "devotees."

It must be a serious, enlightened, doctrinal, Christocentric devotion which proceeds from Jesus and leads to Jesus; which is born of love, confidence, generosity; which stimulates effort, teaches us to be pure, patient, and courageous to please others, and to devote ourselves to their well-being; which struggles and sacrifices itself, if need be, for the cause of Christ and of the Church.

Such devotion must, of course, adapt to the age, sex, and character of each. It must exclude anything that might later cause ridicule or shame.

How might we communicate devotion to Mary?

In order to communicate anything, there must be something to communicate. Whoever has a solid devotion to Mary will find occasions for sharing it. And if occasions are not found, they will be created!

The first and most convincing means is example. We must neither hide our faith in Christ nor our confidence in Mary. It is not that we should manifest it with ostentation. There are many ways of letting those around us see our dispositions relative to the Mother of God. The more we are convinced, all the more convincing will we be.

We preach, of course, not only by example, but also by word of mouth. Priests, catechists, and educators have very natural opportunities for making Mary known, loved, and served. Books especially written for them can provide useful instructions on this Marian apostolate.[239] In addition to special occasions, we can devise ways of communicating our dispositions of confidence and love with regard to Mary to those we seek to convert or to sanctify. Biographies of converts easily provide opportunities.

We must strive to place Mary at the forefront of each of our apostolic enterprises. In order to convert his pagan parish of Ars, Saint John Vianney began by reviving an association in honor of Mary. We mentioned earlier that, at the beginning of his pontificate, Saint Pius X published an encyclical on devotion to Mary, motivated by his conviction that there was no surer means of leading people to Jesus than His Mother. Apostolic persons have instinctively been led to give the name of Our Lady to their works: Our Lady of the Road, Our Lady of the Scouts; Blessed Virgin Mary, sweet Mother of Stout Hearts.

---

239 The work of Pierre Ranwez, S.J., *Présence de Marie* {tr. *Presence of Mary*}, Lumen Vitae, 27 rue de Spa, Brussels, contains a very rich and precious mine on books and methods of initiating others to the knowledge of Mary and devotion to her.

It often happens that the first attempts to introduce a soul to devotion to Mary or into a milieu, prove sterile, at least in appearance, as a consequence of misunderstandings or prejudices. But perseverance in the effort, a better understanding of the obstacles to overcome and prayer, succeed in leading sincere souls to a discovery of Mary; and once Mary is understood, success is assured.

We can go further still! Since every Christian should be an apostle, converts must come to understand that, in our having helped them to find Christ, Mary invites them, in turn, to assist her in helping others to find Him.

It is by spreading devotion to Mary throughout the world, and by giving to each of her devotees an awareness of their obligation to help her in her apostolic mission, that an unlimited army of apostles will be recruited for her. In this way, she will be allowed to fully accomplish her mission of giving Christ to the world: *per Matrem ad Filium,* "through the Mother to the Son."

THE END

Appendix

About the Author

The author of this book, Fr. Emile Nicholas Neubert, was born in Ribeauvillé, France on May 8, 1878. In 1892 he entered the postulancy (minor seminary) of the Society of Mary (Marianists); he entered their novitiate in 1894, and made first profession of vows on Sept. 15, 1895. After further study and work as a teacher in schools of the Society, he made final profession of vows on Sept. 7, 1902. He was ordained a priest in Fribourg, Switzerland on Aug. 5, 1906, and was awarded the Doctorate in Theology from the University of Fribourg in 1907. His doctoral thesis, written under the direction of the well-known patrologist, J.-P. Kirsch, bore the title *Marie dans l'Eglise anténicéene* [Mary in the Pre-Nicean Church; no English translation available], was published in 1908. This study was the first doctoral thesis in patristics on the Mother of God ever to be presented in a Catholic faculty of theology. It initiated the career of one of the Mariologists most responsible for the development of this area of theology over the past century. Still more important to his career was the discovery, around this time, of the spiritual heritage of Bl.

William Joseph Chaminade, founder of the Society of Mary.

Between 1907 and 1921, Fr. Neubert labored in the United States for his Order—for the most part in Missouri and Ohio—serving as Master of Postulants and then of Novices. In 1921 he returned to Europe, taught philosophy briefly in Strasbourg and then, from 1922 through 1949, he acted as Rector of the Marianist Seminary in Fribourg. In 1935, he was one of the founding members of the prestigious Mariological Society of France, and a member of the International Marian Academy in Rome. The immense number of his books and articles, most of which enjoy broad appeal, are a testimony to the influence he exercised on the Marian movement of our times and the spirituality and apostolate associated with it. Among friends and correspondents who promoted his books are such great Marian figures as Mr. Frank Duff, founder of the Legion of Mary, and St. Maximilian M. Kolbe, founder of the Militia of the Immaculate and first City of the Immaculate [Niepokalanów] in Poland. Further bibliographical information can be found in the entry on him by his disciple, Fr. Théodore Koehler, in the *Dictionnaire de Spiritualité*, vol. 11, cc. 151–152 [English translation, Appendix

D of the *Autobiography of Father Emile Neubert, Marianist*, Dayton OH 2007, pp. 81–84].

Fr. Neubert died at Art-sur-Meurthe in France on August 29, 1967.

Fr. Neubert's contribution to Mariology and to Marian spirituality cannot be underestimated. His doctoral thesis is a milestone in the history of Mariology. It not only demonstrated the importance of Mary in the writings of the Fathers and how to go about a fruitful patristic study of her, but it also indicated the true place of Mary in the thought and life of the Church from its beginning. The soundness of this study, published at the height of the modernist controversy, was perhaps the most effective rejoinder to the then fashionable opinion of doctrinal historians, like J. Turmel, that Mary only came to occupy such a position long after Pentecost, with the insinuation that said position was an aberration.

More than this, however, he contributed immensely to the integration of Marian doctrine and Marian spirituality: the doctrine for the sake of Marian spirituality to become saints in and through Mary, and the spirituality grounded firmly in Marian doctrine. Two of his better known works: *Mary in Doctrine* (French edition 1933) and *Who is She?: The Life and Study of the Blessed Virgin* (French edition 1936), illustrate this very clearly. The second of these works inaugurated a series of studies intended to apply this spirituality to various states of life. *Mary and the Priestly Ministry* (2009 Academy of the Immaculate, New Bedford, MA [French original: *Marie et notre sacerdoce*]), is one of these. Others in the series dealt with religious life, Christian educators, the Christian family—all published in France after World War II.

According to Fr. Stanley, translator of *Mary and the Priestly Ministry* [cf. his memoir: *Our Lady's Dolphin*, in the *Autobiography* cited above, pp. 75–76], Father Neubert considered the following as his three most important works: *My Ideal, Jesus, Son of Mary* [French original published in 1933, a veritable best seller with over half a million copies sold in all languages and still in print]; *Mary and the Priestly Ministry* [French original published in 1952 and published for the first time in English (2009 Academy of the Immaculate, New Bedford, MA)]; and *The Life of Union With Mary* [French original published in 1954]. To the latter is closely related *The Soul of Jesus Contemplated in Union With Mary* [French original published in 1957]. Among Father Neubert's other available works in English are: *Living With Mary*; *Mariology of Fr. Chaminade*;

Marian Catholic Action; *Our Gift from God*; *Queen of Militants*. Those desirous to know more about this gifted priest may begin with the *Autobiography of Father Emile Neubert, Marianist*, cited above.

Fr. Neubert was a gifted scholar who devoted his entire life and all his energies to the service of God's Mother and ours. More than this, he was a holy priest and religious—totally consecrated to Mary—who lived the doctrine he proclaimed. The following passage from his *Autobiography* unintentionally confirms what so many who were blessed to enjoy his spiritual guidance realized: his humble, saintly love of the Blessed Virgin and all her children. Fr. Neubert recalls how an old friend from childhood days, after reading his *Life of Union with Mary*, remarked: "You have sucked devotion to Mary along with the milk of your mother." Fr. Neubert comments (p. xii):

> The reality, however, is altogether different. I did not start as a good and pious child. Only toward the end of my fifteenth year did devotion to Mary begin slowly to attract me. I never dreamed to become a Marian author, but thanks to providential circumstances, once I began writing articles and books on Marian themes, I widened my plans. I would include, if I lived long enough, books on the

Blessed Virgin that were proposed to me or that proposed themselves as I wrote. To sum up, my life did not unfold according to an internal logic, but according to another, superior logic. I thank Her who designed it. If my biography is to be written, I want it to be at the same time a book on the Blessed Virgin.

Fr. Peter Damian M. Fehlner, FI

A Selection of Books from the Academy of the Immaculate

A Month with Mary *Daily Meditations for a Profound Reform of the Heart in the School of Mary by Don Dolindo Ruotolo* This little book was written by a holy Italian priest Father Dolindo Ruotolo (1882–1970). Originally written as spiritual thoughts to his spiritual daughter, the work is comprised of thirty-one meditations for the month of May. The month of Mary is the month of *a profound reform of heart:* we must leave ourselves and adorn ourselves with every virtue and every spiritual good.

Jesus Our Eucharistic Love *by Fr. Stefano Manelli, FI* A treasure of Eucharistic devotional writings and examples from the saints showing their stirring Eucharistic love and devotion. A valuable aid for reading meditatively before the Blessed Sacrament.

Who is Mary? *Fr. Gabriele M. Pellettieri, FI* This book is a concise Marian catechism presented in a question/answer format. In this little work of love and scholarship the sweet mystery of Mary is unveiled in all its beauty and simplicity. It is a very helpful resource both for those who want to know the truth about Mary and those who want to instruct others.

Padre Pio of Pietrelcina *by Fr. Stefano Manelli, FI* This 144-page popular life of Padre Pio is packed with details about his life, spirituality, and charisms, by one who knew the Padre intimately. The author turned to Padre Pio for guidance in establishing a new Community, the Franciscans of the Immaculate.

Devotion to Our Lady *by Fr. Stefano M. Manelli, FI* This book is a must for all those who desire to know the beauty and value of Marian devotion and want to increase their fervent love towards their heavenly Mother. Since it draws abundantly from the examples and writings of the saints, it offers the devotee a very concrete and practical aid for living out a truly Marian life.

Do You Know Our Lady? *by Rev. Mother Francesca Perillo, FI* This handy treatise (125 pages) covers the many rich references to Mary, as prefigured in the Old Testament women and prophecies and as found in the New Testament from the Annunciation to Pentecost. Mary's role is seen ever beside her Divine Son, and the author shows how scripture supports Mary's role as Mediatrix of all Graces. Though scripture scholars can read it with profit, it is an easy read for everyone. Every Marian devotee should have a copy for quick reference.

Come Follow Me *by Fr. Stefano Manelli, FI* A book directed to any young person contemplating a religious vocation. Informative, with many inspiring illustrations and words from the lives and writings of the saints on the challenging vocation of total dedication in the following of Christ and His Immaculate Mother through the three vows of religion.

Saints and Marian Shrine Series

edited by Bro. Francis Mary, FI

Padre Pio – The Wonder Worker   The latest on this popular saint of our times including inspirational homilies given by Pope John Paul II during the beatification and canonization celebrations in Rome. The first part of the book is a short biography. The second is on his spirituality, charisms, apostolate of the confessional, and his great works of charity.

A Handbook on Guadalupe   This well-researched book on Guadalupe contains 40 topical chapters by leading experts on Guadalupe with new insights and the latest scientific findings. A number of chapters deal with Our Lady's role as the patroness of the pro-life movement. Well illustrated.

Kolbe – Saint of the Immaculata   Of all the books in the Marian Saints and Shrines series, this one is the most controversial and thus the most needed in order to do justice to the Saint whom Pope John Paul II spoke of as "the Saint of our difficult century [twentieth]." Is it true, as reported in a PBS documentary, that the Saint was anti-Semitic? What is the reason behind misrepresenting this great modern day Saint? Is a famous Mariologist right in accusing the Saint of being in error by holding that Mary is the Mediatrix of all Graces? The book has over 35 chapters by over ten authors, giving an in-depth view of one of the greatest Marian saints of all times.

For a complete listing of books, tapes and CDs from the Academy of the Immaculate please refer to our catalog. Request a free catalog by email, letter, or phone via the contact information given below for the Academy of the Immaculate.

Special rates are available with 25% to 50% discount depending on the number of books, plus postage. For ordering books and further information on rates to book stores, schools and parishes: *Academy of the Immaculate, P.O. Box 3003, New Bedford, MA 02741, Phone/FAX (888)90.MARIA [888.90.62742], E-mail academy@ marymediatrix.com.* Quotations on bulk rates by the box, shipped directly from the printery, contact: *Franciscans of the Immaculate, P.O. Box 3003, New Bedford, MA 02741, (508)996-8274, E-mail: ffi@marymediatrix.com. Website: www.marymediatrix.com.*

THE ACADEMY OF THE IMMACULATE

The Academy of the Immaculate, founded in 1992, is inspired by and based on a project of St. Maximilian M. Kolbe (never realized by the Saint because of his death by martyrdom at the age of 47, August 14, 1941). Among its goals the Academy seeks to promote at every level the study of the Mystery of the Immaculate Conception and the universal maternal mediation of the Virgin Mother of God, and to sponsor publication and dissemination of the fruits of this research in every way possible.

The Academy of the Immaculate is a non-profit religious-charitable organization of the Roman Catholic Church, incorporated under the laws of the Commonwealth of Massachusetts, with its central office at Our Lady's Chapel, POB 3003, New Bedford, MA 02741-3003.